THE
EPIC
OF
EDEN

A Christian Entry into the Old Testament

SANDRA L. RICHTER

IVP Academic

An imprint of InterVarsity Press
Downers Grove, Illinois

InterVarsity Press
P.O. Box 1400, Downers Grove, IL 60515-1426
World Wide Web: www.ivpress.com
E-mail: email@ivpress.com

InterVarsity Press® is the book-publishing division of InterVarsity Christian Fellowship/USA®, a movement of students and faculty active on campus at hundreds of universities, colleges and schools of nursing in the United States of America, and a member movement of the International Fellowship of Evangelical Students. For information about local and regional activities, write Public Relations Dept., InterVarsity Christian Fellowship/USA, 6400 Schroeder Rd., P.O. Box 7895, Madison, WI 53707-7895, or visit the IVCF website at <www.intervarsity.org>.

All Scripture quotations, unless otherwise indicated, are taken from the New American Standard Bible®, *copyright 1960, 1962, 1963, 1968, 1971, 1972, 1973, 1975, 1977, 1995 by The Lockman Foundation. Used by permission.*

Design: Cindy Kiple
Images: landscape with hills: ©Robert Hardholt/iStockphoto
        gate: ©Giorgio Fochesato/iStockphoto

ISBN 978-0-8308-2577-6

Printed in the United States of America ∞

 InterVarsity Press is committed to protecting the environment and to the responsible use of natural resources. As a member of Green Press Initiative we use recycled paper whenever possible. To learn more about the Green Press Initiative, visit <www.greenpressinitiative.org>.

Library of Congress Cataloging-in-Publication Data

Richter, Sandra L.
  The epic of Eden: a Christian entry into the Old Testament/Sandra
  L. Richter.
    p. cm.
  Includes bibliographical references and index.
  ISBN 978-0-8308-2577-6 (pk.: alk. paper)
  1. Bible. O.T.—Criticism, interpretation, etc.   1. Title.
  BS1171.3.R53 2008
  221.6'1—dc22

              2008022661

P 27   26   25   24

Y 28   27   26   25   24   23   22

In memory of

Meredith G. Kline,

who first helped me put my Bible together,

and to all the students with whom

I have learned along the way.

CONTENTS

List of Figures and Tables. 9

Acknowledgments 11

Abbreviations 13

Introduction: *The Dysfunctional Closet Syndrome* 15

1 The Bible as the Story of Redemption 21

2 The Bible in Real Time and Space. 47

3 The Concept of Covenant:
   The "General Law" That Holds Our Facts Together. 69

4 God's Original Intent 92

5 God's Final Intent: *The New Jerusalem*. 119

6 Noah and Abraham 137

7 Moses and the Tabernacle 166

8 David and the Monarchy. 189

9 The New Covenant and the Return of the King 209

Frequently Asked Questions 225
   What Role Does the Law of Moses Play in the Christian's Life?. 225
   What About Modern-Day Israel? 229

Notes 234

Glossary. 255

Scripture Index 260

FIGURES AND TABLES

Figures

1.1   Israelite society

1.2   Footprint of the Israelite four-room pillared house

1.3   Israelite four-room pillared house

2.1   A timeline of biblical chronology

2.2   The Fertile Crescent

2.3   Mesopotamia

2.4   Abraham's migration into Canaan

2.5   Abraham's ridge route in Canaan

2.6   Joseph's journey to Egypt

2.7   The exodus and journey to the Promised Land

2.8   Israel's tribal allotments in Canaan

2.9   David's kingdom

2.10 The divided monarchy

2.11 The exile of the northern and southern kingdoms

3.1   The Hittite suzerain/vassal treaty format of the late 2nd millennium B.C. and the *bĕrît* at Mt. Sinai

4.1   The seven days of creation in Genesis 1

4.2   The cosmos

4.3   Adam's choice

4.4   Adam's world

5.1   The footprint of the tabernacle

5.2   An artist's reconstruction of the tabernacle

5.3   King Ahiram's sarcophagus

5.4   The footprint of Solomon's temple

5.5   An artist's reconstruction of the temple

5.6   A synopsis of redemptive history
5.7   The people of redemptive history
5.8   The timeline of redemptive history
6.1   A synopsis of redemptive history, Noah
6.2   Noah's real time
6.3   Noah's real space
6.4   The cosmos
6.5   A synopsis of redemptive history, Abraham
6.6   Abraham's real time
6.7   Abraham's migration
6.8   The people of redemptive history, Abraham
7.1   A synopsis of redemptive history, Moses
7.2   Moses' real time
7.3   Joseph's journey into Egypt
7.4   The exodus
7.5   The people of redemptive history, Israel
7.5   The footprint of the tabernacle
7.7   An artist's reconstruction of the tabernacle
8.1   A synopsis of redemptive history, David
8.2   The era of the judges
8.3   Philistine and Israelite settlement
8.4   David's kingdom
9.1   Timeline of the new covenant
9.2   A synopsis of redemptive history, new covenant
9.3   The people of redemptive history, the church
9.4   A synopsis of redemptive history, New Jerusalem

Table
4.1   The Two Accounts of Creation in Genesis

ACKNOWLEDGMENTS

I owe many thanks to my friends and colleagues at Asbury Theological Seminary who have made the writing of this book possible. For the granting of a fall 2007 sabbatical leave, I offer thanks to the administration and Board of Trustees. For her tireless efforts to create and refine many of the maps and images found in this text, I owe my gratitude to Kelly M. Myers. And for their kind review of portions of the manuscript I offer my heartfelt thanks to my husband, Steve Tsoukalas, my colleagues Fred Long and Ben Witherington, and Paul Wright of Jerusalem University College. Particular thanks must go to my most excellent editor, Daniel G. Reid, and my colleague Lawson G. Stone for his unflagging enthusiasm for this project.

ABBREVIATIONS

AB   Anchor Bible

ABD   *Anchor Bible Dictionary,* ed. D. N. Freedman, 6 vols. (New York: Doubleday, 1992)

ANET *Ancient Near Eastern Texts Relating to the Old Testament,* ed. J. B. Pritchard (Princeton, N.J.: Princeton University Press, 1954)

ARAB *Ancient Records of Assyria and Babylon,* Daniel David Luckenbill, 2 vols. (London: Histories & Mysteries of Man, 1989)

BA   *Biblical Archaeologist*

BAR   *Biblical Archaeology Review*

BASOR *Bulletin of the American Schools of Oriental Research*

BJRL *Bulletin of the John Rylands University Library of Manchester*

BR   *Biblical Research*

BSac *Bibliotheca Sacra*

BZAW   Beihefte zur Zeitschrift für die alttestamentliche Wissenschaft

CANE *Civilizations of the Ancient Near East,* ed. J. Sasson, 4 vols. (New York: Scribner, 1995)

CBQ   *Catholic Biblical Quarterly*

DOTHB *Dictionary of the Old Testament: Historical Books,* ed. B. T. Arnold and H. G. M. Williamson (Downers Grove, Ill.: InterVarsity Press, 2005)

DOTP *Dictionary of the Old Testament: Pentateuch,* ed. T. D. Alexander and D. W. Baker (Downers Grove, Ill.: InterVarsity Press, 2003)

HALOT *The Hebrew and Aramaic Lexicon of the Old Testament,* L. Koehler, W. Baumgartner and J. J. Stamm, 4 vols. (Leiden: E. J. Brill, 1994-1999)

HSM   Harvard Semitic Monographs
ISBE   *International Standard Bible Encyclopedia,* ed. G. W. Bromiley,
          rev. ed., 4 vols. (Grand Rapids: Eerdmans, 1979-1988)
JAOS   *Journal of the American Oriental Society*
JBL   *Journal of Biblical Literature*
JETS   *Journal of the Evangelical Theological Society*
JNES   *Journal of Near Eastern Studies*
NICOT   New International Commentary on the Old Testament
TDOT   *Theological Dictionary of the Old Testament,* ed. G. J. Botterweck
          and H. Ringgren (Grand Rapids: Eerdmans, 1974-)
VT   *Vetus Testamentum*

INTRODUCTION

The Dysfunctional Closet Syndrome

THE BIBLE, IN ALL ITS PARTS, IS INTENDED to communicate to humanity the realities of redemption. Over the centuries, the church has stumbled when it has forgotten this truth, and has thereby, ironically, damaged the authority of the book from which it has drawn its life. Often the error has run in the direction of making this book less than it is—less than the inspired Word of God, less than the supernatural report of God's doings throughout the ages, less than the definitive rule for faith and practice among those who believe. But just as often, the error has run in the other direction—attempting to make the Bible more than it is. Too often in our zeal for the worldwide influence of this book, we forget that it was not intended as an exhaustive ancient world history, or a guide to the biology and paleontology of creation, or even a handbook on social reform. We forget that this book was cast upon the waters of history with one very specific, completely essential and desperately necessary objective—to tell the epic tale of God's ongoing quest to ransom his creation. And to, thereby, give each generation the opportunity to know his amazing grace. The Bible is the saga of Yahweh and Adam, the prodigal son and his ever gracious heavenly father; humanity in their rebellion and God in his grace. This narrative begins with Eden and does not conclude until the New Jerusalem is firmly in place. It is all one story. And if you are a believer, it is all your story.

So why is it that most laypeople struggle with the study of the Old Testament? Certainly they recognize that the Old Testament is Scripture, are intrigued by its stories and realize that there must be some significance to the first two-thirds of that leather-bound book they are lugging around. Yet if you talk to the typical layperson you will find that they have not been involved in any sort of intentional study of the Old Testament since . . . well, since they can't remember when. Nor can they remember the last time they heard a sermon on the Old Testament. Why is this? In my now many years of teaching the Bible, I've come to believe that the issues that keep the average New Testament believer from their Old Testament can be categorized under three headings. The first, and to me the most heartbreaking, is that most Christians have not been taught that the story of the Old Testament is their story. Rather, they have been encouraged to think that knowledge of the Old Testament is unnecessary to New Testament faith. Worse, many have been taught that the God of the Old Testament is somehow different from the God of the New; that unlike Christ, Yahweh is a God of judgment and wrath. So these folks stick with the part of redemption's story that seems to include them—the New Testament. The second set of issues that make the Old Testament less than accessible is what I have come to call the "great barrier." As the narrative of the Old Testament happened long, long ago and far, far away, it can be very challenging to get past the historical, linguistic, cultural and even geographical barriers that separate us from our ancestors in the faith. As a result, to the typical twenty-first-century Christian, the God of Israel seems foreign, his people strange. The third category, and perhaps the most challenging, is the one that has driven me to write this book. This is what I have coined "the dysfunctional closet syndrome."

THE OLD TESTAMENT AS YOUR STORY

Two-thirds of the story of redemption is known to Christians as the Old Testament. Yet in the decades that I have been teaching Bible, I have found that most Christians, if allowed to answer honestly, might be tempted to dub this section of the Bible the "unfortunate preface" to the part of the Bible that really matters. But the reality is that the Old Testament is the bulk of redemptive history. And the church's lack of knowledge of their own heritage renders much of the wealth of the New Testament inaccessible to them. One of my dear friends and colleagues, Mary Fisher, refers to this widespread condition as a sort of Christian Alzheimer's disease. I realize that this is a painful metaphor for many of us, but it is, unfortunately, appropriate. The great tragedy of Alzheimer's disease is that it robs a person of themselves by robbing them of their memory of their experiences and relationships. Hence, an elderly woman with Alzheimer's can watch her own children walk through the door and need to ask their names. (As a mother, I cannot imagine the agony of such a state.) The church has a similar condition. Just as the Alzheimer's patient must ask the name of her own children, the church watches her ancestors walk through the door with a similar response. Abraham, Isaac and Jacob are unknown and unnamed. The end result? The church does not know who she is, because she does not know who she was.

THE GREAT BARRIER

If our goal is to know our own story, then we first have to come to understand the characters who populate the Old Testament: who they were, where they lived, what was important to them. Hence, the first chapter of this book discusses culture, and the second chapter rehearses the story of redemption through the lenses of real space and time. For those who are still recovering from your junior high geography classes, it is only fair to warn you that there will be maps. But I promise you that the payoff will be well worth the pain. Ultimately my goal as regards the great barrier is to bring the heroes of the Old Testament into focus, such that you can see them as real people who lived in real places and struggled with real faith, just as you do. We are "Abraham's offspring" (Gal 3:29), and his story is our story. I will know that we have successfully navigated the great barrier when you can see your own rebellion in Adam's choice, recognize your own frailty in Abraham's doubting and hear the hope of your own salvation in Moses' cry: "Let my people go!"

THE DYSFUNCTIONAL CLOSET SYNDROME

Over the years I have served in an array of educational and ministry positions from youth to adults, the mission field to the local church, university students to seminarians and lots of steps in between. From "newbies" to doctoral students, I have found that the same ailment affects all of those who aspire to study the Old Testament. The ailment? The dysfunctional closet syndrome.

Everyone has a dysfunctional closet somewhere in their lives. A closet where Jabba the Hut could be living, and no one would know it. The closet is crammed full of clothes slipping from their hangers, accessories dangling from the shelves, shoes piled in disarray on the floor. It is impossible to tell where one item stops and the next begins. You can't find anything; you can't use anything. Perhaps you are one of those very "together" people who has reduced this syndrome in your life to a single cupboard or junk drawer, perhaps a kids' toy chest. But even here, where the twine from last year's Christmas project has permanently entangled itself around the leftover hardware from the kitchen makeover, a person of average courage abandons the quest, closes the door (or drawer or cupboard) and says, "Maybe next summer I'll sort that out."

It has been my experience that the average Christian's knowledge of the Old Testament is much the same. Dozens of stories, characters, dates and place names. Years of diligent acquisition. Yet these acquisitions all lie in a jumble on the metaphorical floor. A great deal of information is in there, but as none of it goes together, the reader doesn't know how to use any of it. Rather, just like the dysfunctional closet, the dates, names and narratives lie in an inaccessible heap. Thus the information is too difficult, or too confusing, to use. So the typical student of the Old Testament closes the door and says, "Maybe next summer I'll sort that out."

Let me offer a personal example—my closet in college. And let me begin by confessing that I have not always been the completely together person I am today. Rather, the clothes that belonged in my closet abandoned their hangers and hooks early on in my college career, such that my room was essentially a heap. So bad was my college dorm room that in desperation my resident assistant finally took pictures and posted them on the lounge bulletin board hoping to humiliate me into reform. A valiant effort, but not an effective one. The result of my dysfunctional closet? Not only did I often look less than "fresh" when I ventured forth onto campus, but even when I made every attempt to plan ahead, I honestly could not find the pieces that went together to form a respectable outfit. And as my college had a dress code (and a 7:45 a.m. chapel!) this situation often resulted in crisis. The crisis? Either I would be forced to give up on the outfit I was attempting to wear, or I had to invest an outrageous amount of time finding the pieces that went together. As I was not exactly a morning person, the typical outcome was that I would rewear whatever clothes I found on the top of the pile. Did I mention that I often looked less than fresh?

Why do I tell you this less-than-flattering story? In my experience this is how most laypeople (and many preachers) handle the Old Testament. Their closet is a mess, and even with a significant time commitment, they cannot put the pieces together. Thus they wind up either spending an outrageous amount of time putting together an Old Testament study (or sermon), or they wind up with one or two texts or stories with which they feel comfortable and ignore the rest (i.e., the clothes on the top of the pile). The end result is that most decide that the Old Testament is just too hard and give their attention to the New Testament where there is some hope of memorizing the characters, places and dates. And all this is in spite of the fact that most Christians are hungry to understand their Old Testament heritage.

My goal in writing this book, therefore, is to deal a mortal blow to the dysfunctional closet syndrome. I am convinced that the key to the problem described above is order. Until a believer is able to organize what they know about the Old Testament meaningfully, they cannot use it. An appropriate quotation whose source I have lost over the years says this: "Facts are stupid things until brought into connection with some general law."

So my goal in this book is to provide structure. Metaphorically speaking, to pick the clothes up off the floor, get some hangers, a pole and some hooks, and help you build a closet of your very own. You already have many (possibly most) of the facts you need; I am going to give you a place to hang them. How will we accomplish this? By identifying a "general law" that gives order to the whole, and then by rearranging the contents of your closet accordingly. And rather than doing what folks have been doing for centuries—attempting to impose their own paradigm upon the text—we will attempt instead to discover the paradigm *within* the text. Contrary to popular opinion, the Old Testament is not a hodgepodge of unrelated materials thrown together by some late, uninformed redactor. Nor has it come to us as the result of an empty-headed secretary copying down verbatim some mysterious message. No, the Old Testament writers were themselves theologians, and, under the inspiration of the Holy Spirit, they have written for us a carefully formatted and focused piece of literature in which there exists an intentional, theological structure. Our goal, therefore, is to discover that structure (our closet) and to hang our facts within it. Essentially, our goal is to discover and employ a biblical theological hermeneutic.

How are we going to accomplish this? We have some hard work to do. First, we need to get past the great barrier that divides us from them— the chasm resulting from millennia of linguistic, cultural and historical changes. Then we must begin to put the book "in order" so that you, the New Testament believer, will be able to get a handle on your Old Testament heritage. When we are done, it is my heart's cry that the story of the Old Testament will come alive to you such that you will recognize your own story in the sweeping epic of redemption. More important, my hope is that you will come to know the God of Abraham, Isaac and Jacob, who delivered the children of Abraham from the slavery of Egypt and has delivered you as well.*

---

*The text of this book is designed for the layperson and should be easily understood by most with little assistance. The endnotes, however, are designed for the student who wants to go further. Often I will offer a reference to an easily accessible help, as well as one to more complex and technical materials. Enjoy!

THE BIBLE AS THE STORY
OF REDEMPTION

OUR OBJECTIVE AS CHRISTIANS IS TO UNDERSTAND the story of redemption, the Bible. More than anything else, we want to hear the words of the biblical writers as they were intended and claim their epic saga as our own. To accomplish this, we need to get past the great barrier—that chasm of history, language and culture that separates us from our heroes in the faith. In this first chapter we take our first step across the great barrier by addressing what I believe is the most profound distinction between "us" and "them": culture.

Regarding the average human's awareness of their own culture, career anthropologist Darrell Whiteman has said that "it is scarcely a fish who would discover water."[1] This is a reliable statement. Humans, rather than recognizing the trappings of their own culture (and that their culture may in fact be very different from someone else's), tend to assume that other societies are just like their own. This is known as *ethnocentrism* and is a human perspective that is as old as the hills. As regards the Christian approach to the Old Testament, consider for example the standard depiction of Jesus in sacred Western art. Jesus is repeatedly portrayed as a pale, thin, white man with dirty blond hair and blue (sometimes green) eyes. His fingers are long and delicate, his body frail and unmuscled. Mary is usually presented as a blond. In medieval art, the disciples may be found in an array of attire that would have rendered them completely anomalous (and ridiculous) in their home towns. I am reminded of the famous "sacred heart of Jesus" image in which Jesus is, again, frail, pale, light-haired and green-eyed, and Marsani's *Gethsemane* in which the red highlights of Jesus' hair glow in the light from above, while his piano-player hands are clasped in desperate prayer. These portrayals are standard in spite of the fact that we are all fully aware that Jesus was a Semite and his occupation was manual labor. So shouldn't we expect a dark-haired man with equally dark eyes? Certainly his skin would have been Mediterranean in tone and tanned by three years of constant exposure to the Galilean sun. His hands would have been rough, probably scarred, definitely calloused; his frame short, stocky and well-muscled. So why is he presented in Christian art as a pale, skinny, white guy? Because the people painting him were pale, skinny, white guys! We naturally see Jesus as "one of us" and portray him accordingly. This is not necessarily a bad thing. Rather, our close association with the characters of redemptive history allows us to see ourselves in their story. And this is as God would have it. But to truly *understand* their story, we need to step back and allow their voices to be heard in the timbre in which they first spoke. We need to do our best to see their world through their eyes.

The flip side of ethnocentrism is a second tendency I have come to speak of as "canonizing culture." This is the unspoken (and usually unconscious) presupposition that the norms of *my* culture are somehow superior to the norms of someone else's. Like ethnocentrism, this tendency is also as old as the human race. And in case you are tempted to think that the members of your culture have evolved past these sorts of presuppositions, let me counter for a moment. As an American, I spent most of my life simply assuming that democracy was somehow morally superior to monarchy, that bureaucratic cultures were more sophisticated than tribal cultures and that egalitarian relationships were more "advanced" than patriarchal. Why? Because these are the norms of my culture and I naturally saw them as "better than" the norms of others'. In fact, until challenged, I would have been hard-pressed to even *separate* the norms of my culture from my values or beliefs. Consider, for example, the early European and American missionaries who wound up exporting not only the gospel but Western culture as they spread across the globe. The New England missionaries to

Hawaii are an example made famous by James Michener's novel *Hawaii*.[2] Here, as the Hawaiians converted to Christianity, they were subsequently also converted to the high-collared, long-sleeved, long-skirted uniforms of the missionaries. Petticoats and suit jackets for a seagoing people living in an island paradise! Why? Because these valiant missionaries were unaware of the distinction between the message of the gospel and their own cultural norms. They had "canonized" their own culture such that they saw their Western dress code as part and parcel of a Christian lifestyle. For the same reason, my senior pastor back in the 1980s would not allow my youth group to listen to Amy Grant or Petra. As their youth leader, I was instructed that if the kids wanted to listen to contemporary Christian music, they could listen to Sandi Patty. Why? It had nothing to do with the message or lifestyle of the respective musicians (my senior pastor did not actually know much about Amy Grant or Petra . . . or Sandi Patty for that matter). It was because Sandi Patty sang slowly, she sang soprano and she had no drums in her accompaniment. In the mind of my senior pastor, her music was "holier" than her more percussion-driven contemporaries because it was similar to the music of his youth and the music that inspired him to faith. My senior pastor, like most of us, was having trouble separating culture from content. But history proves to us that it is impossible to diagnose any human culture as fully "holy" or "unholy." Human culture is always a mixed bag; some more mixed than others. And *every* culture must ultimately respond to the critique of the gospel.

As we open the Bible, however, we find that the God of history has chosen to reveal himself through a specific human culture. To be more accurate, he chose to reveal himself in several incarnations of the same culture. And, as the evolving cultural norms of Israel were not without flaw (rather, as above, there was a mixture of the good, the bad and the ugly), God did not *canonize* Israel's culture. Rather, he simply used that culture as a vehicle through which to communicate the eternal truth of his character and his will for humanity. We should not be about the business of canonizing the culture of ancient Israel, either. But if we are going to understand the content of redemptive history, the merchandise that is the truth of redemption, we will need to understand the vehicle (i.e., the culture) through which it was communicated. Thus the study of the Old

Testament becomes a cross-cultural endeavor. If we are going to understand the intent of the biblical authors, we will need to see their world the way they did.

THE WORD REDEMPTION

But even as we attempt this first step of our journey into the Old Testament, we crash into the great barrier because the very term *redemption* is culturally conditioned. It had culturally-specific content that we as modern readers have mostly missed. In fact, *redemption* is one of several words I have come to refer to as "Biblish"—a word that comes from the Bible, is in English, but has been so over-used by the Christian community that it has become gibberish. So let's begin our crosscultural journey with this word: What does the word *redemption* mean, and where did the church get it? The first answer to that question is obvious; the term comes from the New Testament.

> Blessed be the Lord God of Israel,
> for He has visited us and accomplished *redemption* for His people. (Lk 1:68)

> Knowing that you were not *redeemed* with perishable things like silver or gold from your futile way of life inherited from your forefathers, but with precious blood, as of a lamb unblemished and spotless, the blood of Christ. (1 Pet 1:18-19)

> Christ *redeemed* us from the curse of the Law. (Gal 3:13)

Okay, so the word comes from our New Testament, but what does it mean? And where did the New Testament writers get it? A short survey of the Bible demonstrates that the New Testament writers got the word from the *Old* Testament writers. The prophet Isaiah declares,

> But now, thus says the LORD, your Creator, O Jacob, and He who formed you, O Israel, "Do not fear, for I have *redeemed* you; I have called you by name; you are Mine!" (Is 43:1)

And where did the Old Testament writers get the word? Contrary to what we might assume, they did not lift it from a theological context. Rather, this word and the concepts associated with it emerged from the everyday, secular vocabulary of ancient Israel. "To redeem" (Hebrew *gāʾal*) in its first associations had nothing to do with theology, but everything to do with the laws and social customs of the ancient tribal society of which the Hebrews were a part. Thus if we are to understand the term—and what the Old Testament writers intended when they applied it to Israel's relationship with Yahweh—we will need to understand the society from which the word came.

ISRAEL'S TRIBAL CULTURE

Israelite society was enormously different from contemporary life in the urban West. Whereas modern Western culture may be classified as urban and "bureaucratic," Israel's society was "traditional." More specifically it was "tribal."[3] In a tribal society the family is, literally, the axis of the community. An individual's link to the legal and economic structures of their society is through the family. As Israel's was a patriarchal tribal culture, the link was the patriarch of the clan. The patriarch was responsible for the economic well-being of his family, he enforced law, and he had responsibility to care for his own who became marginalized through poverty, death or war. Hence, the operative information about any individual in ancient Israel was the identity of their father, their gender and their birth order.[4] This is very different from a bureaucratic society in which the state creates economic opportunity, enforces law and cares for the marginalized. In fact, in a bureaucratic culture the family is peripheral—not peripheral to the values and affections of the members of that society, but certainly peripheral to the government and economy. In Israel's tribal society the family was central, and it is best understood by means of three descriptive categories: *patriarchal, patrilineal* and *patrilocal*.

Patriarchal. The first of these terms, patriarchal, has to do with the centrality of the oldest living male member of the family to the structure of the larger society. In his classic work on the topic, Marshall Sahlins states that the societal structure of patriarchal tribalism involves a "progressively inclusive series of groups," emanating from the patriarchal leader.[5] In other words, the layers of society form in ever broader circles, radiating from the closely knit household to the nation as a whole as is pictured in figure 1.1. In Israel's particular tribal system, an individual would identify

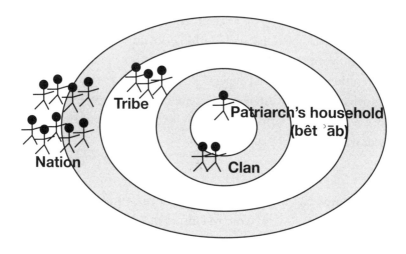

Figure 1.1. Israelite society

their place within society through the lens of their patriarch's household first, then their clan or lineage,[6] then their tribe and finally the nation.[7] Even the terminology for "family" in ancient Israel reflects the centrality of the patriarch. The basic household unit of Israelite society was known as the "father's house(hold)," in Hebrew the *bêt 'āb*. This household was what Westerners would call an "extended family," including the patriarch, his wife(s), his unwed children and his married sons with their wives and children.

In this patriarchal society when a man married he remained in the household, but when a woman married she joined the *bêt 'āb* of her new husband. An example of this is Rebecca's marriage to Isaac in Genesis 24. She left her father's household in Haran and journeyed to Canaan to marry.

Modern ethnographic studies indicate that the Israelite *bêt 'āb* could include as many as three generations, up to thirty persons.[8] Within this family unit, the "father's house(hold)" lived together in a family compound, collectively farming the land they jointly owned and sharing in its produce.[9] This extended family shared their resources and their fate.[10] And those who found themselves without a *bêt 'āb* (typically the orphan and the widow) also found themselves outside the society's normal circle of provision and protection. This is why the Old Testament is replete with reminders to "care for the orphan and the widow." So profound is Yahweh's concern for those who stand outside the protection of the *bêt ʾāb* that he actually describes himself as "the God of gods and the Lord of lords, the great, the mighty, and the awesome God who does not show partiality nor take a bribe. He executes justice for the orphan and the widow, and shows His love for the alien by giving him food and clothing" (Deut 10:17-18). As we will see later in this chapter, there were numerous laws in Israelite society targeted at the protection of "the least of these"—the marginalized of Israel's patriarchal society.

Correspondingly, it was the patriarch of the household who bore both legal and economic responsibility for the household. In extreme situations, he decided who lived and who died, who was sold into slavery and who was retained within the family unit. An example of this from the Bible is the story of Judah and Tamar in Genesis 38:6-26. Here Tamar has become a member of Judah's *bêt ʾāb* by marriage, but is currently a widow. Although she is apparently no longer living under Judah's roof (which is evidence that Judah is not fulfilling his responsibilities to her), she is still under his authority. When Tamar is found to be pregnant, the townspeople report her crime to Judah. It is obvious in this interaction that they expect him as the patriarch of her *bêt ʾāb* to administer justice.[11] And so he does. Judah instructs the townspeople, "Bring her out and let her be burned!" (Gen 38:24). As the head of her household, Judah's words carry the power of life and death for this young woman. We will return to this story a bit later in the chapter.

When the patriarch died, or when the *bêt ʾāb* became too large to sustain itself, the household would split into new households, each headed by the now-oldest living male family member. Consider the description of Abraham's family in Genesis 11:26-32. Here Terah's household consists of his adult sons, their wives and their children. His oldest son Haran "died in the presence of his father Terah" (perhaps while still a member of his household?) but Lot, Haran's son, remains under Terah's care. So when Terah migrates to the city of Haran, he takes Lot with him. When Terah dies, Abram, the eldest, becomes the head of the *bêt 'āb* and therefore takes responsibility for his brother's son. Thus Lot comes to Canaan with Abram.

> Now Lot, who went with Abram, also had flocks and herds and tents. And the land could not sustain them while dwelling together; for their possessions were so great that they were not able to remain together. (Gen 13:5-6)

As a result, Abraham invites Lot to "be separated from upon me" (Gen 13:11). Lot chooses the fertile Jordan Valley and the original *bêt 'āb* becomes two.[12]

Patrilineal. The term *patrilineal* has to do with tracing ancestral descent (and therefore tribal affiliation and inheritance) through the male line. In Israel the possessions of a particular lineage were carefully passed down through the generations, family by family, according to gender and birth order, in order to provide for the family members to come and to preserve "the name" of those gone before.

The genealogies of the Old Testament make this legal structure obvious—women are typically not named. When women *are* named, something unusual is afoot and we should be asking why. A woman might be named in a genealogy if a man had several wives who each had sons, as is the case with Jacob and Esau's genealogies in Genesis 35 and Genesis 36. A woman might be named in the rare and extreme cases in which she might inherit land or goods (Num 26:33; 27:1-11; cf. Num 36:1-12; Josh 17:3-6). But most often, women are named when the biblical writer has something to say.

Note the genealogy of Matthew 1. Here in what comes to be the opening chapter of the New Testament, the information most significant to a first-century Jewish audience regarding one claiming to be the Messiah is announced—his credentials as the son of the promise. Any Jew knew that the Messiah must be the offspring of Abraham; he must be a son of David. This is the bloodline of the Christ. But notice that there are four women named in this crucial register: Rahab, Ruth, the wife of Uriah (Bathsheba) and Mary. Mary's inclusion is an obvious necessity, but what about the others? Why are they here in what ought to be an exclusively male list? Do you remember Rahab's occupation? Ruth's nationality? Bathsheba's claim to fame? Why might the biblical writer have included these women in the *opening* chapter of the New Testament? I believe it is because this writer has something to say about the nature of the deliverance that this Messiah is bringing. This deliverance is for all people. Not just the Jews. Not just the righteous. Rather, the unclean, the foreigner, the sinner—if they will believe as Rahab did—are welcome. Not merely welcome into the new community, but welcome even into the lineage of the Christ.

The genealogies also give us a window into the privileged position of the firstborn in Israelite society. The firstborn male child would replace his father in the role of patriarch upon his father's death. Hence, the firstborn took precedence over his brothers during his father's lifetime (Gen 43:33), and upon his father's death he received a double-portion of the family estate (Deut 21:17; cf. 1 Sam 1:5).[13] I often joke with my classes about the potential impact of incorporating Deuteronomy's law of the double-portion into the typical American home. Picture Christmas morning. The first rays of dawn peek over the horizon. Your offspring leap from their beds and bound down the stairs to find the pile of loot that has come to characterize the celebration of an American Christmas. But rather than finding the carefully apportioned, equal stack of stuff awaiting them under the Christmas tree, your children discover that your firstborn has twice as much as his siblings. Anarchy! Chaos! Bloodshed! In my egalitarian society it is obvious why this apportionment would inspire dispute. Not so in Israel's tribal society. There was a reason that the firstborn received a double-portion: he would become the next patriarch. Thus, during the lifetime of the patriarch, the firstborn was expected to shadow his father, to serve as an apprentice in all his duties. Much more was expected of him than his siblings. As the firstborn came to maturity, he slowly evolved into his father's peer, until upon the patriarch's death he was prepared to assume the weighty responsibility of directing and maintaining the *bêt 'āb*. Obviously, the firstborn would need adequate resources to insure the survival of the family; hence, the double-portion. All firstborns are special to their parents, but because of his pivotal role in Israelite society, the firstborn in Israel was precious.

Consider the stories of Esau and Jacob, Reuben and Judah, David and his seven brothers. In each of these stories the culture demanded that the firstborn male be the one who received the privilege of leading the family into the next generation. But in each of these cases, God chooses a younger son to lead. Thus each of these stories is an example of how God's way of doing things often stands in opposition to the cultural norms of his people and how redemption's story critiques *every* human culture. The choice of David is particularly telling. As the eighth-born son of Jesse, David's inheritance would have fit into a backpack. But after surveying all of Jesse's sons (eldest to youngest, of course), God's spokesman says "no" to those David's society would have chosen and "yes" to the one least likely in the eyes of his own community: "For I have selected a king for *Myself* among his sons" (1 Sam 16:1). Indeed, "people look at the outward appearance, but the LORD looks at the heart" (1 Sam 16:7).

In Israel's patrilineal society, children always belonged to their father's tribe, but when a female child came of age she was married into another *bêt ʾāb*. She became a permanent member of that new household, and her tribal alliance shifted with that marriage. As a result, a woman's identity in Israel—and her link to its economy and civil structures—was always tracked through the men in her life. She was first her father's daughter, then her husband's wife and then her son's mother. The resources and protection of the clan came to her through the male members of her family. This is why it was critical for a woman to marry and to bear children. A woman who was widowed prior to bearing a son was a woman in crisis. And a woman without father, husband or son was destitute; without the charity of strangers, she would starve. Because of this, there were a number of laws in Israelite society targeted at the protection of the widow. Consider, for example, Deuteronomy's gleaning laws, which required that landowners reserve a portion of the produce of their land for those among them who found themselves "on the margins."

> When you reap your harvest in your field and have forgotten a sheaf in the field, you shall not go back to get it; it shall be for the alien, for the orphan, and for the widow, in order that the LORD your God may bless you in all the work of your hands. When you beat your olive tree, you shall not go over the boughs again; it shall be for the alien, for the orphan, and for the widow. When you gather the grapes of your vineyard, you shall not go over it again; it shall be for the alien, for the orphan, and for the widow. (Deut 24:19-21)

Another law concerned with the well-being of widows, and directed at preserving proper lines of inheritance within Israel's tribal culture, is the levirate law found in Deuteronomy 25:5-10. The Latin term *levir* means "brother," and the law dictates the behavior expected when a brother has left a young widow behind. In sum, the levirate law prescribes that in a *bêt ʾāb* that has more than one son, when a married man dies before he has produced a male heir, his young wife is not to be married off to someone outside the household. Rather, it was the responsibility of a living brother to take that woman as his wife (often his second wife) and to father a child with her. The first child of that union would belong to the deceased brother. The child would be legally recognized as the deceased brother's offspring and would receive his inheritance. If there were additional children, those would belong to the living brother. The intent of this law was both to protect the young widow from destitution and to protect her deceased husband's inheritance. The people of Israel considered it a serious offense for a man to fail to fulfill this responsibility to his dead brother.

> When brothers live together and one of them dies and has no son, the wife of the deceased shall not be married outside the family to a strange man. Her husband's brother shall go in to her and take her to himself as wife and perform the duty of a husband's brother to her. And it shall be that the first-born whom she bears shall assume the name of his dead brother, that his name may not be blotted out from Israel. But if the man does not desire to take his brother's wife, then his brother's wife shall go up to the gate to the elders and say, "My husband's brother refuses to establish a name for his brother in Israel; he is not willing to perform the duty of a husband's brother to me." Then the elders of his city shall summon him and speak to him. And if he persists and says, "I do not desire to take her," then his brother's wife shall come to him in the sight of the elders, and pull his sandal off his foot and spit in his face; and she shall declare, "Thus it is done to the man who does not build up his brother's house." In Israel his name shall be called, "The house of him whose sandal is removed." (Deut 25:5-10)

Although this system seems very odd to most Westerners, it worked. The inheritance of the deceased brother was properly conferred upon his legal offspring, and the young widow was secured within the household. Thus her current need for food and shelter was met, and her future need for a child to care for her in her old age was addressed as well.[14]

With this insight into the nuts and bolts of a patrilineal society, let us return to the story of Judah and Tamar in Genesis 38. We have already learned that the widowed Tamar had become a member of Judah's *bêt* *ʾāb* through marriage, and as such Judah is responsible for bringing her to justice after the townspeople announce her out-of-wedlock pregnancy. In agreement with societal norms, Judah orders her execution. But there are details of this story that must be reconsidered. According to Genesis 38:6-11, Tamar had been the wife of Judah's firstborn, Er. When this man died, Judah had instructed his second son Onan to fulfill the "duty of a husband's brother" by marrying Tamar and fathering a child in his deceased brother's name. But because Onan knew that the child would not be his, "when he went in to his brother's wife, he wasted his seed on the ground in order not to give offspring to his brother" (Gen 38:9). The text tells us that for this crime, Yahweh requires his life. Although the law called for Judah now to give this woman to his third son, Judah did not. He was afraid that there was something wrong with this woman (as opposed to something wrong with his sons), and that if his third son Shelah married her, he would die too. So Judah deceived Tamar saying, "remain a widow in your father's house until my son Shelah grows up." The biblical narrator makes it very clear that Judah has no intention of carrying out his responsibilities toward this young woman either by marrying her to his third son, or by making a place for her within his household. Thus, "after a considerable time," when Tamar saw that Judah was not going to fulfill his obligation to her (Gen 38:14), Tamar decided to take matters into her own hands. She "removed her widow's garments," and disguised herself such that when Judah encountered her along the road, he believed her to be a prostitute. Judah propositioned her, and she consented, providing that he leave a pledge of payment with her. The pledge she requested? "Your seal and your cord, and your staff" (Gen 38:18). Tamar's plan worked; she conceived. And when her condition became apparent to her village, they reported it to Judah. Even though this woman was living in her own father's home, Judah ordered her burned. Now consider Tamar's response:

> It was while she was being brought out [to be burned] that she sent to her
> father-in-law, saying, "I am with child by the man to whom these things
> belong." And she said, "Please examine and see, whose signet ring and
> cords and staff are these?" Judah recognized them, and said, "She is more
> righteous than I." (Gen 38:25-26)

"She is more righteous than I"? Hadn't this young woman just tricked
her father-in-law into illicit sex? How could one of the twelve patriarchs
of Israel make such a statement? To answer this question, we have to understand the culture of the people of the Old Testament and resist the
temptation to impose our cultural norms on them. Although in my world
Tamar's actions would be reprehensible, in her own culture it was Judah
who was worthy of rebuke. For it was Judah who had failed to honor the
levirate law and had allowed another household to take responsibility for
the support of his widowed daughter-in-law. In Israelite culture, Judah was
the villain; Tamar was the courageous (albeit a bit audacious!) heroine.

Another important biblical law regarding inheritance addressed land.
Throughout its national period, the bulk of the Israelite populace lived on
small family farms in which the main economy was a mixture of pastoral-
ism and diversified agriculture. The primary goal of that economy was
insuring the survival of the family.[15] As a result, for the typical household
in ancient Israel, the inherited land holdings of the *bêt ʾāb* were the family's lifeline. Thus there were laws in ancient Israel designed to insure that
the family plot (Hebrew *naḥălâ*) remain within the lineage. Based on the
concept formulated early on that the promised land actually belonged to
Yahweh and had been distributed among the tribes as he intended, the
only legally permissible permanent transfer of land in Israel was through
inheritance. And the parcels of land originally distributed by Yahweh were
to pass from father to son in perpetuity. But if poverty or dire life circumstances forced the sale of some portion of the patrimonial estate, the land
was not to be sold permanently. Rather, according to the "inalienable land
law" of Leviticus 25:13-28, it was the responsibility of the seller's nearest
kinsman to step in and buy back what his relative had sold. If there was
no kinsman, but the seller managed to recoup his loss such that he was
able to repurchase his land, the buyer was required to give him that opportunity. And if there was no kinsman, and the seller was incapable of

raising the funds necessary to reclaim his patrimony, "then what he has sold shall remain in the hands of its purchaser until the year of jubilee; but at the jubilee it shall revert, that he [the seller] may return to his property" (Lev 25:28). Although we have no evidence to prove or disprove the actual practice of the widespread restoration of patrimonial lands at the year of jubilee, we do have firm evidence that the kinship-based land tenure described in Leviticus, and the responsibility of the nearest kinsman to restore patrimony when possible, was indeed the expectation of Israelite society (cf. Jer 32:6-44; 2 Kings 8:1-6).[16] Again, this system of land tenure is very different from the capitalist economy in which I have been raised, but, generally, it worked. The end result was that no lineage in Israel was condemned to permanent or inescapable poverty.[17]

Patrilocal. The term *patrilocal* has to do with the living space of the family unit which, as we have come to expect, was built around the oldest living male. Corresponding to the make-up of the *bêt ʾāb* as an extended family, the architectural structure in which the Israelite family lived was not so much a house as it was a compound. Nuclear families were housed in individual units which were clustered together within a larger, walled enclosure, and this living space was also known as the *bêt ʾāb*.

The integration of data gathered via archaeology, modern ethnographic study and the biblical text leaves us with a surprisingly clear picture of this Israelite family compound. Here the individual dwelling places circled a shared courtyard in which the necessary domestic chores were carried out by family members. At any given daytime hour, one might find the women of the household in this courtyard grinding grain into flour, preparing food or baking bread in the standard domed oven known as a *tannûr;* all of this was done with the small children close at hand. A pergola of grapevines for the family's use and animals who had been brought in from the fields to be watered and housed would also be typical courtyard residents. At day's end the family would regather within the security of the walled compound for the evening meal and sleep.[18]

The individual dwelling units of the Israelite *bêt ʾāb* are especially characteristic of Israelite culture and are so consistent in their design that they have come to be known as the "four-room, pillared house." In the States, you might call them the "two-bedroom Cape" of the average Israelite neighborhood. In a rural setting, the houses might be free standing, but frequently (especially in more crowded, urban settings) these houses were more like townhomes—sharing their exterior walls, with their rear walls sometimes doing double-duty as the wall around the compound and/

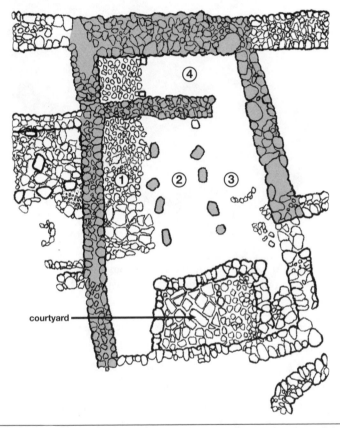

courtyard

Figure 1.2. Footprint of the Israelite four-room pillared house (Courtesy of the Madaba Plains Project excavations at Tall-al-'Umayri, Jordan)

or village.[19] Figure 1.2 offers a diagram of the foundation of such a house, excavated in Tall al 'Umayri (within the territory of the tribe of Reuben). Known as Building B, this is the best-preserved Iron Age I four-room house in the Levant. Figure 1.3 offers a reconstruction of the same.[20]

Notice that this typical Israelite home has two stories, each of which has three long rooms delineated by rows of pillars,[21] and a long room

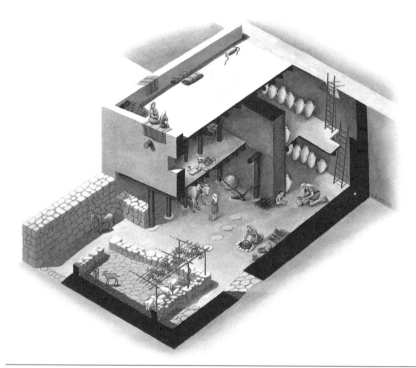

Figure 1.3. Israelite four-room pillared house (Courtesy of the Madaba Plains Project excavations at Tall-al-'Umayri, Jordan. Artist: Rhonda Root ©2001)

which spanned the back of the house. The house was constructed of a mixture of field stone and mud brick, sealed and plastered.[22] The roof was composed of small branches, plastered together with eight to ten inches of tempered clay and mud and/or sod, all of which required a great deal of maintenance. The side rooms of the first floor functioned as stables and were therefore often cobbled. Apparently this warm, protected space was ideal for young or vulnerable animals, as well as the space in which one would house the "stall-fed calf" in order to fatten him up for feast day (1 Sam 28:24).[23] And although the aroma of this shared habitat might be less than ideal, the animals' presence on the first floor provided the family with a cheap source of central heat. The center room often housed a hearth and was used for domestic chores and storage. This center room typically had a floor of beaten dirt or plaster. The long room in the rear was utilized for food storage, often with pits used as grain silos dug into the floor.[24] The family members ate, slept and entertained on the second floor and (during good weather) the roof (cf. 1 Sam 9:25-26; 1 Kings 17:19, and perhaps the "upper room" in Acts 1:13). Based on the now well-known design of the Israelite four-room house, Lawrence Stager has proposed that the story of Jesus' birth in Bethlehem had nothing to do with a stable down the street as we often assume and regularly picture in our nativity sets. Rather, the Bethlehem innkeeper is probably telling Joseph that although he has no room for the laboring woman in the house proper, the little family is welcome to stay on the first floor with the animals. Here, hopefully, they would be warm and safe and the innkeeper's wife would be close at hand in case of trouble. The stone feed troughs that typically separated the stalls from the central room probably served as Luke's "manger" (Lk 2:7).[25]

The design of the family compound helps us see that one of the primary goals of Israel's tribal culture was tribal solidarity—the tribe intended to live *together.* In their unity they found the capacity to prosper under the harsh economic conditions of the highlands, to defend themselves against their Canaanite neighbors and to insure their survival as a people group. This solidarity of the extended family persisted even into death, as is apparent from Israelite burial practices. Archaeology has made it clear that the standard practice was to immediately bury the dead in one fashion or another to allow for the decomposition of the flesh, but then to gather the bones into the family tomb such that the family member was housed permanently with the rest of the clan.[26] The biblical expressions "to sleep with" and "to be gathered to" one's fathers are the literary expressions of this "secondary burial" practice in Israelite culture. Consider the biblical stories surrounding the cave of Macpelah, which Abraham purchased to bury Sarah, and in which Abraham, Isaac, Rebeccah, Jacob and Leah were all eventually laid to rest (Gen 23:1-20; 25:9-10; 49:29-32; 50:13). Here several generations of a single family found their rest *together.* This burial practice also helped to communicate land tenure—the family buried on a plot of ground owned that plot of ground.[27] It is for these reasons that Jacob and Joseph make their sons swear that when they leave Egypt they will take the bones of their ancestors with them, and bury those bones in the land of promise (cf. Gen 47:30; 50:25). The *bêt ʾāb* that lives together, dies together.

LEAVING AND CLEAVING IN GENESIS 2:24

In Israel's patrilocal society, it was the women who did the relocating when marriages were formed. Typically much younger than her fiancé, and probably still in her teens, this young woman was expected to leave her home and family and join her husband's bêt ʾāb. *Can you imagine the relational challenges this young woman faced? Building a new marriage with a man she might hardly have known, relearning how to cook, weave and do laundry according to her new family's habits; navigating the pecking order of this unfamiliar family system . . . all under the watchful eye of her new mother-in-law. Add to this the inevitable homesickness resulting from leaving her own mother and siblings for a group of near strangers, and it is not difficult to envisage some very difficult times for this new wife. Now consider the well-known passage in Genesis 2:24: "For this reason a man shall leave his father and his mother, and be joined to his wife; and they shall become one flesh." Wait a minute. Doesn't the biblical author know that Israel was a patrilocal society? Why is he speaking of the groom doing the leaving? I believe the reason for this apparent "mistake"—like the listing of women in Jesus' genealogy—is that the message of the biblical writer is one of critique. Everyone knew that the relational burden of forming a new household fell upon the women in Israel's society. Everyone knew that it was she who was uprooted and isolated by the process. Yet the earliest and most foundational word we have regarding marriage states that a man shall leave his father and mother and cleave to his wife. They shall become one flesh. I believe this is an intentional reversal on the part of the biblical author. And I think he is intending to communicate something like this: "Young man, although you have all the benefits and comforts in this system, from this day onward you shall live your life as though you too have left. She is now bone of your bones and flesh of your flesh. Your most significant kinship alliance, as of today, is her."*

JESUS AND PATRILOCAL CULTURE: JOHN 14:1-2

The basic patrilocality of Israelite culture and the concept of the family compound survived into New Testament times and serves as a backdrop to many of Jesus' stories and teachings. Consider John 14:1-2. Part of Jesus' "Farewell Discourses," the scene is a private one—Jesus' closest friends have gathered for one last meal together. Just after the meal, Jesus begins telling his disciples about his impending departure and the troubles that will follow. Of course, the disciples are confused and upset. Peter asks the question on everyone's heart: "Where are you going . . . and can we go with you?" (Jn 13:36-37). Jesus responds as follows:

> Do not let your heart be troubled; believe in God, believe also in Me. In my Father's house are many dwelling places,[28] if it were not so I would have told you; for I go to prepare a place for you. If I go and prepare a place for you, I will come again and receive you to Myself; that where I am, there you may be also. (Jn 14:1-3)

Did you notice Jesus' vocabulary? "In my *father's house* there are many *dwelling places*." For generations we in the West have imposed our cultural lens upon this passage such that we have whole songs dedicated to the "mansion up over the hilltop" that is awaiting us in heaven. But what Jesus is saying to his disciples and to us is so far superior to the objectives of a consumer culture that it takes my breath away—our ultimate destination as the newly adopted children of the Father is the family compound! And Jesus, the firstborn of his Father's household, is going back to heaven to get your four-room pillared house ready. Why? "So that where I am, there you may be also." The goal of redemption is not a marbled mansion, but reincorporation into the *bêt 'āb* of our heavenly Father.

In sum, in Israel's earliest culture the tribe and the family were the most important and influential elements of society. Within this tribal system the oldest, closest living male relative held the greatest authority in one's life and the greatest responsibility for one's well-being. And although their culture morphed over the generations with the effects of urbanism, exile, Hellenism, etc., this basic value system endured.

REDEMPTION IN THE BIBLE

So now for the question most central to our chapter: how do these insights into Israelite culture help us in our quest to understand the term *redemption?* As I stated at the beginning of this chapter, whereas we the church have adopted the word redemption from the biblical writers, they adopted it from their everyday, secular world. And rather than entering biblical vocabulary as a theological term as we might expect, the word and concept of redemption actually entered the Bible through the laws and mores of Israel's patriarchal, tribal culture. Specifically, the idea of redemption was intrinsically linked to the familial responsibilities of a patriarch to his clan.

Ruth and Boaz. Consider the story of Ruth and Boaz recorded in the book of Ruth. During the era of the judges, an Israelite woman named Naomi marries a certain Bethlehemite named Elimelech to whom she bears two sons. In her world, Naomi was a blessed woman—a husband and two sons! A local famine, however, prompts Elimelech to abandon their patrimonial estate and relocate to Moab (a neighboring country just across the Jordan River). While in Moab, Elimelech dies, leaving Naomi a widow. This is a grievous event for Naomi, but not a disastrous one as she still has two healthy sons, who subsequently take Moabite women as wives. Naomi's world is stable. Her husband is dead, but her two adult sons are married and the hope of grandchildren (and thus the continuation of her *bêt 'āb*) cannot be far off. But ten years pass and there are no children. Far worse, the men die. Naomi is left far from the patrimony of her husband's family, with no husband, no sons and no grandchildren. In the Israelite mind this family has become an "un-family," and this woman is in dire straights.

Naomi chooses the only course of action left to her, to return to Bethlehem with the hope that a family member will take her in. So she instructs her daughters-in-law to return to their households of origin,[29] hoping that they will find the opportunity to marry again, bear children and secure their own futures. Weeping, the girls beg to stay with her, but knowing that she has nothing to offer them, Naomi says,

Return, my daughters. Why should you go with me? Have I yet sons in my womb, that they may be your husbands? Return, my daughters! Go, for I am too old to have a husband. If I said I have hope, if I should even have a husband tonight and also bear sons, would you therefore wait until they were grown? Would you therefore refrain from marrying? (Ruth 1:11-13)

Without some knowledge of Israel's tribal culture, the reader would have absolutely no idea what Naomi is talking about. But knowing something about patrilinealism, it is obvious that what Naomi is referring to is the levirate law of Deuteronomy 25:5-10. Naomi is reminding her daughters-in-law that she has no means by which to provide for them. She has no sons, and she is too old to have more. And even if by some miracle she found a husband and conceived that very night, would her daughters-in-law wait the twenty-plus years it would take for these unborn sons to come to maturity? Of course not.

No, my daughters; for it is harder for me than for you, for the hand of the Lord has gone forth against me. And they lifted up their voices and wept again; and Orpah kissed her mother-in-law, but Ruth clung to her. (Ruth 1:13-14)

Naomi again instructs Ruth to take the prudent road and follow her sister-in-law. There was no shame in leaving Naomi; they all knew that. But Ruth, as an attestation of her remarkable character, refuses:

Do not urge me to leave you or turn back from following you; for where you go, I will go, and where you lodge, I will lodge. Your people shall be my people and your God, my God. Where you die, I will die, and there I will be buried. (Ruth 1:16-17)

We often hear Ruth's words quoted in marriage ceremonies—which is in some ways appropriate—but these words are in reality plainspoken statements of tribal solidarity. Ruth is announcing that her tribal affiliation is with Naomi. Regardless of the patrilineal mores of their society, Ruth has chosen Naomi as her kin, and she's not leaving.

So the women return to Bethlehem. Here Ruth takes advantage of the local gleaning laws to support them, and her diligent work ethic and tender care for her widowed mother-in-law earn her the attention and kindness of a certain local landowner. Note the subtle aside of the narrator regarding this wealthy (and surely handsome) man: "Boaz, who was of the family [lineage or clan] of Elimelech" (Ruth 2:3). "Aha," the reader says, "I wonder how Boaz will play into all this?" When Ruth returns from her work, she tells Naomi of Boaz's kindness and Naomi responds excitedly, telling Ruth that this man is "one of our relatives," in fact, "he is one of our closest relatives" (Ruth 2:20). At last we begin to see the secular origins of our term. As the story reaches its climax, Naomi instructs Ruth to carry out a daring (and in her day, risqué) plot. Under the cover of darkness, far from town in the harvest fields, after Boaz had enjoyed his fill of wine, a dressed and perfumed Ruth places herself at the sleeping man's feet. The audience is well aware that this is the ideal setting for seduction and sin, and the question in everyone's mind is if Ruth and Boaz are indeed the people of excellence that we have been told they are. Apparently, the answer to that question is yes because rather than the sordid scene we expect, Ruth uses this moment to ask Boaz to "redeem" her. Not only does Boaz generously agree to do all she asks, concerned for her safety and reputation, he sends her home before dawn with a wealth of grain for her mother-in-law.

So what are the practical expressions of Boaz agreeing to redeem this young woman? As the story unfolds, we see that "to redeem" in this situation means that Boaz will marry Ruth, buy back the patrimony of her deceased husband (cf. the inalienable land law of Lev 25), take both Ruth and Naomi into his household, and father a child in Mahlon's name, thereby giving Elimelech an heir to whom the family inheritance will pass (cf. the levirate law of Deut 25). We also learn in chapter four that a relative closer in kinship refuses to do this for Ruth "because I would jeopardize my own inheritance" (Ruth 4:6). This exchange makes it obvious that what Boaz was asked to do was costly. His generous actions put his own resources on the line. But in his integrity, Boaz chooses to embrace the responsibility of a patriarch and become Ruth's gōʾēl—her "kinsman-redeemer."

From this story we learn that the tribal law of "redemption" had to do with a patriarch rescuing a family member who, due to crippling life circumstances, had been lost to the kinship circle, to protect their legal rights. The law demanded that the patriarch protect the individual's legal rights and resolve her debts. Here is a reconciliation of family ties that costs the redeemer. And it is the oldest, closest male relative to whom one looks for help and hope.

Lot and Abraham. A second story illustrating the expectations of tribal law is found in Genesis 14. Lot and Abraham have parted company, and Lot's newly formed *bêt 'āb* is residing in the Jordan Valley, in close proximity to the urban centers of Sodom and Gomorrah. A coalition of kings from Mesopotamia invades the region, and in the process of looting Sodom, takes Lot and his household captive (most likely in order to sell them as slaves). But one of the populace escapes and hurries to Hebron to report to Abraham that a member of his clan has been taken as a prisoner of war. Immediately, Abraham musters the local sheiks as well as the men of his own household to pursue his brother's son. (In case you are picturing a band of ten or twelve, note that there were 318 "trained men" born in Abraham's household [Gen 14:14].) So, Abraham pursues the forces of the eastern kings past the northern boundaries of Canaan (i.e., past the city of Dan), defeats the invaders and rescues his relative and his relative's possessions. Does Abraham do these things simply because he is a good man? Yes and no. Yes, Abraham was a good man, but more significant to our discussion are the mores embedded in his society. A patriarch had responsibilities. If a member of his lineage found himself in need of ransom or rescue, as had Lot, that patriarch was expected to do something about it. So Abraham puts his own household on the line, his own life on the line, in order to rescue his brother's son from a strong enemy against whom he had no defense. This is another expression of "redemption" in Israel's world.

Gomer and Hosea. A final biblical illustration comes from the story of the prophet Hosea and his wayward wife, Gomer. Hosea was a prophet to the northern kingdom of Israel and had the unenviable privilege of being commissioned by Yahweh to live his life as an ongoing visual aid of Yahweh's relationship with Israel. Thus we are introduced to Hosea when he is instructed to "take to yourself a wife of harlotry and have children of harlotry; for the land commits flagrant harlotry, forsaking the LORD" (Hos 1:2). Whether Gomer was a woman with a reputation for promiscuous behavior or a woman professionally employed as a prostititute has been hotly debated over the years.[30] But regardless of how Gomer earned her reputation, we are left with the tale of a local holy man heading down to the "other side" of the tracks (quite possibly the local brothel) to pick out a wife. Pause for a moment to picture this scene. These little Israelite villages rarely numbered more than 250 people. The trip alone would have made the morning gossip column. The fact that this *prophet* returned with a *bride* . . . ? Can you imagine the scuttlebutt in Hosea's village, and the emotions swirling around his soul as he began his life as the husband of a woman he knew had been available to his neighbors . . . possibly for hire? From start to finish, this is a story that grates upon the soul.

And what of Gomer's perspective in all of this? I can assure you that no ten-year-old girl from any culture in any era wakes up one morning and says, "I want to grow up to be a prostitute." Nor have I ever met a young woman who *wanted* the reputation of "tramp." Rather, there must have been some agony in Gomer's history or that of her family that had left this girl in a very bad place. And in Israel's tribal culture, that agony would be ongoing. Gomer had no *bêt ʾāb*. As a woman with a sexual past, she would never have a husband. And whatever children she might bear would be shunned forever by her community. This is Gomer's fate. But then one morning a miracle happens. Hosea, a man of stature and means, asks her to be his wife. Can you imagine the reversal this represented for Gomer? This woman with a past became a woman with a future. Then, blessed be Yahweh, she conceives, and the child that opens her womb is a son! And then she conceives again and again—three children. Gomer's life is transformed, and her world filled with good things.

But chapter two makes it clear that the brokenness of Gomer's soul was not so easily fixed. Rather, this young woman who had gone from nothing to everything repeats the crimes of her past. Consider Hosea's anger and humiliation when he finds that his wife is cheating on him, that in her mind a life of promiscuity is superior to life as his wife (Hos 2:12; 3:1). Although the Bible reports these things in a very restrained fashion, by the opening verses of chapter three it is clear that Gomer is bouncing off of rock bottom, and Hosea's heart is broken. Whereas she had previously enjoyed some measure of income and autonomy, now Gomer is up for sale. Apparently she is now being forced into slavery, auctioned off in the city gate.

So God speaks to Hosea again. "Go and buy her back" (Hos 3:1).[31] Think again of who Hosea is—a holy man in a small town. Think again of what he has given Gomer—a home, children, his bed and probably his heart. And now Hosea finds himself in the public square, in the presence of his neighbors, bidding on the mother of his children . . . his *wife*. "Fifteen shekels of silver and a homer and a half of barley" for his wife (Hos 3:2). This is "redemption."[32]

CONCLUSIONS

So now we have come full circle and are ready to define the word redemption. We are also ready to understand why this word was chosen by the Old Testament writers to describe Yahweh's relationship with his people. In Israel's tribal society redemption was the act of a patriarch who put his own resources on the line to ransom a family member who had been driven to the margins of society by poverty, who had been seized by an enemy against whom he had no defense, who found themselves enslaved by the consequences of a faithless life. Redemption was the means by which a lost family member was restored to a place of security within the kinship circle. This was a patriarch's responsibility, this was the safety net of Israel's society, and this is the backdrop for the epic of Eden in which we New Testament believers find ourselves.

Can you hear the metaphor of Scripture? Yahweh is presenting himself as the patriarch of the clan who has announced his intent to redeem his lost family members. Not only has he agreed to pay whatever ransom is required, but he has sent the most cherished member of his household to accomplish his intent—his firstborn son. And not only is the firstborn coming to seek and save the lost, but he is coming to share his inheritance with these who have squandered everything they have been given. His goal? To restore the lost family members to the *bêt 'āb* so that where he is, they may be also. This is why we speak of each other as *brother* and *sister*, why we know God as *Father*, why we call ourselves *the household of faith*. God is beyond human gender and our relationship to him beyond blood, but the tale of redemptive history comes to us in the language of a patriarchal society. Father God is buying back his lost children by sending his eldest son, his heir, to "give His life as a ransom for many" (Mt 20:28), so that we the alienated might be "adopted as sons" and share forever in the inheritance of this "firstborn of all creation."

For He rescued us from the domain of darkness and transferred us to the kingdom of His beloved Son, in whom we have redemption, the forgiveness of sins. He is the image of the invisible God, the firstborn of all creation. (Col 1:13-15)

Knowing that you were not redeemed with perishable things like silver or gold from your futile way of life inherited from your forefathers, but with precious blood, as of a lamb unblemished and spotless, the blood of Christ. (1 Pet 1:18-19)

THE BIBLE IN REAL TIME
AND SPACE

THE STORY OF REDEMPTION COMES TO US through real time and space—real people, real places, real faith. And if we are going to understand this story, obviously, we are going to need to know something about the time and space our heroes occupied. For most folks, this is where they throw up their hands in despair and head back to the New Testament. The Old Testament is full of so many dates and names and places, how is a person to get their mind around this mass of detail? Again, structure is our friend. Just like a well-ordered closet, we need a few well-designed shelves and hangers to organize what we already know. We need those same shelves and hangers to stand ready to receive the new information we will gather along the way. Be encouraged that even this most dastardly section of the great barrier can be crossed with some good benchmarks and effort. So onward and upward!

REAL TIME

Let us begin with time. We are going to organize the story of redemption as the biblical writers have, around five major eras. Each of these five eras is associated with one key player. Anyone can memorize five names, and most anyone can memorize five storylines that go with those five names. So if you are one of those anyones, you can successfully memorize (and therefore organize) the plot line of the Old Testament.

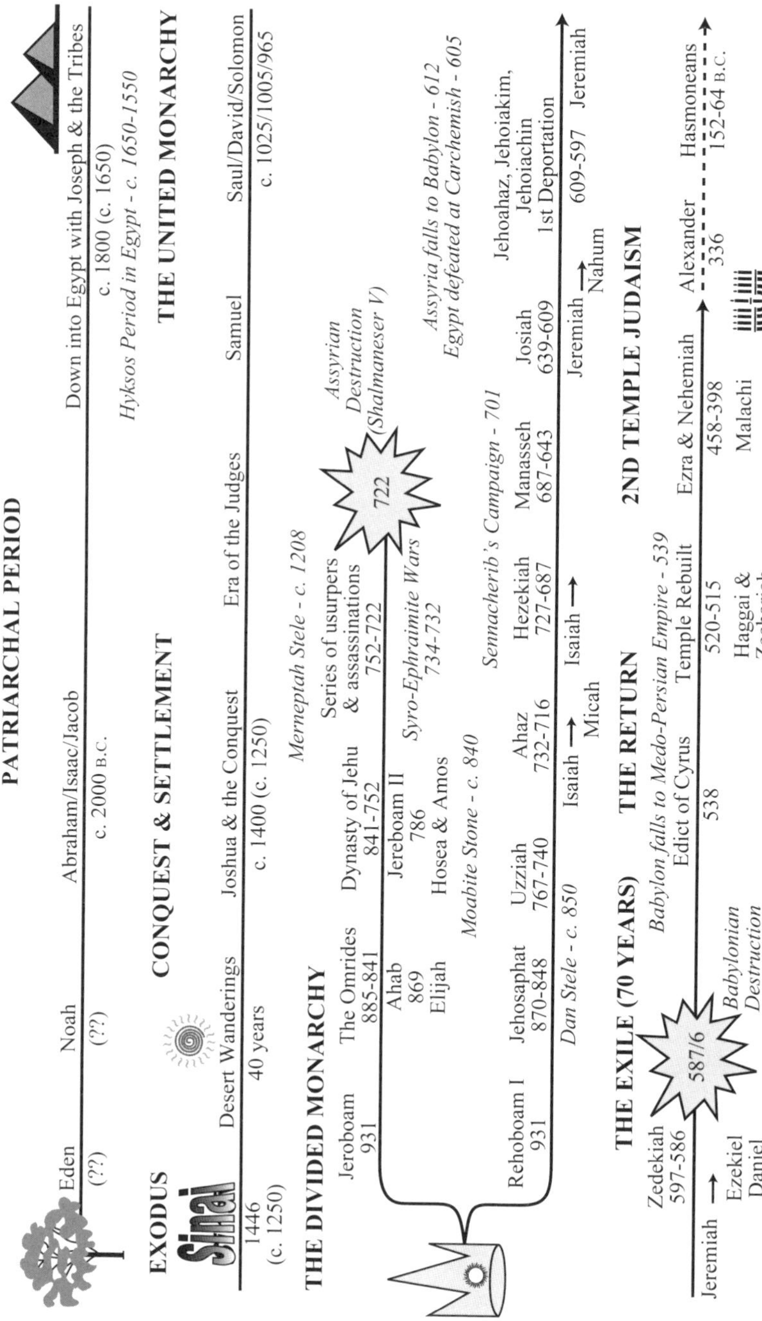

PATRIARCHAL PERIOD

Eden
(??)

Noah
(??)

Abraham/Isaac/Jacob
c. 2000 B.C.

Down into Egypt with Joseph & the Tribes
c. 1800 (c. 1650)

Hyksos Period in Egypt - c. 1650-1550

THE UNITED MONARCHY

Samuel

Saul/David/Solomon
c. 1025/1005/965

EXODUS
1446
(c. 1250)

Sinai

Desert Wanderings
40 years

CONQUEST & SETTLEMENT

Joshua & the Conquest
c. 1400 (c. 1250)

Merneptah Stele - c. 1208

Era of the Judges

Series of usurpers
& assassinations
752-722

*Assyrian
Destruction
(Shalmaneser V)*

722

THE DIVIDED MONARCHY

Jeroboam
931

The Omrides
885-841

Ahab
869

Elijah

Dynasty of Jehu
841-752

Jeroboam II
786

Hosea & Amos

Moabite Stone - c. 840

Dan Stele - c. 850

Rehoboam I
931

Jehosaphat
870-848

Uzziah
767-740

Syro-Ephraimite Wars
734-732

Ahaz
732-716

Isaiah
Micah

Isaiah

Sennacherib's Campaign - 701

Hezekiah
727-687

Manasseh
687-643

*Assyria falls to Babylon - 612
Egypt defeated at Carchemish - 605*

Josiah
639-609

Jeremiah
Nahum

Jehoahaz, Jehoiakim,
Jehoiachin
1st Deportation

609-597   Jeremiah

THE EXILE (70 YEARS)

Zedekiah
597-586

Jeremiah

Ezekiel
Daniel

587/6

*Babylonian
Destruction
(Nebuchadnezzar)*

THE RETURN

Babylon falls to Medo-Persian Empire - 539

Edict of Cyrus
538

Temple Rebuilt
520-515

Haggai &
Zechariah

2ND TEMPLE JUDAISM

Ezra & Nehemiah
458-398

Malachi

Alexander
336

Hasmoneans
152-64 B.C.

Figure 2.1. A timeline of biblical chronology

Take a look at figure 2.1, which is a simplified timeline of the Bible's account of the story. The story starts in the upper left corner in Eden and follows each successive line through the covenant at Sinai, the initiation of the divided kingdom (which splits the story and the timeline to record the saga of both the northern and southern kingdoms), the fall of the northern kingdom to the Assyrians in 722 B.C. (which ends the northern leg of the timeline), and then the fall of the southern kingdom to the Babylonians in 586 B.C. After the star at 586 B.C., the exile of what is left of the south into Babylonia begins. This is followed by the return from exile and the rebuilding of the Jewish community under Ezra and Nehemiah. This ends the Old Testament. But in order to link the Old to the New, I have included the time of Alexander the Great, the era of the Jewish liberation under the Hasmoneans and the subsequent domination by the Romans, which ushered in the time of Jesus in the first century.[1]

I realize that for many, even this simplified version of biblical chronology seems overwhelming. So let's begin to make some benchmarks by means of our five characters. The first character is Adam.

Adam (Genesis 1–5). The story begins in the Garden of Eden. Having orchestrated the magnificence of creation—with all of its amazing creatures, perfect symmetry, order and balance—God offers Adam and Eve everything a human could desire. He installs these two, made in his image, as the stewards of his perfect world. But as we all know, humanity rejects God's plan, choosing autonomy instead, and they are evicted from Eden. Thus Adam's world is birthed with all of its pain and chaos. So too is the story of redemption birthed. For with Adam's choice, God's plan of rescue begins. That, however, belongs to another chapter. For now it is important for you to know that Adam's story is the first segment of redemptive history. Note as well that there are no dates on the timeline for Eden. This is because the Bible does not actually tell us when these events occurred. We know that they were at the dawn of history and were very, very long ago, but these are not *datable* events. We will not step into datable history until Abraham. Now I realize that many folks believe they can date Eden. Early Jewish tradition placed the creation of the world at 3761 B.C., and the famous sixteenth-century scholar, Bishop James Ussher (often spelt Usher) went so far as to name the day of creation: Sunday, October 23, 4004 B.C.[2] Although these dating schemes were created in good faith (and good scholarship for those eras), these early chronographers had very limited information regarding ancient schemes of reckoning time and, particularly important, the function of genealogies in kinship-based societies. Hence, the resulting chronologies were skewed.[3] For example, the medieval scholars (as well as most folks today) believed that genealogies in the ancient world were intended as cumulative records of every generation in a given society. But in fact, these genealogies were intended as contemporary statements regarding group and individual identity. As my colleague Lawson Stone puts it, "genealogies are a filing system for people." They functioned to clarify all sorts of societal relationships— inheritance, legal access to a particular office, geographical location and territory rights, ethnology, or even a group's particular caste or function within a society.[4] Moreover, "[a]ll genealogies, whether oral or written, are characterized by fluidity."[5] In layman's terms, a particular person's genealogy could shift depending on the end goal of the individual recounting that genealogy. Considering all the potential functions of a genealogy, we can anticipate that there was a whole lot of shifting going on. In addition to the array of societal functions, the genealogies we find in the Bible, although derived from older archival records, have been placed into a narrative context and, therefore, have been overlaid with theological and narrative functions as well.

Compare the genealogy of Jesus in Matthew 1:2-17 against his genealogy in Luke 3:23-38. Matthew lists the ancestors of Jesus in blocks of fourteen (a multiple of the frequently cited number seven) and concludes with the statement, "So all the generations from Abraham to David are fourteen generations; from David to the deportation to Babylon, fourteen generations; and from the deportation to Babylon to the Messiah, fourteen generations" (Mt 1:17). The narrative goal here is to make it clear that Jesus is the fulfillment of the promises to Abraham, the messianic promise of David's monarchy, and the true solution to the exile. And Matthew uses his genealogical data brilliantly to accomplish that end. But Luke lists twenty-one generations (also a reflex of seven) between Jesus and the exile (Zerubbabel in Lk 3:27), and twenty-one more to David (3:31). Moreover, the names Luke has selected to represent his generations are almost entirely distinct from Matthew's. We also know from 1 and 2 Kings that Matthew omits Ahaziah, Joash, Amaziah and Jehoiakim in his reckoning of David's line. Should we conclude, therefore, that Matthew and Luke were irresponsible historians? Or, worse, that one was a charlatan? No. We should instead recognize that both of these biblical writers were working from the same pool of information, but that the genre of genealogy was flexible. Thus both authors have adapted the list of Jesus' human ancestors according to their particular narrative and theological goals. R. K. Harrison puts it this way:

> The aim of such genealogies was to establish the general line of descent from given ancestors, and this objective was in no way impaired by the omission of certain generations as long as the line was being traced properly . . . all members of a particular line were not necessarily equal in importance, and because of that principle, as well as for other reasons, certain names and generations could be omitted from family lists without prejudice to either the intent or the accuracy of content of the genealogy.[6]

Note as well that the genealogies of Genesis—which are critical to most attempts to date Eden—have been schematized such that there are ten generations from Adam to Noah, and ten more to Abraham. The narrative goal here is to highlight Adam, Noah and Abraham as major players in the story of redemption, the human representatives of the major junctions in God's relationship with humanity.[7] Notice as well that Enoch, who is special in that he is the only one of the pre-flood heroes not to die, is placed in the seventh slot between Adam and Noah and lives 365 years. Not only is the number seven symbolic, 365 is the same number as the days in a solar year.[8] We also find that both Noah and Terah's genealogies conclude with the report of the birth of three sons to the respective patriarch (Gen 5:32; 11:27). If read without any nuance, the reader would have to conclude that each of these patriarchs had three sons born in the same year! Then, of course, there are the enormous ages which the pre-flood patriarchs of Genesis are recorded to have lived—numbers which we now anticipate from surrounding literature communicated many messages besides simple year tallies and/or calendration.[9] So although it would seem that the date of creation could be identified just by adding up the ages listed in the genealogies in Genesis and tying those totals to dates in the later history of Israel that we can set within our own calendar system, it is actually not that simple at all. Rather, we now know that the genealogies of Genesis are not exhaustive. Moreover the numbers named have very complex messages, and much of what the ancients were doing with their genealogies is simply beyond our current intellectual reach. Bishop Ussher (from whom the 4004 B.C. creation date initially derived) could not have known these things in the sixteenth century.[10] Hence,

> Quite obviously a person such as Archbishop Ussher, who assumed that the Genesis genealogies were complete and proceeded to date terrestrial creation in 4004 B.C., was totally unaware of the rationale of ancient techniques of genealogical compilation, and the consequent pitfalls awaiting uninstructed occidental investigators.[11]

Thus we have to conclude that the Bible is not offering us a date for Eden. And as the Bible offers no date for Eden, we will not attempt to assign a date for Eden either. Rather, we will do our best to read the genealogies of the Bible as they were intended, as a generalized chronological tool that served to highlight key players (cf. the Genesis genealogies) and key themes (cf. the Matthew genealogy) in the story.

Noah (Genesis 6–11). Our next benchmark is Noah. Again, a figure we cannot date, but one whose era was critical to redemptive history. By the time of Noah, the human race had developed to the point of true civilization and had deteriorated to the point where God's only solution was to wash the world clean and start again (Gen 6:5-7). How long it took for humanity to achieve civilization the Bible doesn't say, but it must have been a very long time indeed. As we will investigate in the chapter on Noah, the flood served as the great "epoch divider"—a catastrophic event that marked the transition from the Adamic Age to the current one. With the flood the mysteries of the ancient past end, God's recreational covenant is articulated, and the world casts its eyes to the offspring of Noah's chosen son Shem for the salvation of our fallen race.

Abraham (Genesis 12–50). Abraham is the offspring of Shem and the next step in God's redemptive plan. He is known as "the father of the Jews" because his descendants will become the nation of Israel. With

Abraham we at last step into datable history. At some point around 2000 B.C., Abraham's father Terah decides to leave his home city of Ur (and therefore his clan and patrimony) and migrate to the land of Canaan. Ur is not a fictional site, by the way. Rather, this huge and hugely sophisticated urban center was the political hub of lower Mesopotamia in the late third millennium. In fact, an entire period of Mesopotamian history is named for the city—the "Ur III period" (2112–2004 B.C.). This era of civilization and this urban center experienced a traumatic collapse in 2004 B.C. Perhaps this collapse was the catalyst for a larger migration of which Abraham's family might have been a part. Whatever the catalyst, the Bible tells us that Terah and his extended family left their patrimony and traveled to Haran (Gen 11:31), there Abraham separated from his extended family to bring his own *bêt ʾāb* to Canaan (Gen 12:1). As we will see in the next section on "real space," Abraham's migration followed a very predictable route along the established highways of his day. Eventually, Abraham and Sarah are blessed with the promised son, Isaac. To Isaac is born Jacob (whom God renames "Israel") and Esau. And outside of Jacob's twenty-year sojourn near Haran (Gen 28:10–31:55), Abraham's offspring continue to dwell in Canaan as successful nomadic pastoralists. The family grows. And with Jacob's twelve sons, the clan expands to seventy persons in all (Gen 46:27; Ex 1:5). Not bad for a senior citizen with a post-menopausal wife!

It is these seventy persons who follow Joseph down into Egypt and set up housekeeping in the eastern Nile Delta, a region the Bible knows as Goshen. For several generations Abraham's offspring live in Egypt in peace. But according to Exodus 1:8 there came a day when "a new king arose over Egypt, who did not know Joseph." This shift in leadership marked a harsh transition for Abraham's children. These once welcomed guests are now viewed as a threat to national security. As a result the Israelites are marginalized and subjugated, eventually becoming one of the slave races that make Pharaoh's enormous building projects possible. But God sees their affliction, hears their cry and sends a savior: Moses.

Moses (Exodus–Judges). The child of a Hebrew, but raised with the advantages of Egyptian royalty, Moses becomes God's man for God's hour. Having been driven from Egypt because of his loyalty to his own people,

Yahweh waylays him in the wilderness and sends him back into what most sane people would identify as an impossible situation. But God specializes in such things. You know the story. Confronting the power of Egypt's magicians and priests with the power of the Almighty, making a parody of the authority of Pharaoh by means of the authority of the Lord of the cosmos, miraculously, Moses leads God's people out of slavery and into a new life. And when the sea parts, tens of thousands of the offspring of Abraham step into freedom on dry ground. At Sinai this group is transformed into a nation, and the journey to the Promised Land begins.

The journey is not easy as there is a lot of purging that has to happen before Abraham's offspring are worthy of the land promised. But finally, after a generation in the wilderness, Moses transfers the mantle of leadership to Joshua, and under his command the Israelites enter Canaan. Thus the struggle to drive out the Canaanites and secure the land begins, a struggle that will be ongoing through the era of the judges and will finally reach resolution under the monarchy. Hence, the section of our timeline we will assign to Moses includes the exodus, the wanderings, the conquest and settlement, and the period of the judges. Our next benchmark is David.

David (1 Samuel–2 Chronicles). Most of us have known about the young shepherd boy who challenged a giant since we were young shepherd boys and girls ourselves. His simple confidence in, and unwavering loyalty to, his God is what made this man great. David is born into an era in which Israel has not yet evolved into a centralized government. Rather, the nation is still governed through its tribal leaders, still fighting its wars by means of voluntary conscription, and still living very separate lives within their respective tribal territories. But the people begin to call for a king. Their hope is that a king will end their vulnerability to foreign oppression. Their first choice is a man who looks the part, Saul the Benjaminite. But Saul turns out to be a horrid disappointment, and Yahweh removes him and appoints David the Judahite in his place. With David the actual dynasty begins. He conquers Jerusalem and makes it Israel's capital city. He brings the tabernacle into Jerusalem and starts plans for the construction of the temple—making it clear to all Israel who the true king of Israel is. David is so successful that he becomes the paradigmatic king of Israelite history, as is obvious by the fact that every subsequent king is compared for good or for ill to David. And because of his loyalty to his God, from his ascension to Israel's throne in approximately 1000 B.C. until the demise of the southern kingdom in 586 B.C., one may find a child of David on Jerusalem's throne.

Summary. Thus we have our five benchmarks that lead us through biblical history: Adam, Noah, Abraham, Moses and David. Anyone can memorize these five names, and by doing so a plethora of biblical detail is placed into chronological order. As we will explore in the next chapter, these same benchmarks place the Old Testament into theological order as well. More on that later. For now, let's switch our focus to the story of Israel through the lens of real space.

SPACE

I once heard a student say that they were still recovering from their junior high geography class. Considering that I teach graduate students, whose average age is thirty-something, this is a sad statement indeed. So I want you to know that I understand that geography is a trauma-inducing topic for some folks. My hope is that our excursion into real space in these next few pages will aid you in your catharsis as opposed to adding further damage to an old injury!

Why do geography? Because the biblical stories happened in real space, and that space affected the choices and actions of the players as well as the plot line of the drama. It makes a difference that Sinai is located in no man's land, miles and miles away from any known urban center. It makes a difference that you can drive from Jerusalem to Jericho in a slow car in forty-five minutes, but that your ears will pop all along the way because of the dramatic shift in elevation. It even makes a difference that the Jordan River is neither deep nor wide and "mount" Zion would not qualify as a respectable sledding hill in some parts of New England. For me, it was when a seminary professor required actual map tests (oh, the pain) that these narratives came to life. And I want the same for you (not the pain part). Now please don't panic thinking that the goal is to master all the geographic detail of the Old Testament. But as some basic geographical information will transform the way you read this book, we are going to organize ourselves around three general regions: Mesopotamia (which housed the nations of Assyria and Babylonia), Israel (which is also known as Canaan and Palestine) and Egypt. All of these regions may be found in the Fertile Crescent.

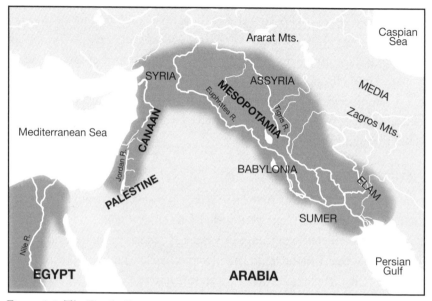

Figure 2.2. The Fertile Crescent

The region you see highlighted in figure 2.2 is the Fertile Crescent. This is where all of the narratives of the Old Testament take place. It is called the Fertile Crescent because—you guessed it—it is fertile and shaped like a crescent. What made this region fertile was water. The Tigris and Euphrates rivers toward the east, the Jordan in the center and the Nile in the west transformed desert and stone into farmland and pasturage. And this swath of habitable and arable land served as the backdrop to the peoples and narratives of the Old Testament. To the east is our first geographical benchmark: Mesopotamia.

Mesopotamia. The name Mesopotamia means "the land between the rivers" (Greek *mesos* = "in the middle" + *potamos* = "river"). Indeed it was the Tigris and Euphrates Rivers that made it possible for this region to host some of the most ancient (and most advanced) civilizations on the planet. The first of these was the nation of Sumer in the south. Here writing was first developed in c. 3200 B.C., and staggering achievements in science and literature were accomplished thousands of years before the Israelites entered the scene. Many historians go so far as to speak of Sumer as the "cradle of civilization." The Bible says the same—this is where the story begins.

As Genesis tells us, Adam and Eve are placed in a garden, "toward the east" where the rivers Tigris and Euphrates may be found (Gen 2:8-9). Although it is probable that the Bible's description of Eden is intended as a microcosm of the entire pre-Fall planet, it is obvious that the biblical writers are thinking about Mesopotamia when they speak of the origins of the human race.

Mesopotamia is also the setting for Noah's flood. Due to the fact that the southern reaches of the (often turbulent) Tigris and Euphrates Rivers were separated only by a low-lying alluvial plain, this region frequently experienced catastrophic flooding. The Sumerian King's List

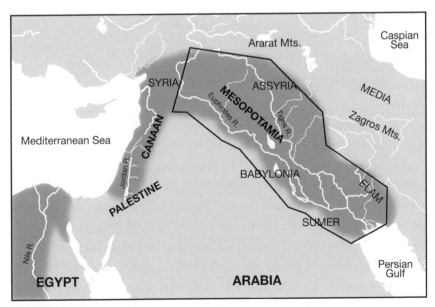

Figure 2.3. Mesopotamia

(an ancient piece of literature we will discuss further in the chapter on Noah) actually organizes Mesopotamia's early history around an epoch-dividing deluge. This same flood is reflected in the famous Gilgamesh

Epic and the stories of Atrahasis. Archaeology has identified several catastrophic floods in Mesopotamia's early history. We also find that the Ararat Mountains (the mountain range upon which Noah's ark finally came to rest in Gen 8:4) are just north of Mesopotamia. So Mesopotamia is also the land of Noah's flood. The biblical writers apparently understand this same region as the setting for the Tower of Babel, as the Bible tells us the tower was built in the "Plain of Shinar" (Gen 11:1-3)—a term broadly recognized as a reference to the plain between the two rivers. So we find that the earliest accounts of the biblical story are set in our first geographical benchmark: Mesopotamia. In fact, the narrative stays in Mesopotamia until a certain citizen of Ur answers the call to migrate west—Abraham.

Departing from his hometown of Ur, Abraham follows one of the major highways of his day (which of course followed the watered areas of the Fertile Crescent) in his migration to a second major urban center, Haran. From Haran, Abraham leaves his clan behind and strikes out toward the Promised Land. This is our second geographical benchmark, the land of Canaan/Israel/Palestine.

Canaan. Canaan is the land that will become Israel and will eventually be known as Palestine. The significance of this region does not come from its size, resources or political history, all of which were unimpressive at best. Rather, the significance of this region comes from its strategic position. Canaan served as the only land bridge between the two great civilizations of the ancient Near East: Mesopotamia and Egypt. Any military activity or trade exchanged between Egypt and Mesopotamia had to pass through Canaan. Thus these larger kingdoms were always interested in controlling this territory both for trade and as a military buffer zone.

The good news about Canaan's identity as a "crossroad" is that the peoples of Canaan were regularly exposed to the newest technologies of their day as Egypt and the nations of Mesopotamia exchanged their goods and services. The bad news is that our heroes regularly got the snot beaten out of them as first this superpower and then that superpower rolled through their territory pursuing an opponent. Interesting is the fact that this land bridge served the animal kingdom as well. Because it was the only natural throughway between the continents where water might be found, ancient

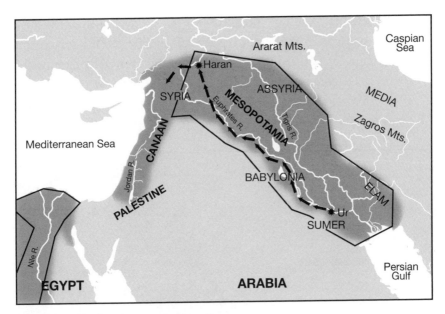

Figure 2.4. Abraham's migration into Canaan

Canaan was populated with an array of exotic species. Prior to extinction (caused by intensive hunting), the lion, tiger, bear, antelope, wild ox, fallow deer, ostrich, crocodile and hippopotamus could be found in this narrow swath of land.

The Bible tells us that Abraham spent most of his life in Canaan as a pastoral nomad. This means that Abraham and his household fed and watered their large flocks of sheep and goats by following the seasonal pasturage of the region in what was probably a carefully planned and annually repeated migratory route. And as was characteristic of the pastoral nomadism of his day, Abraham had regular contact with the urban centers of Canaan. The economic reason for this was trade. Whereas Abraham had animal products to sell, the farmers and craftsmen attached to the cities had grain and other products Abraham's family needed. The cities most often named are Shechem, Bethel, Jerusalem, Hebron and Beer-sheba. When these cities are imposed upon a map of second millennium highways and trade routes, we find that they are all located in the central hill country, upon a watershed route known as the Central Ridge Route or the National Highway (see figure 2.5).[12] Here Abraham and his clan fol-

lowed the seasonal pasturage necessary for the survival of their livestock
and did business with the urban centers named above. One reason this
is interesting to us is that the central hill country eventually became the
backbone of Israelite settlement. Thus the very stretch of land traversed
by Abraham would one day be the heartland of Israel (cf. Gen 15:18; Deut
11:23; Josh 1:4).

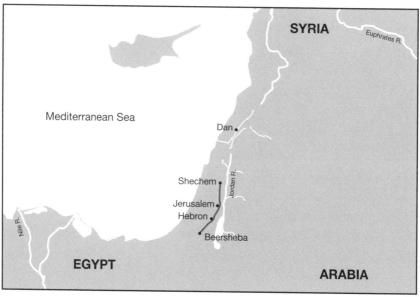

Figure 2.5. Abraham's ridge route in Canaan

Egypt. After several generations in Canaan, Abraham's kin found their
way to our third geographic region, Egypt. Who hasn't heard the story of
Joseph and his special coat? This garment was given to Joseph to demonstrate to the world that Joseph held special favor in his father's eyes. Unfortunately, Joseph's brothers were crystal clear regarding that message.
So when Joseph was sent to check on his older brothers, who were tending
the family's flocks near Dothan (Gen 37:17), his brothers see this as their
chance to get rid of "the little brat" and conspire to murder their brother.
With a little time and conversation, the brothers reconsider their plan and
decide instead upon an equally devastating but less violent plan—to sell
the boy. Dothan was an important junction between the highways of the
East and the major coastal highway to Egypt (the Via Maris). Thus, the

fact that a caravan was passing through (a caravan that might be interested in purchasing a young Semitic slave) is no surprise. So the jealous brothers seize the moment, and Joseph's comfortable life is shattered forever as twenty silver shekels change hands.

Joseph dwells in Egypt for many years—first as the slave of Potiphar, then as a prisoner and finally as the vizier of all Egypt. What an amazing story of God's ability to restore years devoured by bad decisions and bad circumstances. Joseph thought that he had lost everything and every opportunity for anything, but in one sovereign sweep of his hand, Yahweh restores it all: success, reputation, wealth, spouse, children . . . even Joseph's beloved father.

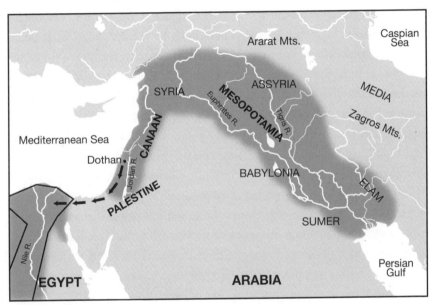

Figure 2.6. Joseph's journey to Egypt

Hear the emotion of this story. When Jacob's ten sons return from purchasing grain in Egypt, they carry a report that their father could not believe: "Joseph is alive and is the ruler of all Egypt!" Jacob's response? "His heart grew numb" (Gen 45:26). This father had lost his child at least twenty years prior with the only clue to Joseph's fate being the torn and bloodied coat Jacob had lovingly bestowed upon him. It is not hard to imagine this heartbroken father sitting evening after evening, staring hopelessly at the horizon, hoping, willing, begging for that familiar silhouette to step over the hill. In my mind's eye I can see him inquiring of every passing caravan, searching in every town, sending messengers to everyone he knew. "Have you seen my child? Do you have any news of his fate?" Joseph was lost, probably dead, and Jacob had not been there to defend him. This ancient story is easily translated into the countless photos each of us has seen of missing children . . . and the desperate parents whose hearts will never rest again. "It is enough," Jacob says, "Joseph is still alive. I will go and see him before I die" (Gen 45:28). And so Abraham's kin, seventy souls in all, came to Egypt (Gen 46:27).

For more than four hundred years, Jacob's offspring live in the land of Egypt. Joseph settles them in Goshen, a region in the eastern Nile Delta. Here a number of Semitic settlements have been identified, settlements in which pastoralists from the land of Canaan had built new lives for themselves in Egypt's primarily agricultural economy (we will discuss this further in the chapter on Moses). But as we have reviewed above, there came a day when a new administration emerged in the land of Egypt, and Jacob's offspring became *personas non grata*. Thus our heroes (and those like them) are renamed "slave," and their lives become progressively intolerable. Eventually we read of Pharaoh's decision to control the growth of his slave race by slaughtering their male children. Pharaoh's program of extermination was so effective that one mother decided that her three-month-old son had a better chance of survival floating down a crocodile-laden river in a homemade basket than in her arms. God delivered the baby . . . and his people. He heard their cry, remembered his covenant with Abraham, and sent Israel a savior, Moses.

By the mighty hand of God, Moses leads his people out of Egypt. Keep in mind that the quickest way out of Egypt would have been north, along the same coastal highway Joseph had traveled. This highway ran from Egypt, through Canaan and on to regions north and east. From Egypt to Canaan it was known as the "Way of the Land of the Philistines" (Ex 13:17). Using this highway, a group such as the Israelites could have reached Canaan easily in three weeks. But as the Bible says, even though this route was "near," it was massively fortified (it was actually the launch point for the Egyptian military).[13] Thus, if they had traveled along a northern route, the Israelites would have had to fight their way out of Egypt, and they simply were not ready for that (Ex 13:17). So God led them east and south.

Now Egypt's eastern frontier was also sealed against entry (and exit), by a series of fortifications—walls, towers, lakes and canals which ran from the Mediterranean to the Red Sea. But by passing *through* the Red Sea (actually "Reed Sea"[14]) Moses circumvents this eastern defense system, setting the Israelites on an unimpeded path south. Thus Moses heads east and south into no man's land and initiates the formation and reformation of the people of God.

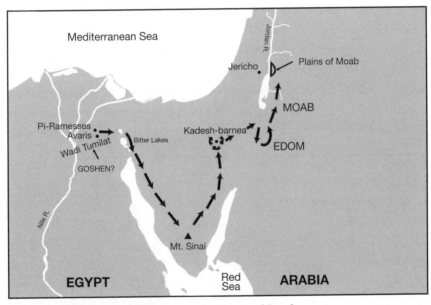

Figure 2.7. The exodus and journey to the Promised Land

After a three-month journey, the children of Abraham reach their goal, Mount Sinai (Ex 19:1). Here they will stay for one full year, receiving and embracing the covenant of Yahweh with all of its stipulations and blessings (Num 10:11). Here a people who were not a people become the people of God. Half of the book of Exodus, all of Leviticus and the first ten chapters of Numbers are dedicated to the sojourn at this mountain.

When it is done, Israel heads north, bound for the Promised Land.

But Israel fails repeatedly in her new commitments, and what should have been a journey of a few weeks turns into a generation of wandering (primarily in the region of Kadesh Barnea; cf. Num 14; Deut 1:2, 34-46). But at last the day dawns when Yahweh says, "You have circled this mountain long enough. Now turn north" (Deut 2:3). So heading north through Edom, Moab and parts of Ammon, they finally settle upon the Plains of Moab to receive Moses' final word to them (captured in the book of Deuteronomy). Here Moses transfers his position of leadership to Joshua, and Israel begins to make preparations for the conquest of the Promised Land.

Canaan revisited. Under Joshua's leadership the tribes of Israel cross the Jordan River and reenter the Promised Land. Their successful assault on Jericho is followed by a central, southern and northern campaign, which carves out territory for the tribes of Israel in the new region. As the books of Judges and Joshua tell us, Israel will spend the next several hundred years wrestling the indigenous people for ascendancy in the land and true control of their tribal allotments. One of the outgrowths of this struggle is the perception that a monarchy (as opposed to the tribal confederation

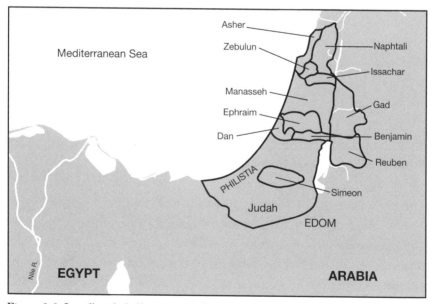

Figure 2.8. Israel's tribal allotments in Canaan

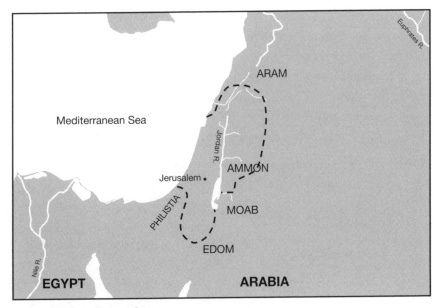

Figure 2.9. David's kingdom

they have been) will tip the scale in Israel's favor. And so in 1 Samuel 8 we read of the people's demand for a king and the appointment of Saul as their first monarch.

Although Saul is called and confirmed as the first king of Israel, it is David who will truly establish Israel's monarchy. Succeeding where Saul failed, David beats back Israel's enemies, expands its territory and brings peace to the land. David's exceptional military talent, followed by Solomon's impressive administrative skill, establish the legacy of the united monarchy. And at last Israel gains control of all the land promised to Abraham "from the river of Egypt as far as the great river, the river Euphrates" (Gen 15:18).

But the success of David's dynasty is fleeting. Under David's grandson Rehoboam the age-old fissure between the northern and southern tribes erupts, and the country is torn apart by civil war. This rupture marks the birth of the divided kingdom (931 B.C.), a breach from which the country will never recover. From 931 B.C. onward there are two countries: Israel in the north ruled by a succession of kings and dynasties, and Judah in the south ruled by the Davidic dynasty. The division weakens both nations and leaves the north (where the temple is not) with a syncretistic form of Israelite religion that inspires the rage of the prophets. As I often tell my students, there is no other period in Israelite history that is more confusing to the typical layperson than the divided monarchy. Most do not even realize that there *were* two kingdoms. So when the average reader reaches 1 and 2 Kings, and the Bible begins to speak of "Israel" (the north) and "Judah" (the south), while referring to both nations together as "Israel"—

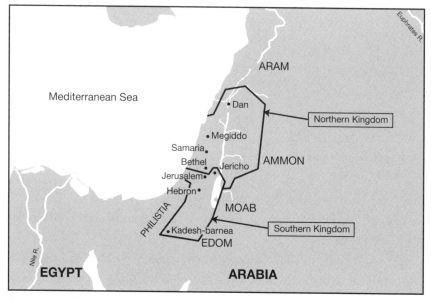

Figure 2.10. The divided monarchy

that reader is lost. Add to this overlapping terminology a steady stream of unpronounceable royal names and a narrative structure that first tells the story of the southern king, then the northern king and then circles back again, and confusion reigns. I hope I can help with that. For now, recognize that there was a divided monarchy. See the division of land in figure 2.10 and know that the temple and David's dynasty continue in the south in Jerusalem.

Mesopotamia revisited. As your timeline illustrates (fig. 2.1), both the northern and southern kingdoms eventually become the victims of conquest and exile. In 722 b.c. the Mesopotamian superpower, Assyria, captures Samaria (the capital city of the northern kingdom), and drags off the populace to the far reaches of the Fertile Crescent. Second Kings 17 reports that this catastrophe was due to Israel's unrelenting rebellion against their God. The result? The ten "lost tribes" of Israel who will never return home again.

One hundred and thirty years later, the southern kingdom suffers a similar fate. By now the superpower is another Mesopotamian nation, Babylonia. After years of warnings through his servants the prophets and a myriad of second chances, at last the covenant curse is enacted, and David's kingdom is swept off into exile by the tidal wave of Nebuchadnezzar II's forces. For nearly two generations the survivors will live as exiles in a foreign land. But unlike the northern kingdom, the remnant of the faithful in Babylonia will return.

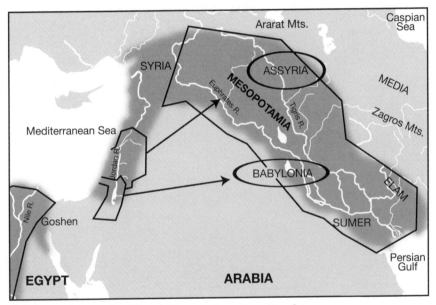

Figure 2.11. The exile of the northern and southern kingdoms

In 538 B.C. the day of promise comes, and those who had once been known as "Israelites," now known as "Jews," are released to go home. Although only a fraction of those who had been taken had the courage to return to the land of Israel, enough came to rebuild the covenant community in and around Jerusalem. And under the leadership of Ezra, Nehemiah and the post-exilic prophets, the Jewish community is reformed and a temple rebuilt. This era of Israelite history is known as the "Second Temple" or "postexilic" period, and it is the era of the birth of the modern religion of Judaism. It is into this community—stripped of so much that it was—that the Messiah will be born.

CONCLUSIONS

Whew! You have just traversed the most treacherous section of the great barrier, the real time and space of the Old Testament. I hope this synopsis has given you a feel for the real people and real places of the story. And if you are still reading, apparently the journey has not done too much injury. Five central characters (Adam, Noah, Abraham, Moses and David) organize the plotline. Three general areas (Mesopotamia, Israel and Egypt) set the stage. How is your closet coming?

THE CONCEPT OF COVENANT

The "General Law" That Holds Our Facts Together

IN THE INTRODUCTION TO THIS BOOK, I promised you a solution to the dysfunctional closet syndrome. Now that we have navigated the great barrier, it is time to start getting organized—get the clothes up off the floor, get some hangers and hooks and get to work. The "general law" we will use to give order to the whole is one of the general laws that the Old Testament writers used to give order to their collection of documents: the concept of *covenant*. As stated in the introduction, the biblical writers were theologians. Contrary to popular opinion, they did not write this amazing book in some haphazard fashion, nor did they function merely as mindless stenographers. No, the biblical writers consciously organized their material in a systematic fashion in order to communicate certain central truths. What we want to do, then, is to rediscover their system and allow *their* system to organize *our* closets.

I stand on the shoulders of many scholars before me when I make the claim that covenant is a major structuring principle of our Scriptures.[1] This is most obvious in the fact that the two divisions of our book are known as the Old and New "Covenants." (Although English speakers know their Bibles as the Old and New "Testaments," the actual term behind our English convention is the Greek word *diathēkē*, which is a

translation of Hebrew *bĕrît*, both of which mean "covenant."[2]) We have
already seen that the real time of the Old Testament narrative is structured around five central figures who stood at critical junctures in the
history of God's people: Adam, Noah, Abraham, Moses and David. In
this chapter we will begin to explore the fact that the *theology* of the Old
Testament is organized around these same five figures. Most specifically,
around five covenantal interactions—the agreement with Adam and Eve
in Eden, with Noah after the flood, with Abraham regarding his descendants and the land of Canaan, with Moses and Israel at Mount Sinai and
with David regarding his dynasty. Indeed, "[t]he literary legacy of ancient
Israel is incomprehensible apart from covenant theology."[3]

So what is a covenant? As with the word *redemption*, this term has
become "Biblish" in the Christian community—so overused and poorly
understood that much of its meaning has been lost. Yet also like the word
redemption, we find that the etymological roots of this term are ancient,
packed with significance and completely secular in their original associations. In its native context a covenant (Hebrew *bĕrît*) was "an agreement
enacted between two parties in which one or both make promises under
oath to perform or refrain from certain actions stipulated in advance."[4]
In other words, a covenant was much like a contract. These agreements
could be made at the individual, tribal or national level. An example of
a covenant at the individual level is Abraham's interaction with a senior
servant of his household in Genesis 24. Isaac and Abimelech's agreement
in Genesis 26:26-33 is an example of a covenant made at the clan or tribal
level—as is Jacob and Laban's pact in Genesis 31:43-54. The treaty between Joshua and the Gibeonites (Josh 9–10) is an example of a covenant
between nations. It is this international level of alliance that is of most interest to us. But before we launch into the details, let's first investigate the
worldview that lay behind the idea of covenant-making in Israel's world.

FICTIVE KINSHIP

The ideological foundation for the concept of covenant-making in the
ancient Near East was an idea we now know as "fictive kinship." As
discussed in chapter one, in Israel's patriarchal culture an individual's
privileges and responsibilities within the *bêt 'āb*, the clan, the tribe and

the larger society were predetermined by their lineage, gender and birth order. The patriarch exercised the highest level of authority within the *bêt ʾāb;* he also bore the highest level of responsibility. Among the children, although all males inherited, the firstborn received a double portion. In return for this privilege came the burden of increased responsibility. This is evident in the New Testament story of the prodigal son. What does the eldest say? "Look! For so many years I have been serving you and I have never neglected a command of yours!" (Lk 15:29). As the eldest, you can be sure that all his life he had pulled the heaviest work detail, the largest share of household chores, the closest scrutiny of his father's watchful eye. No wonder this firstborn is angry with his younger brother who has squandered his part of the family estate and is now further endangering the economic well-being of the *bêt ʾāb* by his return. Or think of Jacob's twelve sons. When the brothers conspire to murder Joseph, who intervenes? Reuben, the eldest (Gen 37:18-22). He convinces the others to leave Joseph in a dry cistern, out of which Reuben intends to rescue him. When Reuben returns to find the cistern empty (as the brothers had sold Joseph to the caravaneers), he tears his garments and cries out: "The boy is not there; as for me, where am I to go?" (Gen 37:30). How will this eldest son explain to his father that he has failed to protect his younger brother? Or think of Boaz's declaration in response to Ruth's request for redemption that "there is a relative closer than I" (Ruth 3:12). You get the picture—one's level of responsibility toward another member of the society (and privilege with that individual) was determined by blood. The more closely related, the greater the responsibility; the more distantly related, the lesser the responsibility.

This was how the ancients ordered their world. Again, we are not called to imitate this culture, but we are called to understand it. And one important question we need to ask in light of this societal organization is: How might a person go about establishing a relationship of privilege and responsibility with someone who was non-kin? Most simply answered, that person would have to *make* kin out of nonkin. This was accomplished by means of fictive kinship. By means of oath the people of Israel's world understood that a fictive kinship bond could be established by which both parties agreed to act like family. Frank Cross puts it this way: "In tribal societies there were legal mechanisms or devices—we might even say legal fictions—by which outsiders, non-kin, might be incorporated into the kinship group."[5] Hence, on the individual, tribal and, eventually, national level, if you needed someone to *act* like a family member, and you were willing to give that person the privileges of family in return, you would invite that individual (tribe or nation) into a covenant agreement which created *fictional* kinship. Perhaps the easiest way for us twenty-first-century types to understand this sort of arrangement is to think in terms of marriage and adoption. Even in our present, nontribal societies we understand the notion of making someone family who was previously non-family, simply by means of a legal agreement. By claiming someone biologically unrelated to me as my child or my spouse, I am also legally binding myself to care for that individual as if they were related to me. Are the legal responsibilities of an adoptive parent any less than those of a biological parent? Of course not. Rather, by means of a legal agreement, two unrelated individuals become family and bear all the responsibilities and privileges that lie therein. This is fictive kinship, and this is the concept which made covenant-making in the ancient Near East ideologically possible. By means of covenant, nations could establish a relationship of fictive kinship, thereby securing from one another the privileges and responsibilities necessary for international relations.

COVENANT-MAKING IN THE ANCIENT NEAR EAST

The political landscape of the ancient Near East was cluttered with dozens of petty kings and kingdoms—so many people groups, so little space, such limited resources. In Israel's day Egypt and Mesopotamia were the superpowers. The nations which evolved in these two regions typically controlled a lot of real estate. In contrast, Israel's territory (also known as Canaan or Palestine) was an area of great political diversity and small landholdings. In the days of the divided monarchy this tiny strip of land housed the Israelites, Judahites, Philistines, Phoenicians, Aramaens, Amonites, Moabites, Edomites and a dozen other smaller tribal groups whose territory we have difficulty delineating. As we learned in chapter two, although small and gifted with few natural resources, this territory was critically important because it served as the land bridge between the two great superpowers. Because of Canaan's significance to international trade and warfare, these larger nations regularly vied for control of the region. Thus Canaan was a region of great political diversity and frequent conflict. Because of this perennially insecure situation, it was not at all uncommon for the smaller kingdoms of the Levant to either unite as allies in order to defend themselves against one of the superpowers or to subjugate themselves to one of the superpowers in order to protect themselves from smaller and larger nations alike. It was also quite common for one of the superpowers to "invite" (translate "force") these lesser kingdoms into an alliance in order to secure their travel/trade routes and to ensure the income of regular tribute. Thus we are left with two sorts of international alliances common to the ancient Near East: the parity treaty (a treaty made between equals) and what the literature names the suzerain/vassal treaty (a treaty made between greater and lesser powers).

In a parity treaty the responsibilities of both parties were typically limited to military alliance against an outsider. Any enemy that attempted to infiltrate the region would be met with an "all for one, one for all" response on the part of the various petty kings and chieftains of that region. If one was attacked, all came to defend. Or if a superpower was on the move, all allied to resist. These treaties might also involve freedom of passage through an ally's territory for the sake of trade, but they rarely infringed on the personal freedoms of any of the covenant partners. In this sort of treaty the covenant partners spoke of each other as "brothers." Here we see the influence of fictive kinship. In order to define the manner in which the partners were bound to one another, the ancients resorted to the metaphor of family: we will behave *as though* we are brothers.

The suzerain/vassal treaty was a horse of a different color. Here one party was clearly more powerful than the other and therefore had the right to demand submission on the part of his weaker ally. As a result, in this sort of treaty the partners referred to each other either as "father and son," or as "lord and servant." Again, the metaphor of family was used to explain the political relationship established. In this sort of covenant the suzerain had authority over the land and people of the vassal nation. Although the suzerain typically allowed his vassal to continue to rule his own people (and thereby maintain his own government and traditions), legally the suzerain owned all of the vassal's land and produce. The responsibilities of a suzerain in this sort of arrangement always involved military protection. If the vassal was threatened by a domestic rebellion or foreign assault, the suzerain was expected to step in and defend. It was also common for a suzerain to initiate this relationship by gifting his vassal with land. Hence, often the vassal owed his territory and even his throne to the suzerain. If the vassal broke covenant, he forfeited his land grant.[6] A highly effective means of insuring loyalty! What did the vassal promise in return? Tribute. A vassal was expected to pay an annual percentage of his gross national product to his overlord. In fact, when a vassal wished to rebel against his overlord, he often did so simply by withholding tribute. The late second-millennium-B.C. treaty between Duppi-Teshub (king of Amurru land) and his Hittite overlord, Mursilis, is an example. Here we see that Duppi-Teshub vowed three hundred shekels of "refined and first-class gold" annually in response to Mursilis' past gifts and promise of ongoing military protection. In the historical prologue of this particular covenant, King Mursilis speaks warmly of Duppi-Teshub's father (the previous vassal) who never failed to bring this same tribute, "year for year; he never refused it."[7]

A vassal also owed his suzerain military assistance. Whenever requested, the vassal was expected to field his army in order to assist in the wars of his overlord and to do whatever was necessary to facilitate the success of his lord's army when in the vassal's territory (i.e., open passage, supplies, housing, etc.[8]). Most critical to these sorts of covenants was the vassal's commitment to consummate loyalty. A vassal could not make a treaty with any other suzerain. Such an arrangement would be, by definition, treason. Hence, Mursilis commands Duppi-Teshub: "Do not turn your eyes to anyone else!"[9] The penalty should Duppi-Teshub make an alliance elsewhere? "May these gods of the oath destroy Duppi-Teshub together with his person, his wife, his son, his grandson, his house, his land and together with everything that he owns!"[10] It was understood that whereas a king might have multiple partners in a parity treaty, a vassal could have only one suzerain. In the Bible, the term for this sort of loyalty is *ḥesed*. This term appears so often in the Old Testament that an array of terms are used to translate it—"love, lovingkindness, mercy, faithfulness, etc." But the best translation of this term is simply "covenant faithfulness."[11] This is the type of loyalty that comes from blood; it is what a firstborn owes his father. If a vassal dared to make a *běrît* with another suzerain—an unthinkable situation within the family metaphor—he had committed high treason, and he would pay.[12]

What examples of this sort of covenant-making do we have in the Bible? Probably the most helpful example of such an international agreement is the story of Joshua and the Gibeonites (Joshua 9–10). Here Joshua has just captured the first two cities on his itinerary for the conquest of the Promised Land, Jericho and Ai. Having heard of Joshua's exploits, the Gibeonites realize that their city-state lies directly in Joshua's path and that they have two options: find a way to make peace with the Israelites . . . or die. So the Gibeonites opt for a ruse. Packing stale bread and worn-out gear, they trick Joshua into believing that they live well outside the Promised Land (as opposed to six miles northwest of Jerusalem) and could therefore be legitimate allies to him (Josh 9:12-14). What they wanted from Joshua was a treaty: "We are your servants; now then, make a covenant [lit. "cut a *běrît*"] with us" (Josh 9:11). Pay attention to the language here. By claiming to be Joshua's "servants," the Gibeonites are inviting Joshua to become their suzerain. Moreover, the Gibeonites use the standard idiom for establishing a treaty—"cut a *běrît*." This language reflects the fact that all covenants were sealed by oath and sacrifice. The "cutting" has to do with the ritual presentation of the sacrificed animal. Joshua fails to consult Yahweh (never a good move) and "made peace with them and made a covenant with them, to let them live; and the leaders of the congregation swore an oath to them" (Josh 9:15). Thus by oath Joshua becomes Gibeon's suzerain and the standard responsibilities are implied.

But it turns out that the Gibeonites had lied to Joshua. They did not live "far away" as they had assured him; rather, they lived right next door. *And* Gibeon was apparently already allied with the kings of central Canaan in a parity treaty. Thus, upon hearing of Gibeon's new alliance with the invading Israelites, the Canaanite lord of Jerusalem does what any king would do in such an instance—he calls upon his allies to attack the defecting treaty-partner. "Come up to me and help me, and let us attack Gibeon, for it has made peace with Joshua and with the sons of Israel" (Josh 10:4). In response, five Canaanite kings march against their previous ally and besiege the city of Gibeon. The king of Gibeon responds as would any endangered vassal: he calls upon his suzerain lord for aid.

> Then the men of Gibeon sent word to Joshua to the camp at Gilgal, saying, "Do not abandon your servants; come up to us quickly and save us and help us, for all the kings of the Amorites that live in the hill country have assembled against us." (Josh 10:6)

Even though his oath had been secured under pretense, Joshua did what a faithful suzerain should—he came to the aid of his vassal.

> So Joshua went up from Gilgal, he and all the people of war with him and all the valiant warriors. The LORD said to Joshua, "Do not fear them, for I have given them into your hands; not one of them shall stand before you." So Joshua came upon them suddenly by marching all night from Gilgal . . . and he slew them with a great slaughter. (Josh 10:7-10; cf. Josh 9:16-21)

Thus we find the substance and language of covenant making as a vehicle for international politics sprinkled throughout the narrative of Joshua 9–10 (see Josh 9:23-27 and 1 Kings 5:15 for the rest of the story). This narrative shows us that the idea of "cutting a *bĕrît*" in order to facilitate international alliances was well-known in ancient Israel.

A survey of the ancient inscriptions emerging from the archives of Israel's neighbors demonstrates that covenant making was broadly known throughout the ancient Near East as well. The most significant of these discoveries is an extensive collection of treaty documents left behind by the Hittite Empire (a people group occupying Anatolia and northern Syria from c. 1400–1200 B.C.). Discovered in the early part of the twentieth century, this collection spurred the modern study of ancient Near Eastern covenants and covenant-making.[13] From Mesopotamia we have the second-millennium West Semitic treaties from Mari and Alalakh, as well as the first-millennium promissory oaths between the Assyrian King Esarhaddon and his eastern vassals.[14] From Egypt the Amarna correspondence (c. 1400–1350 B.C.) provides an insider's view of the covenant relationship between the Egyptian Pharaohs and the kings of pre-Israelite Canaan. Here, the lords of the Canaanite city-states repeatedly (and hysterically) call upon their less-than-attentive Egyptian suzerains for military aid against marauding outsiders and the conspiracies of other traitorous Canaanite kings.[15] In these letters one regularly encounters the covenant language of "lord" and "servant," the assumption that the suzerain owns his vassal's territory and the assumption that the suzerain was responsible to defend his vassal. Although there is much more that could be reported regarding these ancient documents, what is clear is that the practice of covenant-making in order to initiate and define international relations was truly ubiquitous in Israel's world.[16]

THE LANGUAGE AND FEATURES OF A COVENANT

A *bĕrît* always involved oaths that resulted in obligations placed on both parties. Moreover, the oaths were always ratified by the sacrifice of mutually recognized, ritually appropriate animals. As mentioned above, this practice was so consistent that the act of making a covenant was idiomatically expressed by the phrase "to cut a covenant."[17] Often this sacrifice did "double duty" as it also served to communicate the consequences of covenant-breaking. The eighth-century-B.C. treaty between Ashurnirari V of Assyria and *Mati'ilu* of Arpad serves as an example. Here a spring lamb is slaughtered to conclude the treaty, and the treaty states,

> This head is not the head of a spring lamb, it is the head of *Mati'ilu*, it is the head of his sons, his magnates, and the people of [his la]nd. If *Mati'ilu* [should sin] against this treaty, so may, just as the head of this spring lamb is c[ut] off, and its knuckle placed in its mouth, [. . .] the head of *Mati'ilu* be cut off, and his sons [and magnates] be th[rown] into . . . This shoulder is not the shoulder of a spring lamb, it is the shoulder of *Mati'ilu*, etc.[18]

Sometimes this message was actually acted out in the ratification ceremony such that the vassal was required to walk between the bloodied parts of the slain animals while he recited his oaths. In other words, by means of his actions the vassal is stating: "May what has happened to these animals happen to me if I fail to keep my oath" (cf. Jer 34:18-22). A powerful visual aid indeed. After the treaty was concluded the sacrificed animals were typically roasted as the main course of a celebratory fellowship meal shared by the new covenant partners.

In Genesis 15:9 we find Abram participating in such a covenantal exchange. Many years after the initial articulation of Yahweh's promise (Gen 12:1-3), Abram remains a childless sojourner in Canaan. And so Abram, struggling with his faith, asks Yahweh, "O Lord God, how may I know that I will possess [the land]?" (Gen 15:8). Yahweh answers in a fashion that he knows Abram will understand:

> So He said to him, "Bring Me a three year old heifer, and a three year old female goat, and a three year old ram, and a turtledove, and a young pigeon." Then he [Abram] brought all these to Him and cut them in two, and laid each half opposite the other; but he did not cut the birds. (Gen 15:9-10)

Can you anticipate what is about to happen here? Yahweh is inviting Abram to confirm the oaths between them by means of a standard covenant ratification ceremony. How merciful is this God who condescends to Abram's place in time, and *helps him* to have confidence in the promise. The text goes on to tell us that when the sun was going down "a deep sleep fell upon Abram." This is already a clue that something huge is about to happen in that the last biblical character to experience a "deep sleep" (Hebrew *tardēmâ*) was Adam, right before Eve was formed from his side (Gen 2:21). While Abram was under the effects of this supernaturally induced slumber, "immediately a terror of great darkness fell upon him," and God began to reiterate and particularize his promises. Again, the text gives us a clue as to the enormity of this event when it speaks of "deep darkness." A survey of the Old Testament demonstrates that impenetrable darkness is often an aspect of theophany (an appearance of the deity in physical form). Most specifically it is what happens at Sinai when the God of the universe descends upon the mountain in material form to communicate with his people (Deut 4:11; 5:23). We should read these words in Genesis 15:12 with the same intent here: Yahweh is about to visit Abram in physical form. "And so it came about when the sun had set, that it was very dark, and behold, there appeared a smoking oven and a flaming torch which passed between these pieces" (Gen 15:17). The trappings of covenant-making are here. The covenant partners are present, the ritual animals have been slain and laid upon the ground, and the stipulations of the covenant have been recited. "On that day, the LORD cut a *bĕrît* with Abram" (Gen 15:18). But did you notice who it was that "passed between" the torn and bloodied parts of the sacrificed animals? Who by his actions announced, "May what has happened to these animals happen to me if I fail to keep my oath"? Not the weaker party. Rather, the Lord of the cosmos traversed the bloody alley in order to announce to Abram and his offspring that he would not fail. The fact that God would meet Abram's need for reassurance in such a fashion is more than enough to focus our attention. But when we consider this story from a canonical viewpoint and recall that the God of Abram never failed in his promise but the children of Abraham certainly did, we need to ask the question, whose flesh was torn to pay the price for this broken covenant? Now our attention is fully arrested. For indeed it was the God-man, Jesus Christ—the representative of humanity and the embodiment of Yahweh—whose flesh was torn to appease the broken stipulations of the oaths taken. And here in the opening chapters of the Bible, the echoes of the gospel can be heard.

Blessings were another important feature of a *bĕrît*. These were the benefits promised if the contract were maintained. Curses were the consequences if the contract were violated. Covenant loyalty ("lovingkindness" or *ḥesed*) was the objective of the agreement. The parity treaties report that the partners are now brothers; the suzerain/vassal covenants speak of the parties as father/son or lord/servant. To abide by the contract with one's suzerain was to *love* him, and to betray the suzerain or to fail to keep his stipulations was to *hate* him.[19] Is any of this language sounding familiar? It should be! The Bible is riddled with it. Why? Because this is the terminology associated with the international politics of the ancient Near East, and the Bible is describing Israel's relationship to Yahweh in terms of a *bĕrît*. Yahweh has become Israel's suzerain and Israel has become his vassal.

THE FORM OF THE *BĔRÎT*

The international *bĕrît* was so familiar to the ancient Near East, and so broadly applied, that the form in which these treaties appeared became quite standardized. Like a marriage license today, or a bill of sale, this format acquired an international currency recognizable throughout the Fertile Crescent. Let us begin with the form for which we have the most evidence: the second-millennium B.C. suzerain/vassal Hittite treaties.[20] Here the great king initiates the interaction with a **preamble*** which lists all of his names, titles and personal elements of grandeur. For example, in the treaty between Duppi-Teshub and Mursilis III, the Hittite king begins as follows:

> These are the words of Sun Mursilis, the great king, the king of Hatti land, the valiant, the favorite of the storm-god, the son of Suppiluliumas, the great king, the king of Hatti land, the valiant.[21]

Next comes the **historical prologue**. The function of this section was to furnish the basis of obligation—the reason that the vassal should participate in the proposed covenant and accept the suzerainty of the great king. In the treaty cited above, the prologue continues for several paragraphs detailing Mursilis' military faithfulness to Duppi-Teshub's father, his support of Duppi-Teshub's claim to the Amurru throne and his intention to remain loyal to Duppi-Teshub's heir. It is of great interest to us that as far as the present evidence indicates, the historical prologue is found *only* in second-millennium documents, being particularly characteristic of the Hittite treaties.[22] This indicates that the motivational philosophy of the Hittites was, at least in theory, based upon the power of gratitude. Treat a vassal generously and he will remain loyal. This stands in stark contrast to the first-millennium Assyrian treaties in which the historical prologue is conspicuously absent. Scholars assume that the reason for this omission has to do with the Assyrians' well-cultivated reputation for brutality, as well as their insatiable appetite for conquest. Rather than building upon gratitude and a resulting sense of obligation as the basis for covenant fidelity, the basis of obligation expressed in the Assyrian treaties was solely intimidation. Their approach to international influence? Unprecedented savagery. In my classes I often describe the Assyrian Empire as the "Borg" of the ancient Near East: "resistance is futile, you will be assimilated."

The next section of the Hittite treaties would typically be the **stipulations**. Here the suzerain detailed his expectations regarding military and

---

*The terms in bold on the following pages correspond to key terms in fig. 3.1.

economic obedience as well as his expectation of complete loyalty. If these stipulations were kept, **blessings** (i.e., benefits) would result; if they were not kept, **curses**. What sort of curse might a vassal expect? Although the treaties routinely speak of the gods bringing about a long list of plagues and adversities, what typically happened was that the suzerain would express his wrath by turning his military against his disloyal vassal. The disloyal vassal would be stripped of his throne, sometimes his land grant, and depending on how severe or long-lived the rebellion, the vassal state might be annihilated and the populace exiled. In other words, the very one who had sworn to protect, if incited, could also attack and destroy. Finally, **witnesses** were called to validate the contract. These witnesses were always the deities of the covenanting parties; deities who were called upon to ensure the loyalty of the parties involved. This listing of witnesses ensured that there were no loopholes in the treaty, thus the lists could be very extensive. In the second-millennium-B.C. treaty between Hittite Suppiluliumas and Mattiwaza of Mitanni, for example, more than eighty specific deities are named, as well as "the mountains, the rivers, the Tigris and the Euphrates, heaven and earth, the winds and the clouds."[23] After the oaths were made and sacrifices given, a written record of the covenant was sent home with each partner to be **deposited** in the temple of the deity(s) by whom the king had sworn his oath. And finally, a provision for the **periodic reading** of the treaty before the subordinate (and/or people) was provided. Thus the treaty between Suppiluliumas and Mattiwaza states:

> A duplicate of this tablet has been deposited before the sun-goddess of Arinna, because the sun-goddess of Arinna regulates kingship and queenship. In Mitanni land [a duplicate] has been deposited before Teshub, the lord of the KURINNU (a kind of sanctuary or shrine) of Kahat. At regular [intervals] shall they read it in the presence of the king of the Mitanni land and in the presence of the sons of the Hurri country.[24]

THE *BĔRÎT* AT MOUNT SINAI

So how does this ancient vehicle of international politics relate to your Bible and your faith? Turn your thoughts toward Sinai. In 1954, thirty years after the initial publication of the Hittite treaties, George E. Mendenhall

threw open the doors of biblical interpretation by comparing those treaties with the narrative record of the Mosaic covenant in "The Book of the
Covenant" (Ex 19:1–23:19) and the book of Deuteronomy.[25] In this very
important study, Mendenhall demonstrated that the Mosaic covenant was
structured upon the same literary and ideological foundations as were the
secular treaties. In other words, Yahweh did not create the covenant idea;
he co-opted it to communicate his plan of redemption. The modern understanding of Israel's relationship with Yahweh was revolutionized.

So consider Sinai. In the mid-to-late second millennium B.C. there was
no force on earth more powerful than the Egyptian Empire. They ruled
the world. They also happened to "own" a race of people who were the offspring of one to whom Yahweh had promised himself. And so, "God heard
their groaning; and God remembered His covenant with Abraham, Isaac,
and Jacob" and sent to his people a deliverer (Ex 2:24). Born the offspring
of a slave woman and targeted for death, Moses miraculously survived and
matured into a man uniquely prepared and qualified to lead in impossible
circumstances. In the dramatic exchange between Moses and Pharaoh,
Yahweh proved to the world that the Israelites belonged to Yahweh (not
Pharaoh) and that Yahweh was the lord of the cosmos (not the gods of
Egypt). In essence, Moses confronted the gods of Egypt on their own turf
and won. "You yourselves have seen what I did to the Egyptians, and how
I bore you on eagles' wings, and brought you to Myself" (Ex 19:4). It was
here at Mount Sinai that Yahweh extended to the not-yet-nation of Israel a
bĕrît —the vehicle by which a loosely allied tribal coalition would become
a nation. By means of Yahweh's treaty, a rabble of slaves was transformed
into a people, and the most amazing drama of redemption yet known to
human history occurred. "For once you were NOT A PEOPLE, but now you
are THE PEOPLE OF GOD; once you had NOT RECEIVED MERCY, but now
you have RECEIVED MERCY" (1 Pet 2:10).

Keep in mind that the "mixed multitude" that came out of Egypt was
indeed "mixed" (Ex 12:38). Ethnically, it is probable that an array of Semitic (and non-Semitic) groups joined the Israelites in their flight toward
freedom. Theologically, I often describe this group as "polytheists considering monotheism." Monotheism was a brand-new idea in Moses' day,
and not a welcome one. Indeed, most folks would have been baffled by the

idea that there was only one god. What sort of blasphemer would refuse to honor all the gods of heaven? The pious of the ancient Near East were those who acknowledged many gods and exhausted themselves serving each with sacrifice and worship. This was partly an expression of religious zeal and partly an expression of self-preservation. Failing to honor a deity could result in becoming the target of that deity's wrath. In addition to their theological confusion, the people of Israel had been shaped by generations of slavery. Pause to consider the long-term effects of such conditions. Stripped of the opportunity to organize their own lives and society, illiterate, abused and dominated, how would this mob become a nation? By what laws would they rule themselves, structure their religion, organize their calendar? How would they be shaped into a fighting force that had any chance of conquering Canaan? I can only imagine what Moses must have been thinking as he looked out over the factious throng gathered at the foot of Mount Sinai and pondered his new job description.

But God, of course, had a plan. Choosing a vehicle recognizable throughout Israel's world, Yahweh offered himself to Israel by means of a *bĕrît*. "Now then, if you will indeed obey My voice and keep My covenant, then you shall be My own possession among all the peoples . . . you shall be to Me a kingdom of priests and a holy nation" (Ex 19:5-6). How could this be accomplished? God the suzerain of the universe would *make* Israel a nation by making a treaty with them. By means of their association with him as suzerain, Israel would *become* a nation—a vassal nation. And by selecting the *bĕrît* as his medium, Yahweh seizes upon a form through which he can teach Israel volumes about himself and his expectations. Consider the parallels between the Sinai covenant and the second millennium Hittite treaties as shown in figure 3.1.

In Israel's covenant the **preamble** is simple: "I am Yahweh your God." What more needs to be said? It is not every day that the sovereign of the universe introduces himself! Then comes the **historical prologue**. The historical prologue is intended to provide the reason that the vassal should participate in the covenant and accept the suzerainty of the great king. This historical prologue is so important to Israel's faith that you would be hard-pressed to read more than ten pages of the Old Testament without hearing some allusion to it: "I am Yahweh your God, who brought you up

I.   **Preamble/Title**   "I am Yahweh your God . . ."
      Gives title of superior party
      Exod 20:2a; Deut 5:6a

II.   **Historical Prologue**   ". . . who brought you up out of the land
      Furnishes the basis of obligation   of Egypt, out of the house of slavery."
      and the motive for accepting the
      covenant's stipulations as binding
      Exod 20:2b; Deut 5:6b (cf. Deut 1—3)

III. **Stipulations/Obligations Imposed**   "You shall have no other gods before me. . . ."
      Exod 20:3-17; Deut 5:7-21
      (cf. Deut 12—26)

IV.   **Deposition and Provision for Periodic Reading of the Treaty Before the People**
      Treaty text archived in the temple of the
      vassal's chief deity (i.e., the witness to his oath)

      "Then Moses turned and went down from the mountain with the **two tablets** of the testimony
      in his hand . . ." (Ex 32:15)

      ". . . and in the **ark** you shall put the **testimony** which I shall give you." (Ex 25:21; cf. Ex 40:20;
      Deut 10:5)

      "At the end of every seven years . . . when all Israel comes to appear before Yahweh your God at
      the place which He will choose, **you shall read this law in front of all Israel** in their hearing.
      Assemble the people, the men and the women and children and the alien who is in your town,
      in order that they may hear and learn and fear Yahweh your God, and be careful to observe all
      the words of this law." (Deut 31:10-12; cf. Ex 24:7; Josh 8:30-35)

V.   **List of Witnesses**   "I call heaven and earth to witness against
      The deities of both   you today . . ."
      parties are summoned
      to act as witnesses to the oaths taken
      Deut 4:26; 30:19-20; 31:28

VI.   **Curses and Blessings**   "And all these blessings shall come upon
      Deut 27:11–28:68   you and overtake you if you will obey
                                                      Yahweh your God . . . But if you will not
                                                      obey Yahweh your God . . . all these curses
                                                      shall come upon you and overtake you."

      These acts of treaty-making were sealed by means of a **ratification ceremony** involving **oath**
      and **sacrifice** (Ex 24:3-8; cf. Gen 15:17-21; Jer 34:17-20; Mt 27:22-25).[a]

[a]There is a breadth of literature that rehearses this format. Some of the most accessible pieces are
Meredith Kline's *The Treaty of the Great King* (Grand Rapids: Eerdmans, 1963); Kenneth Kitchen,
Ancient Orient and Old Testament, 1st ed. (Chicago: InterVarsity Press, 1966), pp. 90-102; Jon Levenson, *Sinai and Zion: An Entry into the Jewish Bible* (San Francisco: HarperSanFrancisco, 1985),
pp. 26-36; and Beckman, *Hittite Diplomatic Texts*, pp. 2-3. For additional technical bibliography
see n. 6.

**Figure 3.1. The Hittite suzerain/vassal treaty format of the late second millennium
B.C. and the *bĕrît* at Mt. Sinai**

out of the land of Egypt, out of the house of slavery." Hear the testimony of your ancestors in this refrain. "I was a slave, I was in bondage, I was without value until the day that Yahweh found me. He heard my cry, he remembered his covenant, and he set me free." We as Christians use this language to communicate the profound transformation that we experienced the day we said yes to Jesus. But for the children of Abraham, these were not metaphors. Rather, the historical prologue of Israel's covenant recorded the real events by which Yahweh rescued his people from the slavery and death that was Egypt. These are the events that furnished the basis of their obligation to the covenant.

Remembering that not all treaties had an **historical prologue,** the fact that the covenant God designed for Israel does have one is critical to our understanding of who Yahweh is. Remember that the Assyrians relied on fear and intimidation to ensure their stipulations; whereas the Hittites, at least in theory, relied upon loyalty won from past expressions of grace. Like the Hittite treaties, the stipulations of Israel's covenant *follow* the historical prologue. The Israelites were not asked to obey Yahweh's stipulations in order to *obtain* his grace, they were asked to obey Yahweh's stipulations because he had already acted on their behalf. "I am the Lord your God who brought you up out of the land of Egypt, out of the house of slavery, therefore you shall . . . " Sinai teaches the same truth as the gospel: God's actions on our behalf precede our actions on his behalf. We do not obey in order to win his grace; we obey because we have received his grace. Even so, it seems that in every generation God's people manage to enslave themselves (and those under their care) to some form of legalism that demands obedience *before* grace. Something about the fallen human heart compels us to attempt to *make* ourselves good enough for God before we feel free to embrace his offer of love for us. Worse, we feel compelled to force others to be good enough before allowing them access to God's grace. But the truth of redemptive history is that we obey *because* we have been loved; the stipulations follow the historical prologue. Perhaps if we teach this to our children, they might still want to be Christians when they come of age.

The **stipulations** of the secular agreement consisted of the suzerain's expectations of his vassal. Remembering that the most critical of these expectations was the ongoing, exclusive loyalty of the vassal toward the suzerain, note that Yahweh begins his *běrît* with, "You shall have no other gods before me," and then proceeds to detail every possible rationalization of this command.

> You shall not make for yourself an idol, or any likeness of what is in heaven above or on the earth beneath or in the water under the earth. You shall not worship them or serve them; for I, the LORD your God, am a jealous God, visiting the guilt of the fathers on the children, on the third and fourth generation of those who hate Me, but showing *hesed* to thousands, to those who love Me and keep My commandments. (Ex 20:4-6)

Yahweh's point? No other suzerains! Remember that Abraham's kin had been long in the land of Egypt and that their commitment to monotheism was anything but assumed. How would Yahweh make his people understand that they were to worship him alone? By putting the idea of monotheism into terms they would understand: *political* terms. Thus the covenant at Sinai couches the relationship between Yahweh and Israel in the well known conceptual framework of an international political relationship. Just as a nation would never bind itself to more than one suzerain (unless they liked to live dangerously), Israel was not to bind herself to more than one deity.

Built upon the foundation of monotheism, the covenant at Sinai (which we know mostly as "Ten Commandments") goes on to forbid false oaths, to set apart the Sabbath as sacred, to confirm the authority of parents and to prohibit murder, adultery, theft and false witness. Even the desire to take another person's spouse, goods or reputation is prohibited. If these stipulations are kept, **blessings** will result (cf. Deut 28:1-14). And all of these promised blessings can be summarized into a single statement: "If you obey, you will keep the land." The **curses** that will result if Israel violates the stipulations of this covenant are detailed in Deuteronomy 28:15-68. They too can be summarized in a single statement: "If you disobey, you will lose the land." Finally witnesses are called to validate the agreement.

> I call heaven and earth to witness against you today that I have set before you life and death, the blessing and the curse. So choose life in order that you may live, you and your descendants, by loving Yahweh your God, by obeying His voice and by holding fast to Him . . . that you may live in the

land which Yahweh swore to your fathers, to Abraham, Isaac, and Jacob, to give them. (Deut 30:19-20)

As the only deity standing between Yahweh and Israel is Yahweh himself, "heaven and earth" are called as **witnesses**. After the oaths are made and sacrifices performed, the written record of the covenant is **deposited** in the ark. You may recall that Moses came down off the mountain with two tablets in his hands. Tradition has taught us that each tablet held half of the Ten Commandments, with one tablet listing those commandments involving obligations toward God and the other listing obligations toward neighbor. This traditional teaching is very unlikely, however. If the tablets from Sinai contained only the Ten Commandments, they would have taken up very little space and would not have required two tablets. Rather, they would easily have fit onto one tablet.[26] If the written matter on the tablets was instead a full treaty document, then there would have been significantly more on these tablets than the Ten Commandments recorded in Exodus 20 (cf. Ex 32:15 "tablets which were written on both sides"), and the division of material suggested in the traditional teaching would have been quite artificial. No, the most probable reason that Moses is portrayed with *two* tablets is because a treaty required two copies, one for each covenant partner. Each partner was expected to take his tablet home and place it in the presence of the deity by whom he swore his oath.[27] In this case, there is only one deity between the two partners. So the tablets are archived in the ark (best translated "cabinet"), the footstool of Yahweh in the Holy of Holies.

As with the Hittite treaties, a provision for the **periodic reading** of the treaty before the people is dictated in Deuteronomy 31:11: "when all Israel comes to appear before the LORD your God at the place which He will choose, you shall read this law in front of all Israel in their hearing." Not only was this sort of public reading called for at many critical junctures in Israel's history (cf. 2 Kings 23:2; Neh 13:1), but the law of the king in Deuteronomy 17 required that the Israelite king read the covenant regularly:

Now it shall come about when he [the king] sits on the throne of his kingdom, he shall write for himself a copy of this law on a scroll in the presence of the Levitical priests. It shall be with him and he shall read it all the days of his life, that he may learn to fear the LORD his God, by carefully observing all the words of this law and these statutes. (Deut 17:18-19)

We can hear in this law an echo of the second millennium treaty between Hittite Muwattalli II and his vassal Alaksandu, "Furthermore, this tablet which I have made for you Alaksandu, shall be read out before you three times yearly, and you, Alaksandu, shall know it."[28]

All that remains is the **oath** and **ratification** ceremony of Moses' covenant. We pick up the story in Exodus 24:3 just after Moses has come down off of Sinai with the two tablets in his hands. We read that he recounted "all the words of the LORD and all the ordinances; and all the people answered with one voice and said: 'All the words which the LORD has spoken we will do!'" This is immediately followed by a ratification ceremony.

> They offered burnt offerings and sacrificed young bulls as peace offerings to the LORD. Moses took half of the blood and put it in basins, and the other half of the blood he sprinkled on the altar. Then he took the book of the covenant and read it in the hearing of the people; and they said, "All that the LORD has spoken we will do, and we will be obedient!" So Moses took the blood and sprinkled it on the people, and said, "Behold the blood of the covenant, which the LORD has made with you in accordance with all these words." (Ex 24:5-8)

What an amazing moment. By oath and sacrifice the children of Abraham become the nation of Israel. The God of the cosmos becomes their sovereign lord, and a rabble of slaves is transformed into a "kingdom of priests and a holy nation" (Ex 19:6).

THE DATING DILEMMA

Our last topic as regards covenants is the dating dilemma. *When* did Israel assimilate this covenant tradition into their history of redemption? As we have seen, the format of the secular *bĕrît* is quite standardized. It is so standardized that it has been argued that an individual *bĕrît* may be dated by its literary form. Based on this evolving literary form, many have argued that the covenant of Sinai adheres most closely to the form

THE RATIFICATION OF THE NEW COVENANT

Realizing that our New Testament story is chapter two of their story, consider Matthew 26:27-28. The scene is Jerusalem, the last week of Jesus' earthly ministry and his last night of freedom. It is the Passover, and this first-century rabbi and his band of twelve disciples have gathered to celebrate the ritual meal. This was a hallowed night for the Jews. From youngest to oldest, greatest to least, every Jew everywhere was required to gather and commemorate the miracles of the exodus. Most specifically, they were commanded to remember that great and terrible night when the blood of a spotless lamb marked who would live and who would die, when the tenth plague "passed over" the houses of the Israelites but struck down the firstborn of Egypt. It was during this "Last Supper" that Jesus instituted the Communion meal: "And when he had taken a cup and given thanks, he gave it to them saying, 'Drink from it, all of you; for this is My blood of the covenant, which is poured out for many for forgiveness of sins.'"

Do you hear the echo of Exodus 24? Moses said, "this is the blood of the covenant"; Jesus said, "this is My blood of the covenant." This echo is not co-incidental, nor was it missed by its first-century audience. Rather, on that Passover night Jesus announced to his disciples that something greater than the exodus was about to transpire. By means of oath and sacrifice, another rabble of slaves was about to be transformed into God's covenant-people (cf. 1 Pet 2:10). As Moses sprinkled the blood of bulls upon the people of Israel in order to ratify the Sinai covenant, so Jesus distributed his own blood that night to ratify a new covenant. And this time the oaths were not sealed by "the blood of bulls and goats and the ashes of a heifer," but by the blood of God the Son (cf. Heb 9:13-15). Moreover, the slaves who were freed from their bondage by this new covenant were not delivered merely from Egypt, but from death itself. Thus we see that the safe and structured communion meal that you and I participate in according to our liturgies and traditions is actually a most abbreviated representation of the ratification of the new covenant. And in this new covenant the Lord of the cosmos has served as both suzerain and sacrifice.

of the second-millennium treaties, and, therefore, we should look for its origins in the second millennium.[29] Moreover, as the Sinai covenant does *not* adhere to the literary form of the first-millennium Assyrian treaties, many have argued that Israel's covenant could not have emerged from the first millennium. The most distinctive features here are the Sinai covenant's emphasis on the historical prologue and the blessing sections. You will recall that the historical prologue is a standard section in the second millennium Hittite treaties, but it is completely absent in the first-millennium Assyrian treaties.[30] The same is true of the blessings section. Thus the prominence of the historical prologue and blessings section in Israel's covenant (and Israel's resultant theology) is strong evidence that the book of the Covenant and the core of the book of Deuteronomy (or at the very least their ideological foundations) do indeed come from the era from which they claim to come—the second millennium.[31]

CONCLUSIONS

So what are we left with? All in all we see that the secular *bĕrît* served as a critically important element in structuring and informing Israel's relationship with Yahweh. Through the *bĕrît* at Sinai, Israel's self-identity was transformed from aggregate to nation. By means of the political concepts embedded in the *bĕrît*, Israel was introduced to theological concepts far beyond her ideological reach—monotheism being the chief of these.[32] In his covenant, Yahweh declares to Israel who she is (his vassal), what she will do (his law) and when she will do it (his calendar of holy days). If she "loves" Yahweh, she will be blessed with peace and prosperity. If she "hates" him, she will be cursed with exile. Although Israel will be allowed the privilege of ruling themselves (maintaining their own government and many of their own traditions), as with any *bĕrît*, Israel will be expected to pay tribute (the laws of tithe and sacrifice), give unquestioned loyalty to her suzerain, fight his wars, obey his law, teach his stipulations to the next generation and maintain a king who is faithful to the suzerain. Yahweh has become Israel's sovereign lord and Israel is his servant. Although Israel will make use of the land, it is Yahweh who actually owns the land and its produce. And Israel will demonstrate this reality three times a year, every year, when every male is required to appear before Yahweh with his tribute in hand (i.e., the three pilgrim feasts to the tabernacle/temple). Moreover, if Israel fails to obey the stipulations of the covenant, their sovereign lord will surrender Israel to her enemies. But if Israel is faithful, Yahweh will defend her against all military and economic afflictions. In this manner the nation of Israel will retain the land grant of the great king—what we know as "the Promised Land."[33]

In sum, we see that the word *covenant* carries more semantic cargo than most Bible readers would ever guess. And Yahweh, the great teacher, selected this well-known secular image in order to teach his chosen people about himself. So significant is this concept of covenant to the Bible that the biblical writers utilize it as a major structuring principle for both the history and the theology of redemption. We learned in chapter two that the chronology of the text has been intentionally organized around five characters, and we now see that the theology of the text has been organized around these five characters as well. For each of these characters was called to mediate a covenant between God and humanity: Adam, Noah, Abraham, Moses and David. This is not the only structuring principle within the Bible, but it is an important one. Moreover it is a very accessible one. So we will organize our Old Testaments as the biblical writers have—with covenant serving as the general law that coordinates the facts of redemption's story. Adam, Noah, Abraham, Moses and David. Anyone can memorize these five figures, and by memorizing these (in order!) we take our first step toward a useful closet.

4

GOD'S ORIGINAL INTENT

EDEN

In the first three chapters of this book, we've worked hard to get past the great barrier that divides us modern readers from the world of the Old Testament. As a result, you are now a budding expert in the culture of the ancient Near East, the time and space of the Fertile Crescent, and the all-important concept of covenant. Now it's time to get to the story. So let's begin at the beginning: God's original intent for humanity, Eden.

Although there is no specific declaration of covenant making in Eden, we find the profile of *běrît* throughout the narrative. I believe this is so because the concept of *běrît* as it was learned at Sinai so profoundly affected Israel's self-understanding that *běrît* was used to organize the earliest narratives of the Bible as well. Thus in Eden we find Yahweh, the suzerain lord, promising to his vassals, Adam and Eve, the land grant of paradise if they will remain loyal to their agreement. The blessings are many, the stipulations few. In fact, the only negative stipulation of this covenant is "you shall not eat of the tree of the knowledge of good and evil." On the surface this seems like a simple, even silly rule. But in reality this one edict encompasses the singular law of Eden—God is God and we are not. If humanity would simply acknowledge the innate authority of the Creator, would recognize that they were tenants and stewards in God's garden, they would live in paradise forever. But if they had to have access to every part of the garden, if they had to "be free" to choose their own rules and decide for themselves what was "good and evil," if they had to be *autonomous* of the authority of the great King, then they would die. You know the story. The choice was autonomy. The covenant was broken and the curse was enacted.

But before we jump ahead in the story, let us consider the content of God's original plan—his original covenant with humanity. Or to state the topic differently, let's consider how God defined his first *relationship* with humanity as communicated in Genesis 1–2. Note that there are two accounts of creation in these chapters. The first I will refer to as "Genesis 1," but it actually runs from Genesis 1:1–2:3 (or verse 4 depending on which scholar you read); the second runs from Genesis 2:4/5–2:25, and I will refer to this as "Genesis 2." Why, you might ask, do the chapters divide in the middle of the first creation narrative? Good question! The answer is that the chapter and verse delineations in the Bible are not original to the Bible; they were added in the Middle Ages to make it easier to study and cite the text. "The actual marking of each biblical verse with a number was begun only after the Vulgate was divided into chapters by Archbishop Stephen Langton in the thirteenth century."[1] Unless we want to create literary chaos, we can't change those delineations now, but know that if Genesis 1–2 had been divided based on discrete literary units, that division would have come at either Genesis 2:3 or Genesis 2:4.

So we have successfully navigated our first interpretive hurdle, but a far more complex interpretive challenge awaits us. It seems that Genesis 1 and Genesis 2 provide different accounts of God's first plan. Let's take a look at the distinctions between the accounts in table 4.1 and see what we might learn as a result. This comparison shows that although these two accounts of creation are clearly complementary and communicate the same central themes, the order of the distinct creative events is different, the vocabulary shifts and the genre shifts. Simply put, Genesis 1 has a sweeping, panoramic view of creation that emphasizes the transcendence of God; Genesis 2 is more "anthropomorphic" in its approach, portraying God with the human qualities of first a craftsman (Gen 2:7), then a gardener (Gen 2:8), and finally a builder (Gen 2:22). So what do we do with these differences in our effort to identify God's original intent for humanity? First, of course, we read these two chapters assuming that they are indeed complementary (why else would the authors of the Bible have left them side by side?), and together

Table 4.1. The Two Accounts of Creation in Genesis

Genesis 1	Genesis 2
the creation of humanity follows the creation of all of the other creatures in Eden	the creation of humanity precedes the creation of plant life and animals
the Hebrew word *ʾĕlōhîm* is used for God	the Hebrew words Yahweh *ʾĕlōhîm* are used for God
the Hebrew word *bārāʾ* is used for "create"	the Hebrew word *yāṣar* is used for "create"
the narrative is somewhat isolated, not linked to the narrative that follows in any obvious manner	the narrative has a sequel that carries the reader through chapters 3 and even 4; moreover the genre seems to extend through chapter 11
the creation of humanity is accomplished by means of divine decree	the creation of humanity is accomplished by means of divine anthropomorphic involvement: God "forms" (*yāṣar*) Adam from the clay of the ground as a potter would a vessel; he "breathes" life into him; he takes Adam's rib to "build" the second human
male and female are created at the same time	Adam is created first, Eve is created second
the text is highly structured and poetic	the text is a narrative and appears "folkloric" in genre

they communicate the parameters of God's plan. But we also need to think in terms of their distinctions and ask *why* we have two seemingly distinct accounts of creation right here in the opening chapters of the Bible.

My simplified answer to this question is that whereas the creation account of Genesis 2–3 is most likely ancient, ancient material that had been treasured for generations prior to its incorporation into the book we now know as Genesis, Genesis 1 was composed specifically to serve as a grand introduction to the same—not merely as an introduction to Genesis 2–3, but to all the ancient and inherited narratives of Genesis, and even as an introduction to the Pentateuch as a whole. In sum, I believe Genesis 1 was written to provide a *lens* through which to read the rest of the Pentateuch. And since the Pentateuch is the backbone of the entire Bible, ultimately Genesis 1 serves as the introduction to our faith.[2]

Assuming that this assessment of the relationship of Genesis 1 and Genesis 2 is accurate, our next question is, what would have been on this author's mind as he wrote his grand introduction? In other words, what did the author of Genesis 1 feel was necessary to set up the theological and historical lens for his audience as he launched his readers into redemption's story? I must tell you that I do not think he was concerned about the chronological and geological details of the creation event, nor do I think he was occupied with explaining the end of the dinosaur age or the "old" and "young" earth theory.[3] Rather, I think his most central concern was probably educating Yahweh's wayward people as to who this God was and what this God expected of them. And certainly a major point of confusion for the recently liberated, too-long-in-Egypt Israelites was the concept of monotheism. Yahweh was a god unlike the others of the ancient Near East, one who stood outside and above his creation, a god for whom there were no rivals and who had created humanity as his children as opposed to his slaves.[4] Thus I think Genesis 1 was intended as a rehearsal of the creation event (where else would you start the story?) with the all-controlling theological agenda of explaining who God is and what his relationship to creation (and specifically humanity) looked like. Basically, Genesis 1 was written to answer the questions: "Who is God and what is his relationship to us?" Or, as the title of our chapter indicates, "What was God's original intent?"

THE "WEEK" OF GENESIS 1

So what about the "week"? As Henri Blocher states: "Nobody reading the panoramic prologue of Genesis can miss the structural fact which gives the text its most obvious arrangement: the framework of the seven days."[5] The other dominating feature of this chapter is that the magnificent culmination of the seven days of Genesis 1 is the sabbath—the great gift of Sinai. Throughout the years an array of interpretive theories have been applied to this seven-day structure.[6] One that became quite popular at the turn of the century through Scofield's annotated Bible is known as the "gap" or reconstruction theory.

The "gap" or reconstruction theory. According to this theory, there is a narrative "gap" between Genesis 1:1 and Genesis 1:2 which should be filled as follows:[7]

> In the beginning God created the heavens and the earth. *And there was war in heaven, and Satan and a third of the angels waged war against God and his angels. And Satan was defeated and cast down to earth, and as a result* the earth was [became] formless and void [Hebrew *tōhû wābōhû*], and darkness was moving over the surface of the waters.

I bet you haven't found all this in your Bible! The idea here is that the six days of creation found in Genesis 1 are actually six days of *re-creation* that were made necessary by a cataclysmic destruction of the planet that rendered it "formless and void." The cause of this cataclysmic destruction? Satan's fall as extrapolated from Isaiah 14:3-23, Ezekiel 28:11-19 and Revelation 12:12. From an interpreter's standpoint, it is quite odd to insert an entirely new storyline here in the middle of the creation account, literally in the middle of a paragraph. In fact, as nearly all Hebrew language scholars agree, there is no literary or linguistic defense for doing so.[8] So why might an interpreter argue for such an insertion? One contributing factor to the development of this theory is that Hebrew *tōhû wābōhû* ("formless and void") in its other occurrences communicates the destruction of the land, as opposed to mere emptiness (cf. Is 34:11; Jer 4:23). And so the gap theory argues that *tōhû wābōhû* must mean "destruction" in Genesis 1:2 as well. But in these other instances the phrase is communicating destruction so complete that it is *as if* the object of destruction had never been created. This is, of course, the state of affairs in Genesis 1:2—an earth not yet fully formed. We also find that the idea of a God-ordained judgment so severe that the earth reverts back to its pre-created state is a fairly consistent theme in Scripture, the flood being the most obvious example. Thus the contention that *tōhû wābōhû* must communicate the destruction of an already complete creation, as opposed to a not-yet-formed creation, is not a convincing argument.

The other (and far more controlling) motivation for the origination of the gap theory was that this interpretation allowed late nineteenth- and early twentieth-century biblical scholars space to explain the deluge of (then) new scientific data regarding the fossil record and Darwin's theories. If God's story of Adam does not begin until after the destruction of a previous creation, there is now an indefinable period of time between the birth of the earth and the introduction of humanity—a "gap" of time large enough to account for whatever the fossil record might attest.[9]

Geological era theory. A second theory of interpretation for Genesis 1, which first became popular in the nineteenth century and has continued into the modern period with an array of modifications, is the geological era theory.[10] The essence of this argument is that the six "days" of Genesis 1 are actually six "eras" of undefined length. This theory was originally based upon the well-known fact that the Hebrew word for day *(yôm)* is a flexible term and in some instances may be used to communicate an undetermined span of time.[11] When this caveat was noted, nineteenth-century theologians were excited to see that the progression of the six days of creation was very similar to the outline of the evolution of life on this planet which was emerging from contemporary science. "Very similar," however, but not quite similar enough. The biggest fly in the ointment being that the sun, which most scientists would identify as the ultimate source of life on earth, was not created until the fourth day. Moreover, in contrast to current scientific models, trees (day three) precede ocean life (day five), and birds (day five) precede insects (day six).[12] An additional problem was the fact that the chronology of the creation events in chapter 2 differs from chapter 1. Thus, if the geological era theory is correct, we are forced to ask which chapter of the Bible is incorrect?

Obviously, there are literary, linguistic and logical problems with both of the theories summarized above. The biggest issue with these theories, however, is that they attempt to interpret the first chapter of Genesis by asking questions that the author of Genesis 1 could not possibly have intended to answer. What do I mean by this? Think in these terms. If you were to pull out your car owner's manual and ask it where your winter clothes are stored, what sort of answer might you get? Perhaps the manual would tell you that "the hood may be released by pulling lever x." You could spend the rest of your life trying to find your hooded sweatshirt with that answer! But if you were to ask the same question of a letter from your mother, which was written in response to that same question ("Where are my winter clothes stored?"), you would get an answer that actually helped you reach your goal ("Under the stairs in a large, cardboard box . . . your name is on it!"). It would not take you any time at all to find your hooded sweatshirt with that response. Or think in terms of asking two different questions of the same text. If you ask your car manual, "Where are my winter clothes stored?"—no help at all. But if you were to ask the same text a question it was designed to answer, "How often should I change my oil?"—all the help you need. Thinking back to our previous discussion, do we really think that the author of Genesis 1 would have been writing to explain where dinosaurs came from? Do we think that the questions he was intending to answer were the mysteries of paleontology or the geological age of the earth? Would this have been his intent? I can't imagine that to be the case. And just as expecting your car manual to tell you where your winter clothes are stored is going to result in a terribly confusing response, so too is asking Genesis 1 about wooly mammoths. This is not because the Bible cannot answer those questions; it is because, in this case, it did not. This is the bedrock of good biblical interpretation: let the Bible set its own agenda. If we ask questions the text was intended to answer, we will get answers. If we force it to address unrelated questions of our own design, we will wind up confused.

The literal or "twenty-four-hour-day" theory. The most long-lived theory of interpretation of Genesis 1 is the idea that the world was created in six twenty-four-hour days, with each day representing one linear phase in the chronology of that creation. The reason for the longevity of this theory is obvious: this is what the Bible says. And although there have been many people throughout the years who have pointed out the scientific problems with this theory (not the least being no sources of light and therefore no means of measuring a "day" until the fourth day), there are also many wonderful and reasonable Christians who believe that affirming a seven (twenty-four-hour) day creation is a litmus test of true faith. I am not going to argue with either of these groups. But I would like to propose a reading of this text that offers another option—an option that takes very seriously the issue of authorial intent. So my starting point is this question: What might the author of Genesis 1 have intended to communicate by his seven-day framework?

If you have read Genesis 1, you know that the chapter could easily be described as poetry, or even as a song. Each of the seven days is conveyed succinctly with the repeated chorus, "and God saw that it was good, and there was evening and there was morning, a xx day." This continues until the sixth day and the first climax of the piece: the creation of humanity (Gen 1:24-31). The amount of verbiage committed to the sixth day is nearly double that committed to the days previous. So obviously our writer thought something very important was happening on this day. Then comes the final and most important day of the song, the seventh. Although not the longest section, this segment has precedence in that it involves the *seventh* day. This number had symbolic significance among the Hebrews, and more important, it is the *sabbath* day. Note as well that the subject matter of this final day is the Creator, as opposed to the creation.

So we must ask the question: what did the biblical author intend? Did he want us to find chronology here—the sequential order and time frame for God's creation of the cosmos? Or may he have had another message?

The framework theory. It was Augustine (354–430 A.D.), in his piece *On Genesis According to the Literal Sense,* who first articulated the framework theory. Reiterated by many since, the argument is basically that the seven-day structure of Genesis 1, although indeed a literal week, was a literal week being used as a *literary device.* Think in terms of a picture album and a trip to Disney World. A parent might take a hundred pictures of such a grand outing, but when those pictures were narrowed down to the ones that would actually go into the album, and then were organized onto pages, chronology would not necessarily be the organizing theme. Not in my photo albums at least! Rather, I tend to look for an image that somehow captures the "big picture" of the trip for the first page. Then I might put all the photos of my four-year-old meeting Disney characters in a collage on the next page (regardless of what hour of the day she met them). I would probably reserve a page for photos of jubilant faces (and blurred bodies) spinning by on the various rides, and I would likely adorn each page with a group shot reiterating the relatives who had adventured with us. I would reserve a page for the parade (of course!), and the final page might be a close-up of my children waving with their new Cinderella balloons or zonked out in strollers on their way back to the car. The album I'm describing would be a non-linear organization of an actual event and actual people. This is the sort of thing I mean by describing the week of Genesis 1 as a literary device. The seven days are used to organize the details of creation, but like my photo album, the information is being organized according to a theme other than chronology. This idea is better caught than taught. So take a look at figure 4.1.

Here I've presented each of the seven days of Genesis 1 as separate segments of an arrow moving to the right. Days 1-6a are set up as parallel sections within the arrow. The idea is that Genesis 1 is written to commu-

1	2	3	6b	
Day & Night (1:1-5)	Waters Above (the heavens) & Waters Below (the oceans) (1:6-8)	Land & Vegetation (1:11-12)	Man & Woman to rule: land animals, fish, birds, "all the earth."	**7** God to rule: humanity, land animals, fish, birds, "Thus the heavens and the earth were completed... and God rested... God blessed & sanctified that seventh day." (2:2)
4 Sun to rule the day Moon to rule the night (1:16-18)	**5** Birds to rule the heavens; fish to rule the seas "And God said be fruitful, muliply... fill your domain." (1:22)	**6a** Land Animals & Humanity "Let the land produce living creatures." (1:24-26)	"Be fruitful, multiply, fill the earth, subdue it, rule over... every living thing that moves upon the earth." (1:26)	

Figure 4.1. The seven days of creation in Genesis 1

nicate movement toward a goal—the goal being the cosmos in its entirety. As you scan across days 1, 2 and 3, you see that a facet of the cosmos is formed in each. In Day 1 the day and night are created, in day 2, the "waters above" are separated from the "waters below," on day 3 the dry land and all of its vegetation is created.

Returning to day 2, a modern reader is typically confused by the idea of "waters above" and "waters below." To understand what this terminology meant to the ancients, take a look at figure 4.2. This figure illustrates the cosmological worldview of the ancient Near East. They believed that the blue of the sky was an actual solid barrier that held back the "waters above." They called this the "firmament" and believed that when it rained, the "windows of heaven" were opened so that the "waters above" could come through. The "waters below" were the primordial deep (Hebrew těhôm) that lay below the surface of the earth. This was a very scary concept to the ancients because this primordial deep, also known as "chaos," had the ability to break out on occasion, destroying whatever lay in its path (see "Some Thoughts on the Sea" in chapter six). So when the creation narrative reports that Yahweh's spirit is hovering over the primordial deep, it is reporting that chaos is subject to Yahweh—which was very good news to a Hebrew. In sum, in the mind of an Israelite, the sky and the sea were intimately related, and this is why they are both addressed in day 2.

So on these first three days, we find that all the habitats of the planet are created: day and night, sky and sea, dry land. Now consider day 4, which is the parallel of day 1. Here the sun, moon and stars are created "to rule" the day and night, which of course were created in day 1 (v. 16). On day 5, the parallel of day 2, fish and birds are created to populate their habitats as well—the "waters" above and below the earth. On day 6a, the parallel of day 3, land animals are created to populate the dry land. Do you see the logical and literary structure here? First the habitat (or kingdom) is created, and then its inhabitants are created. Could this structure be coincidental? Or was it intentional? And if it was intentional, what does it communicate? Let's take a look at the rest of day 6.

On day 6b, which is also set in parallel to day 3 (the creation of the dry ground with its vegetation), we reach the literary climax of this piece. Humanity is created as a reflection of God himself. But unlike the other inhabitants created, this ruler is told to rule over all that has come before.

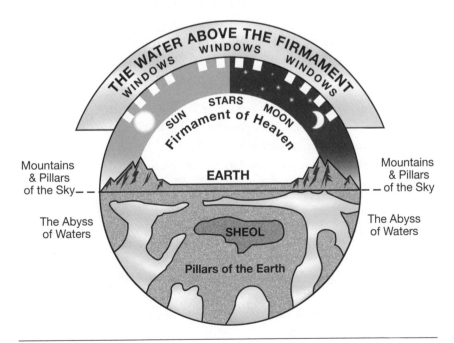

Figure 4.2. The cosmos

Then God said, "Let Us make humanity in Our image, according to Our
likeness; and let them rule over the fish of the sea and over the birds of the
sky and over the cattle and over all the earth, and over every creeping thing
that creeps on the earth." God created humanity in His own image, in the
image of God He created him; male and female He created them. God
blessed them; and God said to them, "Be fruitful and multiply, and fill the
earth, and subdue it; and rule over the fish of the sea and over the birds of
the sky and over every living thing that moves on the earth. . . ." God saw
all that He had made, and behold, it was very good. And there was evening
and there was morning, the sixth day. (Gen 1:26-28, 31)

So what is the structure here, and what is the message of that structure?
Genesis 1 has rehearsed for us the major components of the created order,
first according to their habitats and then according to their inhabitants,
their kingdoms and their rulers. But this structure has also told us that
there is one ruler who stands above the rest. This is ʾĀdām, the collective
Hebrew term for "humanity." This creature, unlike all the others, is made
in the very *image* of God. Male and female, they are God's *representatives*
on earth and have been appointed as his stewards of all the wealth and
beauty of paradise. But the narrative is not over yet. As discussed above,
although in the Middle Ages church leaders separated Genesis 1:31 from
Genesis 2:1, it is universally agreed that this was in error. Rather, the creation account of Genesis 1 should end at 2:3/4.

Thus the heavens and the earth were completed, and all their hosts. By the
seventh day God completed His labor which He had done, and He rested
on the seventh day from all His work which He had done. Then God
blessed the seventh day and sanctified it, because in it He rested from all
His work which God had created and made. (Gen 2:1-3)

So according to the pattern we have seen developing, what is the message of the seventh day? Meredith Kline says it this way:

A hierarchical pattern of dominion can be traced through the creational record, a pattern of ascending consecration with the Sabbath as its capstone.
. . . Within the first three day-frames is described the origin of three vast
spheres over which rule is to be exercised. Then in day-frames four through
six the rulers of each of these spheres is presented in proper turn, each aris-
ing at the divine behest and ruling by divine appointment. But the rising

chain of command does not stop with the six days; it ascends to the seventh day, to the supreme dominion of him who is Lord of the Sabbath.[13]

In other words, whereas birds were created to fill the heavens and fish to fill the seas, and whereas humanity was created to rule sky and sea, bird and fish, *God* rules over all. The movement of figure 4.1 finds its conclusion in the Creator God who "rests" on Day 7. In sum, Genesis 1 tells us of God's first, perfect plan—a flawlessly ordered world infused with balance and productivity. Here every rock, plant and animal had its own designated place within God's design, a God-ordained space in which each could thrive, reproduce and serve the good of the whole. And we see from the structure of Genesis 1 that the force that held this peaceful and productive cohabitation in balance was Yahweh's sovereignty over all. But as Day 6b makes clear, God chose to manage this creation through his representative *ʾĀdām*. Thus humanity is given all authority to protect, maintain and develop God's great gift *under* God's ultimate authority. This is who Yahweh is, who humanity is and how both relate to the creation. And regardless of how you choose to harmonize science and Bible, this message is clearly part of the intent of Genesis 1. I would say it is the primary intent.

EDEN AS A COVENANT

You may have noticed that my description of Genesis 1 sounds a lot like the relationship between a vassal and his suzerain; a relationship in which the vassal is given full autonomy within the confines of his overlord's authority. When this reading of Genesis 1 is wedded to Genesis 2, the profile of covenant becomes even clearer. Here the suzerain (Yahweh) offers his vassals (Adam and Eve) the land grant of Eden with the stipulation that humanity care for it and protect it.

> Then the LORD God took the man and put him into the garden of Eden to cultivate [*ʿābad*] and keep it [*šāmar*]. (Gen 2:15)

In addition to this perfect place, Adam and Eve are given each other (Gen 2:18-25), and as is implied by Genesis 3:8, they are given full access to their loving Creator. The only corner of the garden which was not theirs to use and enjoy was the tree of the knowledge of good and evil:

From any tree of the garden you may eat freely; but from the tree of the knowledge of good and evil you shall not eat, for in the day that you eat from it you will surely die. (Gen 2:16-17)

In essence, Adam and Eve are free to do anything except decide for themselves what is good and what is evil. Yahweh reserves the right (and the responsibility) to name those truths himself.

This was Adam and Eve's perfect world. Not just fruit and fig leaves, but an entire race of people stretching their cognitive and creative powers to the limit to build a society of balance and justice and joy. Here the sons of Adam and the daughters of Eve would learn life at the feet of the Father, build their city in the shadow of the Almighty, create and design and expand within the protective confines of his kingdom. The blessing of this gift? A civilization without greed, malice or envy; progress without pollution, expansion without extinction. Can you imagine it? A world in which Adam and Eve's ever-expanding family would be provided the guidance they needed to explore and develop their world such that the success of the strong did not involve the deprivation of the weak. Here government would be wise and just and kind, resources plentiful, war unnecessary, achievement unlimited and beauty and balance everywhere. This was God's perfect plan: the *people* of God in the *place* of God dwelling in the *presence* of God. Yet, as with all covenants, God's perfect plan was dependent on the choice of the vassal. Humanity must willingly submit to the plan of God. The steward must choose this world; for in God's perfect plan, the steward had been given the authority to reject it.

CONSIDER THE SABBATH

Now what about the language of "rest" in Genesis 2:1-3? In part, this language has to do with the royal imagery of Genesis 1. Rest (in Hebrew typically *nûah*) was something that conquering kings had and did when their enemies were defeated and their domain was fully under their control. This is evident in the story of Joshua and the conquest of Canaan: "The LORD your God gives you *rest* and will give you this land" (Josh 1:13; cf. Josh 1:13-15; 11:23; 14:15). And in David's success during the early monarchy: "Now it came about when the king lived in his house,

and the LORD had given him *rest* on every side from all his enemies"
(2 Sam 7:1). In the ancient Near East, a king who had proven himself a
king "rested." In the same manner, Yahweh, who had proven himself the
lord of the cosmos by his acts of creation, rests. The image is of a king
enthroned above his peaceful and productive domain—an ideal image for
Yahweh's place in the seven-day structure of Genesis 1.

But in Genesis 2:2-3, the verb *šābat* is used instead of the more standard *nûaḥ* for Yahweh's resting after his six days of creation.[14] I believe
that the reason for this somewhat distinctive vocabulary is that Genesis 1
is making use of wordplay. The goal of the wordplay is first to catch our
attention, and second, to direct it somewhere else. The "somewhere else"
is another important moment in the Israelite experience: the giving of the
sabbath ordinance on Mount Sinai.

> Remember the sabbath day, to keep it holy. Six days you shall labor and do
> all your work, but the seventh day is a sabbath of the LORD your God; in it
> you shall not do any work, you or your son or your daughter, your male or
> your female servant or your cattle or your sojourner who stays with you. For
> in six days the LORD made the heavens and the earth, the sea and all that
> is in them, and rested on the seventh day; therefore the LORD blessed the
> sabbath day and made it holy. (Ex 20:8-11; cf. Ex 31:14-16)

Can you imagine what the gift of the sabbath meant to the Israelites
standing at the foot of Mount Sinai? A few months prior they had been
slaves. Slaves who had been born of slaves. Slaves whose only value was
the quantity of labor they could produce before their backs gave way and
their strength failed. Slaves who, outside of a holy day or two, worked
every day of their lives—from the tenderest days of their childhood until
their broken bodies were laid in the ground. And now this God, who has
claimed them as his "treasured possession," is announcing that one day out
of every seven will be set apart for *rest*. It is once again obvious that the
content of Genesis 1 has been deeply impacted by Sinai. And how does
this Sabbath ordinance offered to Israel on Mount Sinai tie into God's
perfect plan for humanity? Blocher expresses it this way:

> Now what is the meaning of the Sabbath that was given to Israel? It relativ-
> izes the works of mankind, the contents of the six working days. It protects

mankind from total absorption by the task of subduing the earth, it antici-
pates the distortion which makes work the sum and purpose of human life,
and it informs mankind that he will not fulfill his humanity in his relation
to the world which he is transforming but only when he raises his eyes
above, in the blessed, holy hour of communion with the Creator. . . . The
essence of mankind is not work![15]

This message is as necessary in this generation as it was in theirs. In our
driven, workaholic world, in which we are trained to think that the only
measurable value of our lives is the quantity of labor we can produce before
our broken bodies are laid in the ground, our Creator says, the essence of
the one made in the image of God is not work.

ADAM'S CHOICE

God's perfect plan (and humanity's perfect world) was a matter of choice.
Did ʾĀdām want this world? Or one of their own making? The ones made
in the image of God could not be forced or coerced, but instead were
called upon to *choose* their sovereign. And choose they did. Whenever I
think of this moment, the lyrics of Don Francisco's old folk song echo in
my mind: "And all their unborn children die as both of them bow down to
Satan's hand."[16] God's original intent was sabotaged by humanity, stolen
by the Enemy. ʾĀdām rejected the covenant, and all the cosmos trembled.
Genesis 2:17 makes it painfully clear what the consequences of such an
insurrection would be: in that day, "you shall surely die." But amazingly,
mercifully, even though Yahweh had every right to wipe out our rebellious
race, he chose another course—redemption. In a move that continues to
confound me, God spared the lives of Adam and Eve (and their unborn
children) by redirecting the fury of the curse toward another—the battered flesh of his own Son. This is the one the New Testament knows
as "the last Adam" (Rom 5:14; 1 Cor 15:22, 45). And although the first
Adam did not die, the second surely did. But we are getting ahead of ourselves. As we consider Genesis 3, what were the consequences of ʾĀdām's
choice? For each of the human partners we find not just the removal of
blessings, but the *reversal* of blessings. What had been a blessing now
becomes a curse, a benefit becomes a burden, paradise is exchanged for
prison. Let's begin with Eve.

THE IMAGE

In Genesis 1:26-27 God announces his intent to create humanity in his "image"—Hebrew ṣelem (cf. Gen 5:3; 9:6). It may surprise you to learn that ṣelem (with its cognates) is the standard ancient Near Eastern word for "idol." When a polytheist from the ancient world set out to make an earthly representative of their deity (understood as the incarnation of that which could not be fully incarnated, a lifeless object that must be animated by the deity), that polytheist fashioned a ṣelem.[a] When the language of Genesis 1:26-27 is combined with the images of Genesis 2:7, we see that Yahweh is presenting himself to us as a divine craftsmen, who is making an idol of/for himself, which he himself must animate. And that idol is us. Within the worldview of the ancient Near East the message here is clear: we are the nearest representation of Yahweh that exists.[b]

What aspects of the human being reflect the divine original? The clues are in the text. Note the deliberative plural: "Let us make . . . in our image . . . male and female he created them" (Gen 1:26-27). It seems that the plurality of humanity (male and female in relationship) reflects the plurality of the original; and humanity, like deity, is created to live in relationship. Note as well that Adam and Eve are given dominion; like its divine analogue, humanity is creative, productive, judicial and authoritative.[c] Distinct from the animals, humanity is also self-aware and empathic. Similar to their Creator, humanity is also eternal; our immaterial and material selves will live forever somewhere. And what about the physicality of pre-fallen humanity? Genesis 5:1-3 and Luke 3:38 make it clear that the image of God in humanity is like the image of a parent in a child—there is some sort of physical resemblance. It has been argued that one aspect of this physical resemblance was radiance. Kline claims that light is a physical manifestation of God's glory.[d] The many

---

[a]For the rituals associated with this process, see Michael Dick, *Born in Heaven, Made on Earth* (Winona Lake, Ind.: Eisenbrauns, 1999), pp. 54-121.

[b]This is why Israelite religion is anti-idol ("aniconic" being the technical term). God has already made an image of himself, and for humanity to attempt to replace that with one of their own design would be blasphemy (cf. Is 44:9-20; Jer 16:20).

[c]Meredith Kline states: "As image of God, man is a royal son with the judicial function appertaining to kingly office" (*Images of the Spirit* [Meredith G. Kline, 1986], p. 29).

[d]See in particular the Akkadian concept of *melammu* and Kline, *Images of the Spirit*, pp. 13-34.

descriptions of God and his angels clothed in light (Ps 104:2; Is 60:19; Mt 28:3; cf. Ps 8), and the presence of God filling the New Jerusalem with light (Rev 21:10-11; 22:5) encourage us toward this idea. The periodic invasions of God's kingdom into ours as manifested in Moses' shining face (Ex 34:29-33) and Jesus' transfiguration (Mt 17:2) seem to confirm it. Thus it is quite possible that in their pre-fallen state, Adam and Eve, like their creator, were "clothed in light."[e]

---

[e]Cf. Henri Blocher, *In the Beginning*, pp. 79-94.

Eve.

To the woman He said, "I will greatly multiply your pain in childbirth, in pain you will bring forth children. Yet your desire will be for your husband, and he will rule over you." (Gen 3:16)

The first aspect of Eve's curse involves childbirth. According to Genesis 3:20, Eve's special blessing was to be "the mother of all the living."[17] Think about this. Eve was commissioned to be either the mother or grandmother, or great-(great-great-)grandmother of all who live. And this in a world without the standard dysfunctions of the standard family! What a joy; what a privilege. As someone who has recently experienced the miracle of becoming a mom, I can tell you that there is nothing else in my life that even plays in the same arena. Coming to know your unborn child as she grows inside you, witnessing the first moment she draws breath, holding her tiny body in your arms knowing that your calling in life is to protect her, teach her and then let her fly . . . nothing can touch it. And I have it on good authority that being a grand-mom is even better! This was Eve's blessing. But now this woman, who was called to be the source of *life*, will enter this experience only through severe pain and often severe injury. In truth, the leading cause of *death* for the daughters of Eve prior to the industrial age (and still in many parts of the world) is childbirth. Eve, the one blessed to mother the human race, will now die in the process of bringing forth life. With the Fall, she who held the unique privilege of producing the heirs of Adam's race finds instead that her chief source of injury and death would be that very act.

And what of the second aspect of Eve's curse? Genesis 1 makes it clear that Eve was designed as Adam's coregent. Made in the image of the Creator, Eve was also to "rule over the fish of the sea and over the birds of the sky and over the cattle and over all the earth, and over every creeping thing that creeps on the earth" (Gen 1:26). In every fashion, Eve is presented as Adam's equal in Genesis 1. But with the Fall, this mutuality is shattered.

> Your desire ["urge, craving, impulse," Hebrew *tĕšûqâ*] will be for your husband, and he shall rule over you. (Gen 3:16)

I know of only one parallel to this language in the Bible—God's curse of Cain just after his murder of his brother Abel.

> But if you do not do well, sin is crouching at the door; and its desire ["urge, craving, impulse" Hebrew *tĕšûqâ*] is for you, but you must master it. (Gen 4:7)

No one is exactly sure what this language means, but it surely isn't good! My best interpretation is that whereas Adam and Eve's relationship had been all that they could need or want in Eden, with the Fall, this ideal partnership is transformed into the competitive grappling of two hungry souls. In the coregency of Eden, Adam and Eve's creative ambitions had been fully satisfied, their needs for partnership and intimacy, affirmation and admiration had found full satisfaction in the "helper suitable" (Gen 2:18). They saw in each other "bone of my bones, and flesh of my flesh" (Gen 2:23). But with the Fall, although Adam and Eve still desperately need and desire one another, they are no longer able to live their lives together with the same mutuality. Rather, they are now locked into a competitive relationship, each vying for control of the other, contending for the resources that now appear so transient. As Adam had the advantage of size and strength, and Eve was still constrained by her desire for hearth and home, the centuries testify to the fact that Eve's longing for her husband will too often result in her willing participation in her own oppression and abuse. A relationship that should have been characterized by mutual self-sacrifice, productivity and joy will create instead the deepest of frustration and pain . . . and yet she will still yearn for this relationship. There is not a marriage on this planet that has not felt the aftershock of this curse. Yet even in the midst of all this loss, a word of hope remains. The woman is promised that her union with her husband will produce an heir who, in the end, will slay the one who deceived her (Gen 3:15). Even in her fallen state, it is Eve who will bring forth the Christ.

Adam.

> Then to Adam [ʾādām] He said, "Because you have listened to the voice of your wife, and have eaten from the tree about which I commanded you, saying, 'You shall not eat from it'; cursed is the ground [ʾădāmāh] because of you; in toil you shall eat of it all the days of your life. Both thorns and thistles it shall grow for you." (Gen 3:17-18)

To understand Adam's curse, first we need to recognize the word-play in the passage. Adam (ʾādām) had been created for the ʾădāmāh ("cultivatable land"). Adam was a farmer. His special blessing was to tend and cultivate the ground such that it brought forth its very best. And, the ground was designed to respond to Adam's direction with eager abundance. For anyone who has ever planted one of those lifeless little "dry root" catalog seedlings, and after endless months of watering, staking and fertilizing seen it grow into an actual *tree*, you know what I'm talking about. If you've ever transformed a barren patch of earth into a shady patio garden, or even grown a particularly splendid tomato, you've caught a hint of Adam's joy. You would know his full joy if every plant you touched, every inch of soil you tilled, bore exactly the harvest you desired, and tenfold. The ʾădāmāh was created for Adam, to submit to his authority and to provide abundantly for his family. Moreover, just like his Creator, Adam was designed to love his work and his work was designed to prosper. But with the Fall, Adam's authority over the ʾădāmāh is shattered. Now Adam's careful and creative tilling of the earth will become toil, toil that at times will be more than he can bear. And worse, the land will be fruitless. "Thorns and thistles it shall grow for you." The ʾădāmāh was designed to serve ʾĀdām, but now it will rebel against them. Designed to respond and supply, now it will deceive and withhold. Notice as well that it is not work that is Adam's curse here, it is *fruitless* work. I often remind my students that even in our fallen world, the only difference between work and play is who is making you do it. For me to be able to get up at dawn and run five miles is pure joy—as long as I got a good night's sleep and my husband agrees to watch the kids. That same five-mile run is transformed into torture if the person waking me at dawn is a drill sergeant and he's running behind me yelling the whole way! We who are created in the image of God are designed to love to create and produce, but when that work is forced upon us or is fruitless, then it becomes toil and our will is broken.

> By the sweat of your face you shall eat bread, till you return to the ground
> [*ădāmāh*], because from it you were taken; for you are dust, and to dust
> you shall return. (Gen 3:19)

This last bit of the curse is particularly poignant. Most read the phrase "by the sweat of your face" as having to do with difficult physical labor. But an article by Daniel Fleming of New York University has demonstrated that this phrase is actually an old ancient Near Eastern idiom having nothing to do with hard work.[18] Rather, this idiom speaks of anxiety—perspiration-inducing *fear*. Where does anxiety fit into God's curse upon us? What we find in Genesis 3 is that because of the rebellion of the earth and the expulsion of Adam and Eve from God's presence, humanity will now live their lives in an adversarial world with a constant, gnawing undercurrent of dread that there will not be enough, that their labor will not meet the need. What if the crop fails? The livestock die? A fire, storm or drought? Can you relate? What about groceries this week? Rent, mortgage and car payment? College tuition? Retirement? What if I get sick? What if my kids get sick? I am a citizen of the richest nation in the world, I have a secure position at a well-endowed seminary and still I worry. And so do you. This is the curse of ʾĀdām—limited resources, an insecure future and a world that no longer responds to my command. Any Adams out there?

And now for the most horrific aspect of this word against humanity: "For you are dust, and to dust you shall return" (Gen 3:19). This aspect of the curse introduces something previously inconceivable: the image-bearers will now die like the beasts. And whereas ʾĀdām had been made to rule the ʾădāmāh, now they will rot in it. To put it even more bluntly, the ones made to rule the cultivable earth will now become fertilizer for it. God's perfect order has been turned upside down.

The loss of the presence.

Therefore the LORD God sent [*sālaḥ*] him out from the garden of Eden . . . So He drove man out; and at the east of the garden of Eden He stationed the *cherubim* and the flaming sword which turned every direction to guard the way to the tree of life. (Gen 3:23-24)

The final scene of this heartbreaking drama is that Yahweh drives his children from his presence, and the place that Adam and Eve were privileged to protect is now protected from them. This final curse embodies all that has gone before. ʾĀdām has lost Yahweh, and now the people of God will live in exile from both his place and his presence. The verb in verse 23, *sālaḥ* is the same verb one uses to divorce a wife or disown a child. As we think back to chapter one and what the word "redemption" actually means, we see that a divorce or disowning is indeed an appropriate metaphor for this event. By their own choice, Adam and Eve are separated from their Creator.

THE SEVEN DAYS TURNED UPSIDE DOWN

So let's return to the literary and theological structure of Genesis 1 for a moment. What we've seen in the curses of Genesis 3 is not merely the spewing of random penalties in response to a bad decision, but the *reversal* of intended benefits. Those made in the image of God and designed to live eternally will now die like the animals; the earth, which was designed to serve, will now devour; the bringing forth of life will now produce death. In other words, the perfect seven-day structure of Eden has been turned upside down, thrown into a tailspin by the treason of God's stewards.

Take a look at figure 4.1 again. Remember the slot in this framework given to humanity? Humanity was designed to rule over all creation (the sixth day) under the rule of God (the seventh day). But Adam and Eve refused this plan; in essence, they rejected the seventh day. They chose

1	2	3	
Day & Night	The Waters Above (the heavens) & The Waters Below (the oceans)	Land & Vegetation	**6b** Man & Woman
4	**5**	**6a**	
Sun & Moon	Birds to rule the heavens Fish to rule the seas	Land Animals	

Figure 4.3. Adam's choice

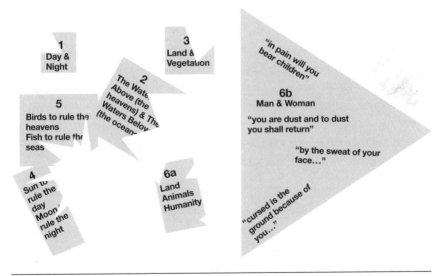

Figure 4.4. Adam's world

figure 4.3 instead, in which the seventh day (Yahweh's ultimate sovereignty) is deleted from the framework. And although Adam and Eve had authority to *make* this choice, they did not have the agency to hold the cosmos in check after making it. Rather, with the removal of day seven, the structure cannot be maintained. The days break apart like a mighty fleet in a terrible storm, and what had been held in balance by Yahweh's supreme authority is cast into terrible, tragic disarray (fig. 4.4).

Thus what humanity had previously ruled erupts in rebellion against them just as they broke out in rebellion against Yahweh. And in an instant, God's perfect world becomes ʾĀdām's broken world. Like a fractured mirror, only distorted images of perfection remain. Who would heal this broken world? Humanity, having erected the veil, is now powerless to remove it. And whereas Yahweh's world was one of life, joy and beauty, ʾĀdām's world is one of loss, anxiety and violence. And the greatest grief of all is that this twisted existence is not merely ʾĀdām's heritage. Rather, because of their strategic place in the created order, *all* of the cosmos is subjected to the agony of ʾĀdām's choice.

Romans 8. Nowhere is the brokenness of the cosmos more apparent in Scripture than in Romans 8. Read it carefully.

> For the anxious longing of the creation waits eagerly for the revealing of the sons of God. For the creation was subjected to futility, not of its own will, but because of Him who subjected it, in hope that the creation itself also will be set free from its slavery to corruption into the freedom of the glory of the children of God. For we know that the whole creation groans and suffers the pains of childbirth together until now. And not only this, but also we ourselves, having the first fruits of the Spirit, even we ourselves groan within ourselves, waiting eagerly for our adoption as sons, the redemption of our body. (Rom 8:19-23)

This text is reiterating what Genesis 1–3 has already taught us, that God's first perfect plan was cast into futility by ʾĀdām's choice. Therefore the entire creation (over which humanity had been given authority) was consigned to fruitlessness and confusion, "not of its own will" but because of ʾĀdām's. And just as you and I are longing for release, so too is creation. When will creation's anxious longing be fulfilled? This is Paul's addition to what we already know. The redemption of the cosmos will come with the redemption of humanity, and that by means of the Christ. In sum, when the stewards of Eden are returned to their proper place in God's perfect seven-day structure by means of the re-creative power of redemption, when their treasonous choice is reversed, so too will the cosmos be "freed from its slavery to corruption," and returned to its pre-fallen state.

Folks, we are not merely waiting for our personal deliverance, we wait for the day when all of creation will be "born again."

And what is the "freedom of the glory of the children of God"? The passage tells us it is "our adoption as sons, the redemption of our body." In other words, the sign that our redemption is accomplished is the moment that our death-ridden bodies are resurrected into the ongoing state of eternal life. Not only will this be the trumpet blast of freedom for us, it is the trumpet blast for all creation. "For we know that the whole creation groans and suffers the pains of childbirth together until now." What pains of childbirth? According to Kline, this text communicates that the 'ădāmāh is as repelled by 'Ādām's presence within it as are we. The very dust of the earth longs for this wrong to be made right, for the soil to be free of its accursed state as the recipient of Adam's children, for humanity to be delivered from their role as fertilizer. So like a mother bringing forth a child, the 'ădāmāh is groaning in childbirth even now, longing for the day when the child is delivered, when 'Ādām is raised up from the dirt, "our adoption as sons, the redemption of our body." Romans 8 makes it clear that the goal of redemption is far broader than the simple salvation of the individual. Redemption is a cosmic plan of cosmic proportions. God's plan is that *all* creation will be "saved" from the effects of sin.

What did Adam lose? With the Fall, humanity loses their identity as God's people, their place in his paradise and their access to his presence. Intimacy with God, which was the essence of humanity's existence, is shattered. Rather than being casually welcomed into God's presence like a child by her parent, now an armed *cherubim* stands between humanity and their Creator. The paradise that had been their home is now inaccessible to them. Thus Adam and Eve lose the opportunity to be what they were designed to be; they lose a secure world in which the safety of their children and the next meal were *never* in question; they lose their dominion over a willing earth.

In addition the bodies of these made in the image of God are cursed with death. Not immediate death, but their bodies become mortal and are thereby invaded with the sickness and deformity that lead to death. Although I am still alive (at this printing at least!), I am very sad to say that gray hairs and wrinkles have made their appearance. I have a knee that worked a lot better four surgeries ago. I am no longer able to dive for a volleyball without ibuprofen-inspiring results. In other words, my body is already rotting around me. And so is yours. We inherited this state of affairs from our ancestors, and unless the process is interrupted by the return of Christ, then as with all who have gone before us, the death already resident in our bodies will have its way. Adam and Eve were the biological and legal representatives of our race, and they have passed on the legal and biological consequences of the curse to their children's children's children.

’Ādām's breach with the Father has also fractured humanity's relational world. Self-centeredness and competition are now the relational norms. A healthy relationship, at any level, is hard to find. Rather, in ’Ādām's world the strong use the weak to obtain their objectives, be they parents or presidents. Moreover, our fallen race has used its superior skills and intellect to strip and despoil the garden. Thus a world that once provided only good now trembles under ’Ādām's rule. Unable to produce, even poisoning its inhabitants, the garden is dying as well.

Adam's world (or "Why do bad things happen to good people?"). This is ’Ādām's world, and the ironic thing about this picture is that it is exactly what Adam and Eve asked for. They wanted a world of their own making, a world without the seventh day. And that is what they got . . . and what we now have. In light of this picture, reflect with me on a question I am frequently asked: "Why do bad things happen to good people?" By this question people usually mean why do babies die, why are young parents struck with cancer, why are good citizens killed by drunk drivers? Sometimes people who ask this question are thinking more globally: "Why do tyrannous governments thrive? Why does terrorism reproduce itself? Why are tens of thousands of children on this planet orphans?" I am intrigued by the frequency of this question for many reasons. The foremost is because the very voicing of this question demonstrates to me that ’Ādām remembers. Our DNA seems to know that it is *wrong* for babies to die, for disease to pillage our bodies, for governments to abuse those they are called to protect. The earliest literature we possess speaks of humanity's quest for immortality. Humanity somehow knows that it should not die, even though in all remembered experience humanity has died. And this sixth sense is not restricted to those who believe. No, all of the sons of Adam and daughters of Eve somehow know that ʾĀdām is not what they are supposed to be, that there is something profoundly wrong with the world as it is. I believe this sense is evidence of the residual presence of the image of God in humanity. The image is broken and marred, but it remains. And it is this aspect of humanity that recognizes the "wrongness" of this world and continues to cry out for the world as it should be—Eden.

So how do I go about answering this question? Well, the answer typically comes in two parts. The first part of the answer is that there are no good people. Most folks are a bit shocked at this statement. But reality is that in comparison to what we were designed to be, we are a broken, twisted, evil race. The finest deeds among us are, before the Father, "filthy rags" (Is 64:6; cf. Rom 3:9-18). So although in comparison to the folks I see on the news, I might appear a fairly "good" person; in comparison to what I was designed to be, I am wholly corrupted—both morally and physically. Like the female wraith in C. S. Lewis's *The Great Divorce* who foolishly preened and primped her rotting body to charm the saints in heaven, my degree of degeneracy escapes me, but is wholly obvious to the one who created me.[19]

The second part of the answer has to do with the fallenness of our world. No longer ordered according God's perfect seven-day structure, no longer subjected to his ideal authority, this world is at war with itself. Our gene pool is flooded with death and disease, our relationships are consumed by self, our resources are limited, our planet is poisoned, death is everywhere, anxiety abounds, and sin reproduces itself at every level. In essence, God has yielded this world to the authority of his stewards, and his guiding grace has been withdrawn. The reason bad things happen is not because God lets them happen in our generally good world, but because the *nature* of Adam's world is evil—bad is now the norm.

I will never forget a lecture I heard in seminary in which my teacher nearly shouted, his voice breaking: "We should not be surprised that in this fallen world babies die or marriages fail; we should be surprised that some babies live and some marriages thrive." What my teacher was trying to communicate is that the world is fallen, the flesh is rotten, the fabric stained, the water foul. So although our tendency is to ask why God does not step in to stop one particular instance of abuse, one murder or one corrupt official, in truth, the only way to fix this cycle of sin and death is to stop it, tear it down and build again. So although sometimes God does step in and interrupt human history by taking out that one corrupt official, know that the evil of our world will not be fixed until our world is unmade and made again (2 Pet 3:7). Know as well that it is actually *mercy* that holds back the hand of God. Because once he intervenes to stop injustice, this entire system will end and another will begin . . . and not one more of the lost children of Adam will have the opportunity to enter heaven's gate. But that belongs to the next chapter. In sum, the answer to the question "Why do bad things happen to good people" is this: every child starving in Darfur, every young Arab woman slaughtered in an "honor killing," every body laid to rest because of 9/11 is the victim of ʾĀdām's choice.

CONCLUSIONS

We have learned in this chapter that Genesis 1–2 essentially provides a blueprint to God's original intent for humanity: God's people dwelling in God's place with full access to his presence. You will hear this little triplet many times throughout the course of this book. Yahweh planned a perfect world in which the sons of Adam and the daughters of Eve would live eternally, stretching their cognitive and creative skills to the uttermost, building their civilization within the protective boundaries of their relationship with him. But treason bred tragedy—a broken covenant, a broken race. The end result was that God's people were driven from God's place and forever separated from his presence. The only hope in this wretched state of affairs was God's redemptive mercy. Indeed, redemptive history starts right here. For it is with ʾĀdām's choice that the saga of redemption begins. Who will pay the price for ʾĀdām's rebellion? How will ʾĀdām's race be held accountable and delivered all the same? How do we get Eden back? Although Christians too often think that the story of salvation begins with Jesus, the story actually begins with Adam and Eve. I know for myself that I am unable to share the gospel without speaking of Eden. Because when we ask the salvation question, what we are really asking is, what did the first Adam lose? And when we answer the salvation question, what we are really attempting to articulate is, what did the Second Adam (i.e., Jesus) buy back? Let the story begin!

GOD'S FINAL INTENT

The New Jerusalem

For as through the one man's disobedience the many were made sinners, even so through the obedience of the One the many will be made righteous. . . . That, as sin reigned in death, even so grace would reign through righteousness to eternal life through Jesus Christ our Lord. (Rom 5:19, 21)

WHEN WE LEFT EDEN, WE LEFT A FRUIT-FILLED paradise animated by a cosmic river and graced by the Tree of Life. This paradise, which was once the shared dwelling place of God and humanity, is now defended *against* Adam's race by means of *cherubim*. The city of man and the kingdom of God are now separated; Adam and Eve now live in exile from their heavenly father. How will this wretched state of affairs be righted? What is God's plan of redemption? Or should we say, what is God's final intent for humanity?

THE ICONOGRAPHY OF EDEN: OF CHERUBIM, TREES AND RIVERS

There are many ways to approach the questions voiced above, but the one I like best is to ask these questions by tracing the iconography of Eden throughout redemption's story. Let's start with the cherubim, the fearsome creature armed with a double-edged sword, stationed at the entrance of the garden. Who (and what) is this dire creature?

Cherubim. In the Bible we find that cherubim appear only in particular contexts. After Eden, the first reappearance of the cherubim is the divinely dictated design of the tabernacle in Exodus 25–26 and Exodus 36–37. Here on Mount Sinai, God instructs Moses to build a habitation for the Holy One among his people.

"Let them construct a sanctuary for Me, that I may dwell among them" (Ex 25:8). The text tells us that the reason God wants this sanctuary is "*so that* I might live among them." Do you hear the echo of Eden here? This will be the first time since the garden that God has dwelt with ʾĀdām. Perhaps I am overly sentimental, but I hear in this passage the longing of a father for his children. Whereas with the Fall humanity was forbidden from God's presence, with the Mosaic covenant God commands a meeting place so that he may cohabit with his children once more. In order to help get our bearings for the following discussion, I've included figure 5.1, which provides the footprint of the sacred tent-structure we know as the tabernacle, and figure 5.2, which is an artist's reconstruction of the same.

Notice that whereas the Holy Place and Holies of Holies were concealed under tent curtains, the outer court of the tabernacle (where the altar and laver were located) was open to the sky. The outer court was open to worshippers, but only priests were allowed to enter the Holy Place. The innermost sanctuary, the Holy of Holies, was only visited once a year by the High Priest on the Day of Atonement. This is where God lived and where the Ark of the Covenant was housed.

And according to God's instructions, the curtains of the Holy of Holies (where God actually dwelt) and the sacred veil that divided the Holy of Holies from the Holy Place (the place in which the priests served him) were to be decorated with cherubim.

> You shall make a veil of blue and purple and scarlet material and fine twisted linen; it shall be made with cherubim, the work of a skillful craftsman. You shall hang it on four pillars of acacia overlaid with gold, their hooks also being of gold, on four sockets of silver. You shall hang up the veil under the clasps, and shall bring in the ark of the testimony there within the veil; and the veil shall serve for you as a partition between the holy place and the holy of holies. (Ex 26:31-33; cf. Ex 36:8-13; 1 Kings 6:32-35)

The Ark of the Covenant, which housed the tablets of the covenant within the Holy of Holies, is also adorned with cherubim.

You shall make two cherubim of gold, make them of hammered work at the two ends of the mercy seat. Make one cherub at one end and one cherub at the other end; you shall make the cherubim of one piece with the mercy seat at its two ends. The cherubim shall have their wings spread upward, covering the mercy seat with their wings and facing one another; the faces of the

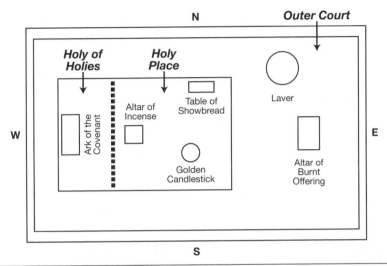

Figure 5.1. The footprint of the tabernacle

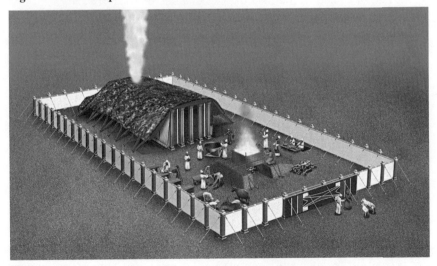

Figure 5.2. An artist's reconstruction of the tabernacle (copyright 2003, The New Life Mission)

cherubim are to be turned toward the mercy seat. You shall put the mercy seat on top of the ark, and in the ark you shall put the testimony which I will give to you. (Ex 25:18-21; cf. Ex 37:1-9; 1 Kings 6:23-29; 8:6-7)

Very interesting to us is the *function* of the ark's golden cherubim.

There I will meet with you; and from above the mercy seat, from between the two cherubim which are upon the ark of the testimony, I will speak to you about all that I will give you in commandment for the sons of Israel. (Ex 25:22; cf. Num 7:89; 1 Sam 4:4, 6:2).

So what in the world are cherubim? Obviously the Israelites knew what one was, or these texts would have been unintelligible to them. When we search the Scriptures, we find that Ezekiel and John the Revelator actually describe these creatures. One of Ezekiel's descriptions reads as follows:

And this was their appearance: they had human form. Each of them had four faces and four wings. Their legs were straight and their feet were like a calf's hoof, and they gleamed like burnished bronze. Under their wings on their four sides were human hands. As for the faces and wings of the four of them, their wings touched one another; their faces did not turn when they moved, each went straight forward. As for the form of their faces, each had the face of a man; all four had the face of a lion on the right and the face of a bull on the left, and all four had the face of an eagle. Such were their faces. (Ezek 1:5-11; cf. Rev 4:5-11; 2 Sam 22:11; Ps 18:10-11)

Ezekiel's fearsome figures are not at all like the chubby, flying babes so popular on postcard art today. And when we broaden the circle further we find that these creatures, so mysterious to us, were actually well known to the ancient Near East. In Mesopotamia, Egypt and Canaan we find repeated presentations of huge, intimidating creatures with the wings of an eagle, the face of a man and the body and feet of either a lion or a bull. Their composite bodies have been interpreted by modern scholars as pointing to "a union of the highest powers (strength, speed, sagacity)" of the human and animal kingdoms.[1] Examples of such composite creatures include the sculpted column bases guarding the entryway to Barrakub's palace in Zinjirli (Neo-Hittite, late eighth century B.C.), the winged Sphinx well known in Egyptian art and architecture, and the *enormous* winged bulls and lions stationed outside the throne room and palace entrances of the great Assyrian monarchs.[2] According to Othmar Keel, these creatures served as semi-divine guardians: "The emplacement of guardian genii was motivated by the belief that they would repel, or even kill the wicked, and thus protect the holy precincts from defilement."[3] Stationed at the entrances of palaces, throne rooms and temples, these creatures were intended to intimidate visitors and to make them think twice about doing any sort of damage or showing disrespect to the king/deity or his palace/temple. And so they did. And when you stand in the British Museum next to one of the winged lions of Ashurbanipal and your head barely reaches its knees, you quickly come to understand why these things were used as royal and sacred sentries!

Why is all this significant to us? Because the cherubim of the biblical text also show up at the entrance of a throne room, and they too were intended to defend the Great King from any who would attempt to enter unworthily. Indeed, the cherubim stationed at the entrance of Eden and embroidered on the curtains of the Holy of Holies let us know that Eden and the Holy of Holies should both be understood as the throne room of God. And this throne room is now defended from *ʾĀdām* by the armed sentries of heaven.

And what of the cherubim that adorn the ark (Ex 25:18-25)? Turning back to archaeology for a moment, we find that one of the most amazing portrayals of cherubim coming out of the ancient world is the frequent Late-Bronze/Early Iron-Age depiction of cherubim thrones.[4] One of these is carved into the tenth-century-B.C. limestone sarcophagus of Phoenician King Ahiram of Byblos.[5]

In this sketch of the carved panel of the sarcophagus, Ahiram is portrayed as seated upon his cherubim throne, participating in a banquet. There are *ten* similar images from ancient Canaan.[6] When we recall that Exodus 25:18-25 commands

Figure 5.3. King Ahiram's sarcophagus

Moses to position two cherubim above the ark, and that God's plan was to meet and speak with the Israelites from that spot ("from above the mercy seat, from between the two cherubim," Ex 25:22), and that Yahweh is repeatedly described as the one "enthroned above the cherubim" (2 Sam 6:2; 2 Kings 19:15; 1 Chron 13:6; Ps 80:1; 99:1; Is 37:16), it seems that archaeology has provided us with a *picture* of what the Bible is describing. These analogues show us that the cherubim on the Ark of the Covenant were to serve as the actual *throne* of Yahweh, and the ark as his footstool (1 Chron 28:2). And Yahweh, like all kings, intends to utilize his throne room as a place of audience with his people. Thus the cherubim of the ark and of Eden are best understood as Yahweh's watchers, his sentries, his armed guards. But the distinction between Eden and the Holy of Holies is that whereas ʾĀdām was driven from Eden with no hope of reentry, the Holy of Holies is designed to function as God's outpost in ʾĀdām's world. Here, although guarded by his cherubim and set apart by means of the mediation of sacrifice and a priestly staff, God once again dwells among his people.

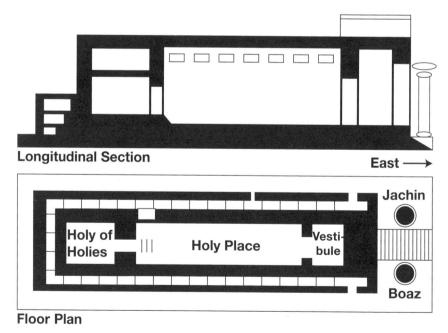

Figure 5.4. The footprint of Solomon's temple

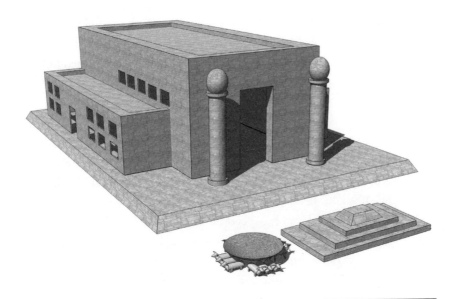

Figure 5.5. An artist's reconstruction of the temple

Trees. When Israel became a settled people under David's monarchy, they began to think in terms of a more permanent sanctuary. So with God's direction, Solomon built the temple. Formatted and decorated in the same fashion as the tabernacle, we find the same floor plan, furniture and appliances, as well as the same decorative motifs. But here the curtains are replaced with walls and roofs, dimensions are amplified and the adornment is far more elaborate.

In 1 Kings 6 and 7 we read a description of the temple.

Then he [Solomon] carved all the walls of the house round about with carved engravings of cherubim, palm trees, and open flowers, inner and outer sanctuaries. He overlaid the floor of the house with gold, inner and outer sanctuaries. For the entrance of the inner sanctuary he made doors of olive wood, the lintel and five-sided doorposts. So he made two doors of olive wood, and he carved on them carvings of cherubim, palm trees, and open flowers, and overlaid them with gold; and he spread the gold on the cherubim and on the palm trees. So also he made for the entrance of the nave four-sided doorposts of olive wood and two doors of cypress wood. . . . He carved on it cherubim, palm trees, and open flowers; and he overlaid them with gold evenly applied on the engraved work. (1 Kings 6:29-35)

So as in the tabernacle, we encounter cherubim in the temple. But now another motif of Eden has been added—trees, flowers and fruit. Apparently this place in which God and his people cohabitate is designed to turn the heart toward Eden (1 Kings 6:29, 32, 35; 7:15-26, 36).[7]

Rivers. Our next stop is Ezekiel 47. This chapter is embedded in the prophet's larger vision about the rebuilt and restored temple (Ezekiel 40–48). Whereas Ezekiel had lived through the period of the exile in which Jerusalem was captured and the temple razed, in these chapters he is seeing with the eyes of vision the restoration of this beloved temple at the end of all things.[8] In his vision, the temple has subsumed all of Jerusalem; the entire city has become the temple. And the temple is now a perfect square (Ezek 48:35). This becomes very significant when we remember that the only part of Solomon's temple that was perfectly square was the Holy of Holies. Thus, in Ezekiel's vision, the Holy of Holies (the place God actually *dwelt*) has enveloped the city of man. "He said to me, 'Son of man, this is the place of My throne and the place of the soles of My feet, where I will dwell among the sons of Israel forever'" (Ezek 43:7). In sum, Ezekiel's vision of the "rest of the story" is God and humanity dwelling together within a city that has become a temple.

Then suddenly in Ezekiel 47 we are introduced to something wonderfully new—a river. It begins as a trickle in the Holy of Holies but eventually becomes a raging river flowing east through the desert toward the Dead Sea. The river transforms the deserts of Judah into a garden, and even turns the Dead Sea (which can support no marine life) fresh.

> Then he said to me, "These waters go out toward the eastern region and go down into the Arabah; then they go toward the [Dead] sea, being made to flow into the sea, and the waters of the sea become fresh." (Ezek 47:8)

The supernatural nature of this vision becomes fully apparent when we read the next verse. For although this river will transform the heavy, mineral-laden water of the Dead Sea so that it will support "very many" fish (Ezek 47:10), it will not turn the *marshes* of the Dead Sea fresh. This is because those salt marshes were an important source of income in Ezekiel's day! So this river brings all that is good and nothing that is evil. Rather, this river is a river of *life:* "everything will live where the river goes" (Ezek 47:9l cf. Is 66:12).

So what does this have to do with Eden? You may recall that Eden was characterized by a cosmic river that split into four and "watered the entire garden" (Gen 2:10). In Ezekiel's heaven, this river does the same. Originating in the throne room of God (i.e., the Holy of Holies), it brings life back to a fallen earth. Pause for a moment over Ezekiel 47:12.

> By the river on its bank, on one side and on the other, will grow all kinds of trees for food. Their leaves will not wither and their fruit will not fail. They will bear every month because their water flows from the sanctuary, and their fruit will be for food and their leaves for healing.

Hmmm . . . when did we last encounter a Tree of Life?

THE NEW JERUSALEM

This brings us at last to Revelation 21–22, the end of the story.

> Then I saw a new heaven and a new earth; for the first heaven and the first earth passed away, and there is no longer any sea. And I saw the holy city, new Jerusalem, coming down out of heaven from God, made ready as a bride adorned for her husband. And I heard a loud voice from the throne, saying, "Behold, the tabernacle of God is among men, and He will dwell among them, and they shall be His people, and God Himself will be among them, and He will wipe away every tear from their eyes; and there will no longer be any death; there will no longer be any mourning, or crying, or pain; the first things have passed away." And He who sits on the throne said, "Behold, I am making all things new." (Rev 21:1-5)

What John is describing here is what Christians call "heaven." But unlike the images common to our imaginations—disembodied spirits, clouds and wings, harps and chubby cherubs—the biblical author is describing heaven as a *new* earth. The garden has been restored, the primordial deep ("chaos") has been defeated, and Ezekiel's city/temple is being lowered from the heavens to serve as the residence of the redeemed.[9] Hear the voice from the throne ringing out into the silence and grief of ʾĀdām's wasted world: "I am making all things new!" (Rev 21:5). The Creator speaks and the earth and its inhabitants are finally free (cf. Rom 8:21).

Healing has come; mourning is passed; death is no more. This is the *New Jerusalem*, purified and whole. And with the New Jerusalem comes the Presence, "and God Himself shall be among them" (Rev 21:3; cf. Rev 21:22-27). Glory to his name.

> Then he showed me a river of the water of life, clear as crystal, coming from the throne of God and of the Lamb, in the middle of its street. On either side of the river was the tree of life, bearing twelve kinds of fruit, yielding its fruit every month; and the leaves of the tree were for the healing of the nations. There will no longer be any curse; and the throne of God and of the Lamb will be in it, and His bond-servants will serve Him; they will see His face, and His name will be on their foreheads. And there will no longer be any night; and they will not have need of the light of a lamp nor the light of the sun, because the Lord God will illumine them; and they will reign forever and ever. (Rev 22:1-5)

This New Jerusalem (what we know as "heaven") is all that the city of man in Eden was meant to be. In fact, it *is* Eden—a fruit-filled paradise animated by a cosmic river and graced by the Tree of Life. Here, once again, the unhindered presence of God and the unhindered maturation of a sinless humanity coexist. The most significant difference between the New Jerusalem and Eden is that there was no city in Eden; ʾĀdām had not gotten that far. But now the city built in our fallenness has been redeemed and restored. God and ʾĀdām live under the same roof once again. Moreover, the icons of Eden are now multiplied and expanded. The Tree of Life lines *both* sides of the river in the New Jerusalem, and now the tree and the river bring healing to a wounded race. All of this because what had been the "outpost" of God's presence has become the whole. Whereas the Holy of Holies had served as a small-scale locus of connection, a "bubble" in ʾĀdām's world in which the two dimensions of God's place and humanity's place could be the same place, in the New Jerusalem the two dimensions are rejoined:

> I saw no temple in it, for the Lord God the Almighty and the Lamb are its temple. And the city has no need of the sun or of the moon to shine on it, for the glory of God has illumined it, and its lamp is the Lamb. The nations will walk by its light, and the kings of the earth will bring their glory into it. In the daytime (for there will be no night there) its gates will

never be closed; and they will bring the glory and the honor of the nations into it; and nothing unclean, and no one who practices abomination and lying, shall ever come into it, but only those whose names are written in the Lamb's book of life. (Rev 21:22-27)

This city will need no temple, because it will not need to *house* God, he will live there. Its gates will never be closed because there will be no enemies to threaten it. And who will live there? "Those whose names are written in the Lamb's book of life."

And where are the cherubim in the New Jerusalem? As there is no longer any need to defend the throne room of God from ʾĀdām ("they will see His face, and His name will be on their foreheads"; Rev 22:4), we find no cherubim here either. God has taken back the garden, Adam's children are home, and the seven days of Genesis 1 have been put back in their proper order.

GOD'S FINAL INTENT

So what is God's final intent for humanity? As is obvious from tracing the iconography of Eden through redemptive history, God's original intent *is* his final intent. Eden was the perfect plan, and God has never had any other. His goal was that the people of God might dwell in the place of God, enjoying the presence of God. This is all our heavenly Father has ever wanted for us. And everything that lies between Eden's gate and the New Jerusalem, the bulk of our Bibles, is in essence a huge rescue plan. In fact, we could summarize the plot line of the Bible into one cosmic question: "How do we get ʾĀdām back into the garden?" In Genesis 3 humanity was driven out; in Revelation 21–22 they are welcomed home.

My years in the classroom tell me that at this point some readers are asking, "Wait, I'm confused. Then where is heaven?" Heaven is the same place it has always been . . . where God is. More specifically, heaven is the place where the people of God dwell in the place of God with full access to the presence of God. But this insight must be balanced by the fact that ʾĀdām is a creature; humanity was not designed to float about in the heavenlies as is so often portrayed in popular theology. No, ʾĀdām was designed for Eden. And the new heavens and the new earth (which are the new Eden) is where God intends for us to spend eternity. Because of this, Eden-past is actually our best picture of what heaven-future will be. This portrait of heaven should help out a lot the next time your seven-year-old asks you where relatives go when they die.

So if Eden and the New Jerusalem are God's original and final intent for humanity, what of all that lies in between? Take a look at figure 5.6. This simple little chart offers us a synopsis of redemptive history. The tree in the top left-hand corner is our icon for Eden. Start here. Although designed to live out their lives in Eden, humanity chose rebellion instead. The result was the Fall with all of its horrible repercussions. Like a rock climber having fallen from a great height, ʾĀdām now lies broken and bloody on the ledge of the cliff—too far from top or bottom for a simple rescue. It will take a series of rescues to bring this climber to safety. Let's pursue this metaphor for a moment. A climber who has experienced this sort of accident is too injured to do anything to help himself; he is probably unconscious. So someone is going to have to rappel down that precipice to reach him in his need. That someone will need to do emergency first aid, brace the climber's neck and strap his battered body into a litter so that he can be hoisted back up or down the face of the cliff. But this is only the beginning of the rescue. An airlift will be needed to get this man to a hospital. Emergency surgery will be necessary to stop the bleeding, remove the irreparable organs and splint the bones. And now the real vigil begins. Placed in ICU on a respirator and IV, will our climber recover? This is only a metaphor, but it's one that has a lot to teach us because the rescue of ʾĀdām is much the same. The Bible teaches us that redemptive history did not happen in one fell swoop. Rather, God has been leading humanity back to Eden by means of a sequence of steps, a series of rescues, a series of covenants. To mix metaphors, with the covenant of Noah the paramedic successfully reaches the fallen climber; with the covenant of Abraham triage is done and the climber is lowered down the cliff; with the covenants of Moses and David the airlift is accomplished and surgery begins; with the covenant of Jesus the surgery is successful and the vigil begins—will our rescued climber endure to the end?

The rest of this book is dedicated to detailing each of the covenantal administrations of this great rescue plan. As promised, we will find that the "general law" that will organize the facts for us is *covenant*. Each step

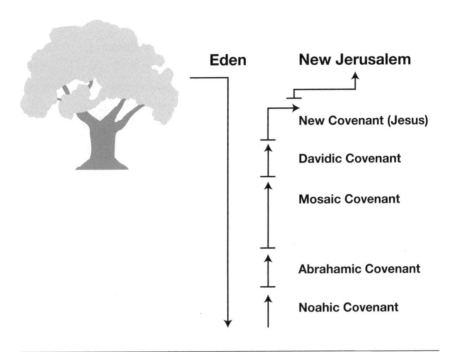

Figure 5.6. A synopsis of redemptive history

of the story, each stage of the rescue may be organized under one of six covenants. Let me summarize. The first post-Eden covenantal administration is with Noah. This covenant reestablishes contact between Adam's race and Yahweh, and it speaks to all creation. Thus we will speak of Noah's covenant as a "cosmic" and "re-creational" covenant. The Abrahamic covenant begins the hard work of restoring a people for God's own possession. Do you remember our little triplet? The people of God dwelling in the place of God with full access to the presence of God. The Abrahamic covenant addresses the first two components of this equation by promising Abraham offspring and land: the *people* of God (Abraham's offspring) and the *place* of God (Canaan). The covenant with Moses comes next. When the New Testament writers speak of the "Old Covenant," this is the one they mean. This covenant takes up the lion's share of the Old Testament, and in it the promises offered to Abraham are fulfilled. But they are fulfilled only in a typological fashion. We will get to the idea of "typology" later; for now understand that under Moses the *people* of God are the citizens of the nation of Israel and the place is the real estate that belongs to that political entity. Moreover, under this covenant, for the first time since Eden, the Presence is restored to the people. God dwells among his people by means of the tabernacle and then the temple. Although in a limited (typological) fashion, under Moses the people of God dwell in the place of God with access to the presence of God. David's covenant will add to this picture the capstone of a human leader whose first ambition is to lead his people in their service to God. David is, in essence, the ideal vassal. And unlike Adam, David welcomes the seventh day into his kingdom. Thus David becomes the prototype of the coming Messiah who will be the *ultimate* human mediator, the perfect vassal, the Word incarnate. With Jesus comes the new covenant. In Jesus, the types of the Mosaic and Davidic covenants are fulfilled in an "already" and "not yet" fashion. The "already" is what we live today: restored but waiting, free but bound, born again yet still experiencing death. The "not yet" is what we live for. This is the promise of the New Jerusalem in which the people, place, and presence are restored in full and forever—where death has been defeated and the curse forever repealed.

In its simplicity, figure 5.6 illustrates that Eden and the New Jerusalem are the bookends of redemptive history. God's original intent is his final intent, and everything that lies between is one extraordinary rescue plan. To use another metaphor, the rescue plan is much like a series of overhead transparencies. In the days of overhead projectors, when I needed to illustrate a region of Israel in my classes, I would start with a backdrop transparency showing the topography of the land; I would then overlay that with a second transparency illustrating the national boundaries of the region and then overlay that with a transparency showing the towns and highways in which I was particularly interested. Thus, whereas each transparency was correct in and of itself, the picture was not complete until each had been laid upon the other. This is redemptive history as well. Each of the stages in the story brings ʾĀdām one step closer to full deliverance; each serves to reeducate humanity as to who the God of Eden was and is. But the picture is not complete until the New Jerusalem descends from heaven, God reestablishes his dwelling place among humanity, and humanity is home.

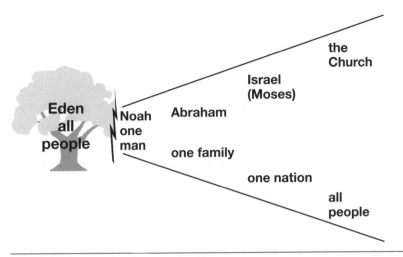

Figure 5.7. The people of redemptive history

Another way to picture this story is illustrated in figure 5.7. Here you see the ever-expanding embrace of redemptive history. Whereas in Eden all humanity was welcomed into relationship with God, with the Fall, that relationship was broken. With Noah, one man and his immediate family reenter God's plan. With Abraham, an extended family that eventually becomes a tribal confederacy is welcomed home. With Moses, an entire nation experiences the grace of God. Finally with Jesus, as in Eden, every son of Adam and daughter of Eve is offered the opportunity for relationship with their Creator.

A final illustration of the trajectory of redemptive history is found in figure 5.8. Here a simplified timeline is offered. According to the Bible, human history begins with Eden and may be tracked and organized around the six covenantal administrations until it finds its great culmination in the New Jerusalem in which "there will no longer be any curse" (Rev 22:3). This is the big picture, and it is in every way amazing. We are

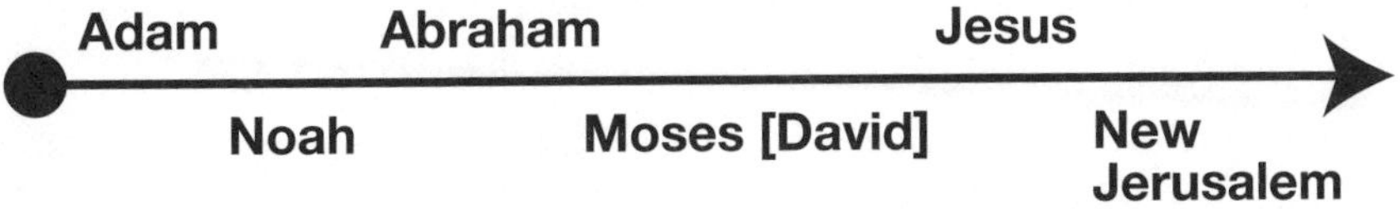

Adam   **Abraham**   **Jesus**
Noah   **Moses [David]**   **New Jerusalem**

Figure 5.8. The timeline of redemptive history

headed back to Eden, with all of heaven urging us on! To use a New Testament metaphor, the table is prepared and our Father awaits our return.

CONCLUSIONS

In sum, redemptive history is all about fixing what went wrong in the garden. What went *wrong* in Eden is what must go *right* in redemption; what was *done* in the garden must be *undone* in Christ. In the garden humanity made a choice for autonomy. That choice cast the entire cosmos into disarray. Moreover, that choice birthed in our race the power of sin which has been passed down to every son of Adam and every daughter of Eve. Thus you and I stand guilty on two fronts: (1) we are guilty because our forefather represented us in a sinful choice; but (2) we are also guilty because we have followed our forefather in that choice with our individual choices. Thus we need to be delivered on two fronts as well. First, we need a representative who will stand in for us in making a different choice; and second, we ourselves need to make a different choice. But as we do not have the power on our own to free ourselves from our depraved state (inherited from Adam and Eve) and make the right choice, we need to be somehow lifted from our depravity long enough to say "yes" to God.

How in the world will God save his people from this impossible state of affairs? Glory to his name, the solution to all of this and more was accomplished in the life and death and resurrection of Jesus. Although there are volumes that could be written, the essential points are these. When Jesus came to this fallen planet as the "Last Adam," he was born in the same state as was the first Adam, sinless. As a result, he had the same opportunities and the same weaknesses as our forefather in the flesh. Thus, when Jesus successfully resisted Satan's temptation to throw off the Father's authority and use his own authority as he pleased (Mt 4:1-11), and when he chose to participate in the crucifixion by taking the wrath of God upon himself on our behalf, he did two things. One, he proved that the first Adam could have succeeded in his charge. Two, he bore in his own body the curse of Eden, so that the children of Adam would not have to. And when Jesus *rose* from the grave, he *defeated* death; he eradicated the curse of Eden. And because Jesus was both human and God, his death and resurrection was of such a nature that it could be vicariously applied to all of Adam's children. Thus Jesus became that right representative of our race who made the right choice. In his victory over the grave, this same Jesus suspended the power of death in our lives such that you and I could be given the same opportunity given to Adam and Eve . . . the chance to choose. Thus, when you said "yes" to God at that altar rail years ago, or last week as you knelt at the side of your bed, what you were doing was "undoing" the choice of Adam in your own life. Whereas Adam said "no" to the sovereignty of God, you said "yes." What is the prayer? "Jesus, be *lord* of my life."

> If you confess with your mouth that Jesus is Lord, and believe in your heart that God raised Him from the dead, you shall be saved. (Rom 10:9)

Saved from what? The curse of Eden with all of its ramifications. In sum, in the work of Christ, the rebellious heart is softened, the choice is "un-made," the broken relationship is healed, the curse is lifted, and the lost inheritance regained. All this because the second time around, Adam did not fail.

> For as in Adam all die, so also in Christ all shall be made alive. (1 Cor 15:22)

> Therefore, just as through one man sin entered into the world, and death through sin, and so death spread to all men, because all sinned—for until the Law sin was in the world, but sin is not imputed when there is no law. Nevertheless death reigned from Adam until Moses, even over those who had not sinned in the likeness of the offense of Adam, who is a type of Him who was to come. But the free gift is not like the transgression. For if by the transgression of the one the many died, much more did the grace of God and the gift by the grace of the one Man, Jesus Christ, abound to the many. The gift is not like that which came through the one who sinned; for on the one hand the judgment arose from one transgression resulting in condemnation, but on the other hand the free gift arose from many transgressions resulting in justification. For if by the transgression of the one, death reigned through the one, much more those who receive the abundance of grace and of the gift of righteousness will reign in life through the One, Jesus Christ. So then as through one transgression there

resulted condemnation to all men, even so through one act of righteousness there resulted justification of life to all men. For as through the one man's disobedience the many were made sinners, even so through the obedience of the One the many will be made righteous. (Rom 5:12-19)

So also it is written, "The first MAN, Adam, BECAME A LIVING SOUL." The last Adam became a life-giving spirit. (1 Cor 15:45)

NOAH AND ABRAHAM

IN THE LAST FEW CHAPTERS WE HAVE BEGUN to put our closets
in order by outlining God's original and final intent for humanity. To our
joy, we have found that these are the same and that Eden and the New
Jerusalem may be understood as the bookends of redemptive history. This
is the clothes rod in your new closet. We have also discussed how all that
lies in betwixt and between Eden and the New Jerusalem is, in essence, an
enormous rescue plan. Each stage of this grand story is organized around
one of six covenantal administrations: Adam, Noah, Abraham, Moses,
David and Jesus. These are your new shelves. This chapter is dedicated
to the first two stages of the rescue plan: Noah and Abraham. By means
of Noah's covenant, God redefines his relationship with humanity for the
first time since Eden. With Abraham, the reidentification of people and
place begins. Let the closet clean-up begin!

NOAH AND THE RE-CREATIONAL COVENANT

As Genesis 6 opens, the first epoch of human history (the Adamic Age)
is drawing to a close. And as we would anticipate from what we know of
the Fall, the human race has managed to completely corrupt itself and
the earth: "Then the LORD saw that the wickedness of man was great
on the earth, and that every intent of the thoughts of his heart was only
evil continually. . . . Now the earth was corrupt in the sight of God,
and the earth was filled with violence" (Gen 6:5, 11). Do you hear the
all-inclusive language here? *Every* intent of every thought was *only* evil

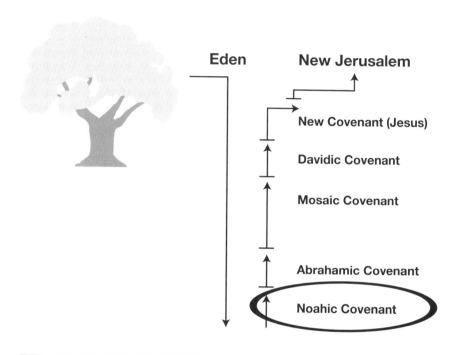

Figure 6.1. A synopsis of redemptive history, Noah

continually. Murder, violence and corruption characterize Noah's world. What is God's response to this complete and widespread depravity? He decides to start again—a choice which results in both worldwide catastrophe and a second chance. And so into this degenerate world a champion is introduced, Noah, whose name means "rest" (Hebrew *nōaḥ;* cf. Gen 5:29). Noah's role in this cosmic drama will be to rescue enough of the created order that a new start is possible and to reintroduce *'Ādām* to their Creator.

Noah's real time. How many years lie between Adam and Noah? As the genealogies of Genesis are not intended to be exhaustive,[1] there is no way to say. But I anticipate it was a very long time indeed. In fact, it is likely that thousands of years have passed since the days of Adam and Eve. I suggest this for two reasons. One, because humanity has had enough time to multiply, civilize, develop, deteriorate and decay. This sort of expansion and corruption takes time. The second reason has to do with a major New Testament parallel, Matthew 24:37-39:

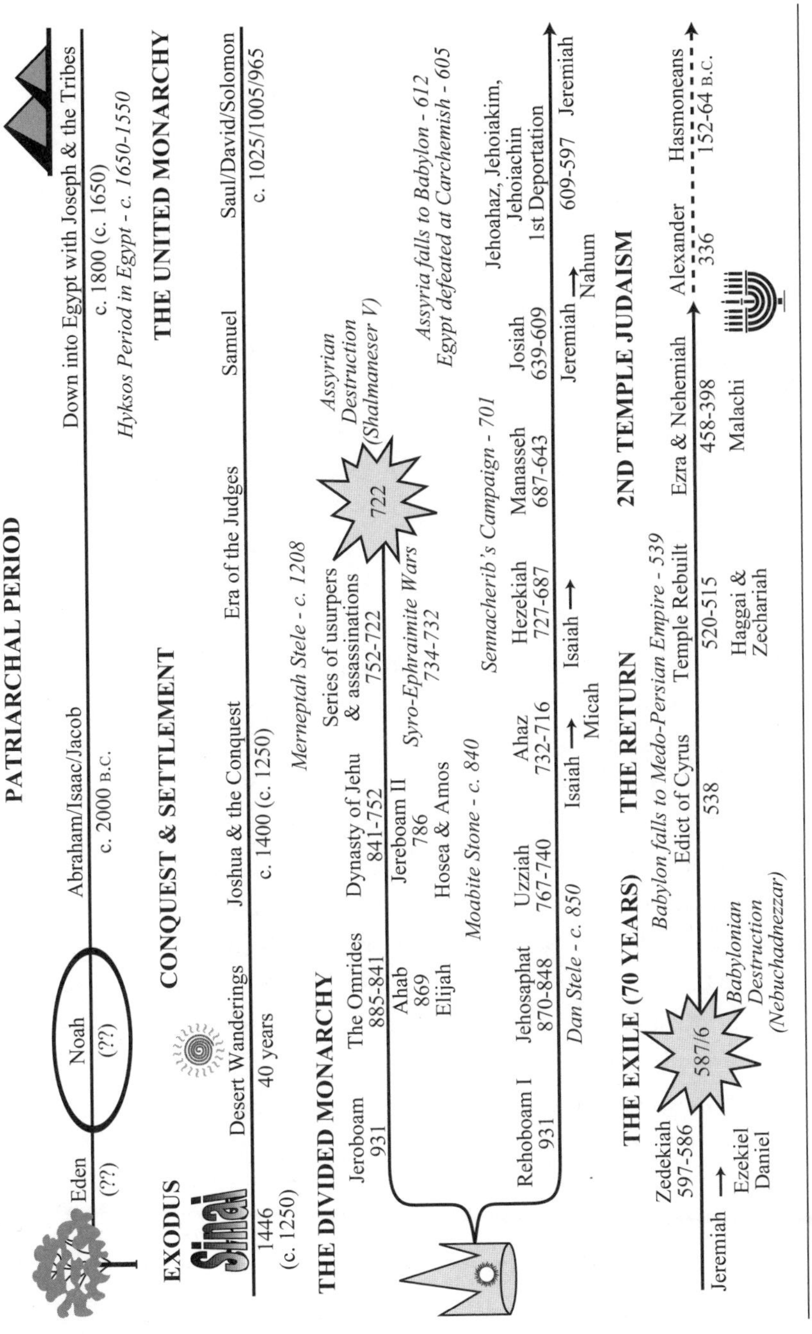

PATRIARCHAL PERIOD

Eden (??)

Noah (??)

Abraham/Isaac/Jacob c. 2000 B.C.

Down into Egypt with Joseph & the Tribes c. 1800 (c. 1650)

Hyksos Period in Egypt - c. 1650-1550

THE UNITED MONARCHY

Samuel

Saul/David/Solomon c. 1025/1005/965

EXODUS 1446 (c. 1250)

Desert Wanderings 40 years

CONQUEST & SETTLEMENT

Joshua & the Conquest c. 1400 (c. 1250)

Era of the Judges

Merneptah Stele - c. 1208

Series of usurpers & assassinations 752-722

Assyrian Destruction (Shalmaneser V)

722

THE DIVIDED MONARCHY

Jeroboam 931

The Omrides 885-841

Dynasty of Jehu 841-752

Ahab 869

Elijah

Jeroboam II 786

Hosea & Amos

Syro-Ephraimite Wars 734-732

Sennacherib's Campaign - 701

Assyria falls to Babylon - 612

Egypt defeated at Carchemish - 605

Jehoahaz, Jehoiakim, Jehoiachin 1st Deportation 609-597

Jeremiah

Nahum

Moabite Stone - c. 840

Dan Stele - c. 850

Rehoboam I 931

Jehoshaphat 870-848

Uzziah 767-740

Ahaz 732-716

Hezekiah 727-687

Manasseh 687-643

Josiah 639-609

Isaiah Micah

Isaiah

2ND TEMPLE JUDAISM

Ezra & Nehemiah 458-398

Malachi

Alexander 336

Hasmoneans 152-64 B.C.

THE RETURN

Babylon falls to Medo-Persian Empire - 539

Edict of Cyrus 538

Temple Rebuilt 520-515

Haggai & Zechariah

THE EXILE (70 YEARS)

Zedekiah 597-586

587/6

Babylonian Destruction (Nebuchadnezzar)

Jeremiah

Ezekiel Daniel

Figure 6.2. Noah's real time

> For the coming of the Son of Man will be just like the days of Noah. For as in those days before the flood they were eating and drinking, marrying and giving in marriage, until the day that Noah entered the ark, and they did not understand until the flood came and took them all away; so will the coming of the Son of Man be.

Here we see that Jesus' second coming is compared to "the days of Noah." In other words, just as in the days of Noah humanity had succeeded in so corrupting themselves that the only option was to wash the world clean and start again, so too at the time of Jesus' return, humanity will have succeeded in so corrupting themselves that judgment will be the only option. Again, how much human time these developments demand is difficult to say. But we would be wrong to think that just because there are only a few chapters between Adam and Noah, there were only a few years as well.

Noah's real space. Just like everything else in Genesis 1–11, the story of Noah is set in Mesopotamia, in the fertile alluvial plain between the Tigris and the Euphrates. This is the area most historians identify as the birthplace of civilization, and it is the area in which the Bible reports that humanity multiplied and expanded after Eden. This area was thoroughly urbanized in ancient times and was well-known for catastrophic flooding.[2] We know this from both material remains and written records. In the 1920s Sir Leonard Wooley excavated the city of Ur (Abraham's hometown) and discovered a twelve-foot-thick layer of flood deposit dating to the middle of the fourth millennium B.C.[3] The city of Kish also has a large flood layer from the mid-third millennium, and the city of Shuruppak from the early third millennium. So the material remains of Mesopotamia let us know that floods of ruinous proportions were common in this area.

Even more interesting is the fact that this region of the world boasts several accounts of a great deluge that wiped out the race and became an epoch divider in the local histories. The Gilgamesh Epic is the most famous of these accounts.[4] The hero of the tale is Gilgamesh, an ancient Mesopotamian champion who sets out on a quest to acquire immortality. His quest brings him to Ut-napishtim (meaning "he has found life"), who is the only divine-human in Gilgamesh's world. Gilgamesh ques-

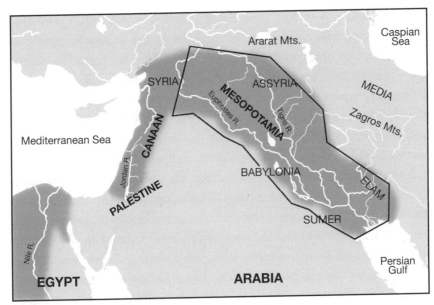

Figure 6.3. Noah's real space

tions Ut-napishtim as to how he gained immortality so that he can get it too. In response to his questions, Ut-napishtim reports that many years before, the Mesopotamian god Ea had warned him that the other gods intended to rid themselves of the noisy and bothersome humans by sending a flood. So with Ea's help, Ut-napishtim built a great boat and rescued his family and all of the animal kingdom, and for his courageous efforts was rewarded with immortality. In addition to Ut-napishtim's account in the Gilgamesh Epic, there is another, more complete version of the same story in which Atrahasis (meaning "exceedingly wise") is the hero.[5] And there are fragments of a third Sumerian version in which the hero's name is Ziusudra.[6] In each of these Mesopotamian accounts the gods attempt to rid themselves of humanity by means of a great flood. A hero builds a boat to save a remnant of the living, and the gods repent afterwards because they realize that they've overdone it, and they actually need humanity as a slave core.[7]

Obviously, these flood stories sound more than a little familiar. In fact, some of the parallels are as detailed as Ut-napishtim sending a dove and a raven from the boat to check for dry land as the flood subsides.[8] So there is a lot of overlap. But there is a lot of difference too. Interestingly, the dif-

ference is not so much the event, but the interpretation of the event. Unlike the Mesopotamian versions, in Noah's story the catalyst for the flood
is not the whim of the gods, it is the wickedness of humanity. In Noah's
story Yahweh saves because of mercy and his long-term redemptive plan,
not because one god defects from the will of the council and "leaks" the
plan. In Noah's story Yahweh does not repent of his plan because he real-
izes he is hungry and needs a slave race (see n. 7). Rather, the salvation of
humanity and the land creatures had always been his plan.

There is a fourth Mesopotamian text known as the Sumerian King
List that also speaks of a great flood. This important document claims to
date to the very first days of the existence of monarchy in Sumer, "when
kingship was lowered from heaven," and lists 140 kings with the location
and lengths of their reigns.[9] The reason this list is so interesting to us is
that it divides ancient Mesopotamian history between those kings who
ruled before "the flood swept over the earth," and those who ruled "after
the flood."[10] Obviously, this flood was pretty important to these peoples'
perception of their history. Even more interesting is that the antediluvian
era (i.e., the era before the flood) is understood as a golden age when each
king ruled at the bequest of the gods for tens of thousands of years. In
Eridu, for example, two kings reign for a total of 64,800 years. In Bab-
tibira three kings rule for 108,000 years! But after the flood, the reign of
each king drops to approximately 1,000 years. If this reminds you of the
life spans attributed to the heroes of Genesis who lived before the flood
and how those life spans change after, it should.

So what do all these parallels between the Bible and the Mesopotamian
literature teach us? For one thing, they let us know that this flood story in
Genesis 6—9 is not mere fancy. When two or more people groups record
the same event, and particularly when that event becomes a significant
benchmark in the way those peoples track their history, historians notice.
Add to this literary witness the fact that the Tigris/Euphrates plain is well
known for devastating floods, and suddenly the idea of a great deluge that
wipes out the race is not as notional as it first seemed. Rather, the geography, climate, archaeology and epigraphy of ancient Mesopotamia all point
the same direction—long, long ago there was a catastrophic flood that
deeply embedded itself in the memory of the people of that region.

Even more important to our interpretation of Noah's story is that in all of these ancient narratives, the flood was understood as an epoch divider. The flood marked a definitive shift in world history in which one era (and one race) was replaced by another. Again, the interpretation of this epoch divider is different in Mesopotamian memory than in biblical revelation, but the concept is shared in all accounts. In the Bible the elongated life span of the antediluvian race (Adam's race) begins to decline after the flood, eventually reaching a length more recognizable in our modern world (cf. Gen 6:3). As we will see later in the chapter, whereas the Mesopotamians viewed this drop in longevity as a move away from the "golden age" prior to the flood, the Bible sees things differently. In fact, Genesis 6:3 may indicate the exact opposite—it was because of the corruption that humanity achieved with their long lives before the flood that God ordained a shortened life span. Alternatively, many have theorized that the length of life of the early humans was the result of their post-Edenic gene pool. In other words, it took many generations for the death resident in our bodies to reproduce itself such that it overcame the perfection of our original state. I'm afraid I cannot offer a definitive answer to the "why" of the pre- and post-flood lifespans recorded in Genesis. But I can say that there is a consistent testimony as to what happens after the flood. The antediluvian race is replaced, and the life span of humanity drops significantly. More on this later.

The flood. In Genesis 6:13-22 God details his plan: "everything that is on the earth shall perish" (Gen 6:17). But in the midst Yahweh promises Noah that he will establish a covenant with him: "and you shall enter the ark—you and your sons and your wife, and your son's wives with you" (Gen 6:18). And so the drama begins. In Genesis 7:10-24, "all the fountains of the great deep burst open, and the floodgates of the sky were opened" (Gen 7:11). Figure 6.4 reminds us of the worldview of the ancient Israelite. You will remember from our creation discussion that the ancients understood the "waters below" (Hebrew *těhôm*) to be the primordial deep, the "chaos" that every Hebrew feared. They understood the "waters above" as originally part of this primordial deep, but placed in the heavens and restrained by the firmament. God had confined and ordered these waters as part of the creation event (Gen 1:2, 6-9; cf. Job 38:8-11).

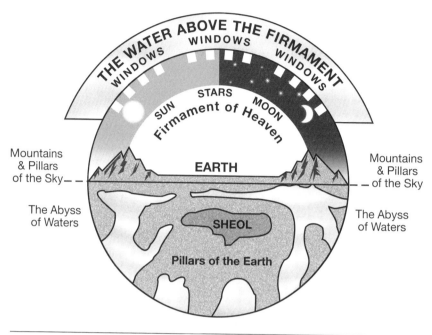

Figure 6.4. The cosmos

But in the deluge, on a specific day, God unloosed chaos. The fountains of the *tĕhôm* erupted, and the windows of the firmament of heaven were thrown wide so that the earth was once again consumed in the violent watery chaos of the pre-creation. In other words, what we see in the flood is not merely a natural disaster intended to bring about God's judgment on humanity, but a *de-creational* event. What had been done at creation is undone with the flood. The world is brought back to its pre-creation state—"formless and void." To use the words of the Gilgamesh Epic, "all mankind had returned to clay."[11]

So unlike the fun and cheerful images we often associate with Noah—the decorations in our nurseries and children's classrooms, the toys and camp songs, "the animals they came on, they came on by twosies, twosies"—the story of Noah is completely terrifying. Think of the deadly tsunami that hit Asia in December of 2004. The news reports said that once the earthquake struck, the waves traveled faster than the communications warning system could, 500 miles per hour. The disaster caught hundreds of thousands of people unaware, wiping out whole towns and villages, killing, injuring and displacing unimaginable numbers of people.[12] Put this sort of disaster into the terms of one man and his family escaping to start again, and you begin to get a feel for this epoch-dividing event.

Some thoughts on the sea. As we've discussed, for a Hebrew, the *těhôm* was a majestic but dangerous entity. Job captures some of this Hebrew ambivalence in his magnificent verse.

> Who enclosed the sea with doors when, bursting forth, it went out from the womb; when I made a cloud its garment and thick darkness its swaddling band, and I placed boundaries on it and set a bolt and doors, and I said, "Thus far you shall come, but no farther; and here shall your proud waves stop"? (Job 38:8-11)

Why such a mixed report? The mythology of the surrounding cultures gives us some insight because the Israelite's ambivalence was in some measure a reflection of the worldview of which they were a part. In an important creation myth named Enuma Elish, the Mesopotamians tell the story of the origins of the heaven and the earth. Here the chief deity of first millennium Mesopotamia, Marduk, defies the older gods (think "Titans") of Mesopotamia in his quest for ascendancy over the gods. The climax of his victory is the defeat of the mother goddess Tiamat, who personifies the primordial deep. He slays her, and then "he split her like a shellfish into two parts"—half of her carcass he used as the waters of the sky; half the waters of the deep.[13] Like the flood stories of Gilgamesh and Atrahasis, there is some obvious overlap between the Mesopotamian literature and the biblical account. But like the flood account, we find the interpretation of events very different in the Mesopotamian literature versus the Bible. In Enuma Elish the premise is that supremacy over the gods (and therefore control of the created order) was dependent on the defeat of "Sea." This idea was deeply imbedded in the mind of the ancients,[14] as was the resulting idea that "Sea" could break out at any moment and destroy the order of creation. Perhaps this ongoing fear had been birthed from the experience of the flood, I don't know. But for the Israelites, Yahweh corrects this misperception throughout the Bible. He lets his people know that there is only one god, he has no rivals, and therefore his sovereignty throughout creation is unchallenged and unrivalled. Likewise, Genesis 6–9 makes it clear that the primordial deep does not break loose on its own. Rather God in his sovereignty sets it loose in order to accomplish his purposes. All the same, in the mind of the Israelite, the sea evoked a mixture of myth and theology, fear and wonder.

Is the Israelite perception of the sea a result of their yielding to the fears of their age? Is it the result of a great mystery only partly understood? Again, I don't know. But I do know that God makes use of the Israelite perception in his carrying out of redemptive history. Throughout the story there is a recurring theme of Yahweh rescuing his people by delivering them from the sea. First there is creation, in which God contains and directs the sea such that its great power is harnessed to serve the needs of the created order. Then there is the flood, in which God makes use of the ark (Hebrew *tēbat*) to rescue his people from the sea and therefore from judgment. Then the great deliverance under Moses in which God parts the Red Sea such that his people pass through on dry ground. (Note as well that the basket into which the baby Moses is placed in the Nile River is called an "ark" [Hebrew *tēbat*]—an obvious and intentional association with Noah's *tēbat*.) Next Joshua leads the children of Abraham into the Promised Land by parting the Jordan River—and again God's people pass through safely on dry ground.

And then there is this young rabbi from Nazareth who finds himself on the *Sea* of Galilee on a stormy day. His friends—who, by the way, were career fisherman and had navigated hundreds of squalls during the course of their lifetimes—become terrified at the ferocity of this particular storm. Like their ancestors, they find themselves panic-stricken that the sea will break loose and destroy them. And then a very odd thing happens. The young Nazarene, seeing the fear in the eyes of his friends, stands up and speaks to the sea. And the sea, as it had on the morning of creation, obeys him. What do the witnesses to this stunning event say? Just what they ought: "What kind of a man is this, that even the winds and the sea obey Him?" (Mt 8:27). The answer, of course, is that this is Yahweh the Son. And this event is one of the clearest declarations of Jesus' deity in the New Testament. It is Yahweh who said at the dawn of creation: "thus far you shall come, but no farther"; and it is only Yahweh the Son who could stand and remind the Sea of Galilee of the same.

ON BAPTISM, FLOODS AND GRANDMOTHERS

Peter continues the theme of victory over the sea in his comparison of the waters of baptism and Noah's ark. He teaches us that "eight persons were brought safely through the water" by the ark, and so too the waters of baptism deliver us from eternal death (1 Pet 3:18-22). Years ago, I attended my Catholic grandmother's funeral. She was one of those rare and fortunate souls who had lived her entire life in one town, in one parish. As a result the parish ledgers contained the record of her life. So when the thirty-year-old priest, who could only have known my grandmother for a few years, stepped forward to give her eulogy, he was able to speak of her baptism, her first holy communion, her confirmation, her marriage, her children's baptisms and even her children's marriages as though he had witnessed them himself. It was powerful. And as he stood behind her casket, his arms raised in blessing and prayer, he spoke a line from the ancient liturgies that I will never forget: "We are confident regarding our sister, Lauda, because we know that for her the waters of baptism have parted the waters of death." Hallelujah. Sea has been defeated; the enemies of the people of God are no more.

The defeat of the *sea* finds its grand culmination in Revelation 21:1: "Then I saw a new heaven and a new earth; for the first heaven and the first earth passed away, and there is no longer any sea." Amen. God's people are safely home, and life is come!

The re-creation. Back to the flood. As we've already discussed, the bursting forth of the great *tĕhôm* in Genesis 7:10-11 is a reversal of God's good work in Genesis 1:1, 6. This epoch-dividing judgment is therefore best described as a *de-creational* event. The cataclysmic result is a world returned to its pre-creation state—"formless and void." But we also find here a world given a second chance. God's first, perfect world has been "washed" clean of the effects of the sin of Adam's generation, and what appears to be complete emptiness will be repopulated by the passengers on the ark. Thus God begins afresh with his fallen children. The vehicle of this fresh start being God's *re-creational* covenant with Noah. Take a look at the language of Genesis 9:1-17.

> And God blessed Noah and his sons and said to them, "Be fruitful and multiply, and fill the earth. The fear of you and the terror of you will be on every beast of the earth and on every bird of the sky; with everything that creeps on the ground, and all the fish of the sea, into your hand they are given. Every moving thing that is alive shall be food for you; I give all to you, as I gave the green plant. Only you shall not eat flesh with its life, that is, its blood." (Gen 9:1-4)

Can you hear in these words the echo of Eden? Remember the words of Genesis 1.

> God blessed them; and God said to them, "Be fruitful and multiply, and fill the earth, and subdue it; and rule over the fish of the sea and over the birds of the sky and over every living thing that moves on the earth." Then God said, "Behold, I have given you every plant yielding seed that is on the surface of all the earth, and every tree which has fruit yielding seed; it shall be food for you; and to every beast of the earth and to every bird of the sky and to every thing that moves on the earth which has life, I have given every green plant for food"; and it was so. (Gen 1:28-30)

The command to be "fruitful and multiply" that had been issued to Adam and Eve is now reissued to Noah's family (Gen 9:1). The dominion granted to Adam and Eve over the animal kingdom is now, in an altered fashion, bestowed on Noah's offspring (Gen 9:2). The instruction regarding what may be eaten is now reconferred as well . . . but the profile of this command has changed (Gen 9:3). Do you hear the reiteration of the commands of creation? And do you see the shift as well? The mutation of the Edenic instructions becomes more dramatic in the verses that follow.

> Surely I will require your lifeblood; from every beast I will require it. And from every man, from every man's brother I will require the life of man. Whoever sheds [*ʾĀdām's*] blood, by [*ʾĀdām*] his blood shall be shed, for in the image of God He made humanity. As for you, be fruitful and multiply;

populate the earth abundantly and multiply in it. (Gen 9:5-7)

The change here is that although God has indeed started again with the same players, he has started again in a *fallen* world. Whereas in the covenant of Eden the gift was dominion, with Noah the gift is fear (and in all likelihood this fear is not given to protect humanity from raging wildlife, but to protect vulnerable wildlife from their insatiable predator, humanity). And whereas with Adam and Eve the gift was abundant food in the form of fruits and vegetables, with Noah the gift includes the flesh of other living things. And although Adam and Eve would never have thought of eating an animal while it still lived, in the post-Fall world, apparently such legislation is necessary (Gen 9:4). An even more unfathomable shift from the pre-Fall world is that God must now legislate regarding murder: "Whoever sheds ʾĀdām's blood, by ʾĀdām his blood shall be shed for in the image of God He made humanity" (Gen 9:6). Even in their fallen state humanity is made in the image of God, and this image cannot be violated without consequence.[15]

And so God reestablishes his relationship with fallen humanity by means of covenant. And like Eden, the nature of this first step in the rescue plan is cosmic—in other words, this covenant is with all creation.

> Then God spoke to Noah and to his sons with him, saying, "Now behold, I Myself do establish My covenant with you, and with your descendants after you; and with every living creature that is with you, the birds, the cattle, and every beast of the earth with you; of all that comes out of the ark, even every beast of the earth. . . ." God said, "This is the sign of the covenant which I am making between Me and you and every living creature that is with you, for all successive generations; I set My bow in the cloud, and it shall be for a sign of a covenant between Me and the earth . . . to remember the everlasting covenant between God and every living creature of all flesh that is on the earth." (Gen 9:8-16)

Thus God cleanses the world of the first, sinful race and starts again in a fallen world with a cosmic covenant that applies to all humanity and all the earth as well. And he seals his oath with the sign of his bow in the clouds.

The curse of Canaan: Genesis 9:24-27. The final episode in the story

of Noah story involves a little too much wine, a little too much nakedness and a blessing and curse that would shape the political profile of the
Promised Land.

> Now the sons of Noah who came out of the ark were Shem and Ham and
> Japheth; and Ham was the father of Canaan. These three were the sons of
> Noah, and from these the whole earth was populated. Then Noah began
> farming and planted a vineyard. He drank of the wine and became drunk,
> and uncovered himself inside his tent. Ham, the father of Canaan, saw the
> nakedness of his father, and told his two brothers outside. But Shem and
> Japheth took a garment and laid it upon both their shoulders and walked
> backward and covered the nakedness of their father; and their faces were
> turned away, so that they did not see their father's nakedness. When Noah
> awoke from his wine, he knew what his youngest son had done to him. So
> he said, "Cursed be Canaan; a servant of servants he shall be to his broth-
> ers." He also said, "Blessed be the LORD, the God of Shem; and let Canaan
> be his servant. May God enlarge Japheth, and let him dwell in the tents of
> Shem; and let Canaan be his servant." (Gen 9:18-27)

This event has mystified commentators for generations. What was it that
Noah's son "had done to him"? Many hypothesize that Ham's sin was
some sort of perverse sexual act. The author does not say. But the contrast between the behavior of the three sons is clear—two honor their
father by covering his nakedness; one does not.[16] The result is a blessing
and curse that predicts and defines the good guys and the bad guys of
Israel's world. The children of Shem will become Israel (as well as all the
other Semitic people groups). Shem's name means "name" (appropriate
for those who will bear the Name), and this word becomes the root of the
modern term *Semite*. The children of Japheth will become the numerous
gentile peoples living north of Canaan (Anatolia and the Aegean region).
Japheth's name seems to derive from a verb meaning "to make spacious,"
and most hypothesize that this meaning is connected to his large territory.[17] His blessing is to live in peace and cooperation with the children
of Shem (Gen 9:27). The children of Ham, on the other hand, become
the peoples of Egypt and Canaan. Canaan (Ham's son who is specifically
cursed) is the ancestor of the indigenous peoples of the land of Canaan
whom the Israelites will one day drive out of their homeland. His name,

predictably, means "to have to submit; to be humbled."[18] Thus the identity of God's future people and their territory is laid out in this brief prophetic etiology.[19] More important, we leave this first stage of redemptive history with contact reestablished between God and humanity and the first of our triplet restored: God's people will be the children of Shem. The place and presence are yet to be identified.

    The sons of God and the daughters of men: Genesis 6:1-4. And now for the question I am most frequently asked regarding this section of Scripture: "What about the 'sons of God,' the 'daughters of men,' and their *něpilîm* offspring?" The interpretation of this narrative is quite enigmatic, due in large part to a lack of clarity and consensus as regards the identity of the principle players. The most popular (and sensational) reading is that the "sons of God" are male angels who, due to the fall of Satan, were resident on our planet and procreating with human women, "the daughters of men." The identification of the "sons of God" as angels is inferred from Job 1:6; 2:1; and 38:7 where angels are spoken of as "sons of God," and their sexual sin is inferred from Jude 1:6.[20] The offspring of these unions (the *něpilîm*) are therefore understood as semidivine, super-human creatures—similar to Hercules and Achilles in Greek mythology. As the Hebrew word *něpilîm* comes from the verb *nāpal*, meaning "to fall," the idea here is that these creatures are morally "fallen" individuals due to their ancestry as fallen half-angels. A second interpretation of this story claims that the "sons of God" are human royalty (upper class) and the "daughters of men" are commoners (lower class), and their union results in some sort of impurity in the race. This ancient Jewish reading finds support in that "son of God" is used periodically in the Old Testament as a reference to a God-ordained, human leader (Ps 2:7; 82:6; and 2 Sam 7:14).[21] A third interpretation is that the "sons of God" are the sons of Seth and the "daughters of men" are the daughters of Cain whose intermingling is endangering the survival of God's chosen, covenant line. This was John Calvin's proposal, and it derives from the genealogies in Genesis 5 which separate the line of Adam into these two lineages.[22] All of these interpretations share the idea that it was the ongoing spawning of the *něpilîm*, who were in some fashion corrupt because of the intermingling of classes, that made the annihilation of the race by means of the flood necessary.

Let me propose another reading. John Sailhamer has demonstrated that the standard interpretations reviewed above are derived from reading Genesis 6:1-4 as the *prologue* to the flood story—as if it is the narrator's introduction to and rationale for the flood.[23] Thus in each of these standard interpretations, the great new sin that necessitates the destruction of the race is the intermingling of the "sons of God" with the "daughters of men." In contrast, John Sailhamer suggests that Genesis 6:1-4 was intended as an *epilogue* to Genesis 4–5, a concluding paragraph to the Adamic Age. With this understanding, the flood account begins with Genesis 6:5: "Then the LORD saw that the wickedness of man was great on the earth, and that every intent of the thoughts of his heart was only evil continually." This is a compelling suggestion, as Genesis 6:5 offers the reader all the explanation needed for the catastrophe about to occur. What is more, this would mean that what we have in Genesis 6:1-4 is no longer the *reason* for the flood, but simply a paragraph intended to bridge the age of Adam to that of the flood.

> If we read 6:1-4 as a summary of chapter 5 . . . there is little to arouse our suspicion that the events recounted are anything out of the ordinary. As a summary of the preceding chapter, this little patch of narrative is a reminder that the sons and daughters of Adam had greatly increased in number, had married, and had continued to have children. The impression it gives is that of an interlude, a calm before the storm.[24]

With this suggested interpretation of Genesis 6:1-4, who then are "the sons of God," "the daughters of men" and the *nĕpilîm?*

Let's start with the *nĕpilîm*. As I have already mentioned, this Hebrew noun comes from the verb *nāpal*, meaning "to fall." Taking its form into account, the term should mean "ones having fallen."[25] Our first school of interpretation identifies this group as superhuman, half-breed angels who are wiped out in the flood. But problems with this interpretation abound. For one, it is at odds with Matthew 22:30—in which resurrected humanity is compared to the angels in that they no longer copulate or reproduce.[26] In addition, we find that the *nĕpilîm* were *not* wiped out in the flood, but they (and their descendants, the "sons of Anak") reappear in later texts (Num 13:22, 28, 33; Deut 9:2; Josh 15:13-14; 21:11; Judg 1:20). More important,

Genesis 6:4 specifically describes the *nĕpilîm* as "the mighty men who were of old, men of renown" (literally "men of the name").[27] Thus the Bible tells us that what sets this group apart is not their half-breed, superhuman status, but their unique ability in battle. In fact, later biblical passages speak of the *nĕpilîm* as some sort of unassailable warrior class who intimidate and paralyze their opponents by their superior skills.[28] Moreover, we find that in the ancient Near East as a whole, the verb *nāpal* typically has to do with wreaking havoc. More than a quarter of its biblical occurrences have to do with "falling" in death, most specifically falling "by the sword."[29] Hence, if we read *nĕpilîm* within its broader usage, we find that the term has something to do with assault and battle. And from its immediate context in Genesis 6 it would seem that the best interpretation is some sort of warrior. So perhaps Genesis 6:1-4 is not about wicked, superhuman half-angels, but the infamous "heroes" (i.e., warriors) of the pre-flood era. And perhaps this passage is not as sensational as it appears at first blush.

If so, what do we make of the phrases "sons of God" and "daughters of men"? I would like to suggest that these phrases are nothing more than an idiomatic way to refer to the first race of humanity (one might think of C. S. Lewis's terminology "sons of Adam and daughters of Eve" as an analogue). I would also like to suggest that the talk of marriage in this section is intended (1) to explain the spread of the race, and (2) to notify the audience as to exactly how unprepared this generation was for the coming judgment of God. Think of our parallel passage in Matthew 24:36-39:

> But of that day and hour no one knows, not even the angels of heaven, nor the Son, but the Father alone. For the coming of the Son of Man will be just like the days of Noah. For as in those days before the flood they were eating and drinking, marrying and giving in marriage, until the day that Noah entered the ark, and they did not understand until the flood came and took them all away; so will the coming of the Son of Man be.

Noah's generation was so completely unaware of the depth of their sin that they were "marrying and giving in marriage" right up to the final hour. In other words, life before the flood continued as normal without a hint of what was to come. This is exactly how Jesus describes the second coming.

So if Genesis 6:1-4 is indeed an epilogue to Genesis 5, and we define the vocabulary as I have above, what function does this section of Scripture serve? I believe it serves to conclude the Adamic Age and to answer the oft-repeated Sunday-school question, "Teacher, where did the girls come from?" In other words, Genesis 5:1–6:4 explains how Adam and Eve and their three named sons birthed an entire civilization. And Genesis 6:5 introduces the next age. A last and very significant point here is how the biblical author views the Adamic Age. Important to us is that whereas the Mesopotamian documents we've reviewed (the Sumerian King List and the Gilgamesh Epic) speak of the first age as a sort of Camelot, a golden age in which the men were mighty and the women fair, the biblical writer identifies it as an age of depravity. Although the *něpîlîm* (the famous men of old) lived in those days, it was not a *heroic* age. It was an age of violence, blood-lust and corruption. Thus, rather than the flood being seen as an event that introduced an inferior era (as the Mesopotamian literature infers), the flood is seen as an act of God that rescued humanity from themselves and offered our corrupt race a second chance.

ABRAHAM, THE FATHER OF THE JEWS

As we pass from the story of Noah, through the Babel story and into Genesis 11, we find that the bloodline of the chosen leads us from Shem, the one called to bear God's name, to Abram. With the genealogical interlude of Genesis 11:10-32, the primeval prologue of Genesis concludes and we step into what I identified earlier as "datable history." Here we are introduced to the "Father of the Jews," Abraham, and for the first time we begin to hear of a chosen nation. As you can tell from your Bibles, the genre of the text seems to change with this juncture as well. We pass from stories that seem very foreign to us about gardens, floods and towers reaching to heaven into a story about a fairly regular guy living a fairly regular life, which is interrupted by the call of God.[30] As I introduced in chapter two, "The Bible in Real Time and Space," there really is no way for us to know how much time has passed. But what we do know is that with Genesis 12 a new era opens. With this second step in redemptive history the plan begins to come into focus. Having laid the groundwork for his relationship with his fallen people in Noah's covenant, God is now

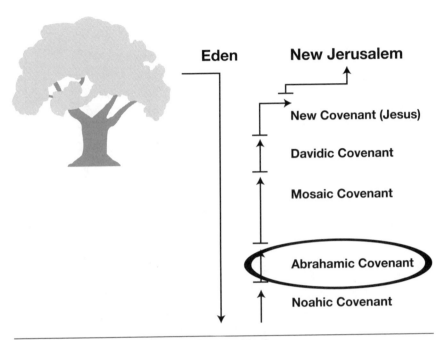

Figure 6.5. A synopsis of redemptive history, Abraham

ready to begin identifying a place, a people and a means of Presence.

Abraham's real time. Our story begins with the migration of Terah's household (Hebrew *bêt ʾāb*) from the city-state of Ur in southern Mesopotamia to the Syrian city of Haran. If we are reading the Bible's dating of this event correctly, we should place Terah's migration somewhere around 2000 B.C.—which also happens to be the approximate date of a major upheaval in that region, the collapse of the Ur III civilization. But as I've said before, biblical dating is a tricky thing, and it is very possible that Abraham actually lived several hundred years after this date.[31] And as we are not yet sure that we know what the biblical writers meant by the dates and numbers they *seem* to be communicating, it is best to hold this sort of thing loosely. So heuristically speaking, we will look for Abraham's migration *about* 2000 B.C. This is an easy benchmark to keep in your mind and a good place to start.

This general dating places the patriarchs in what is known as the Middle Bronze Age. And although we will probably never find direct evidence of Abraham's individual existence by means of archaeology or

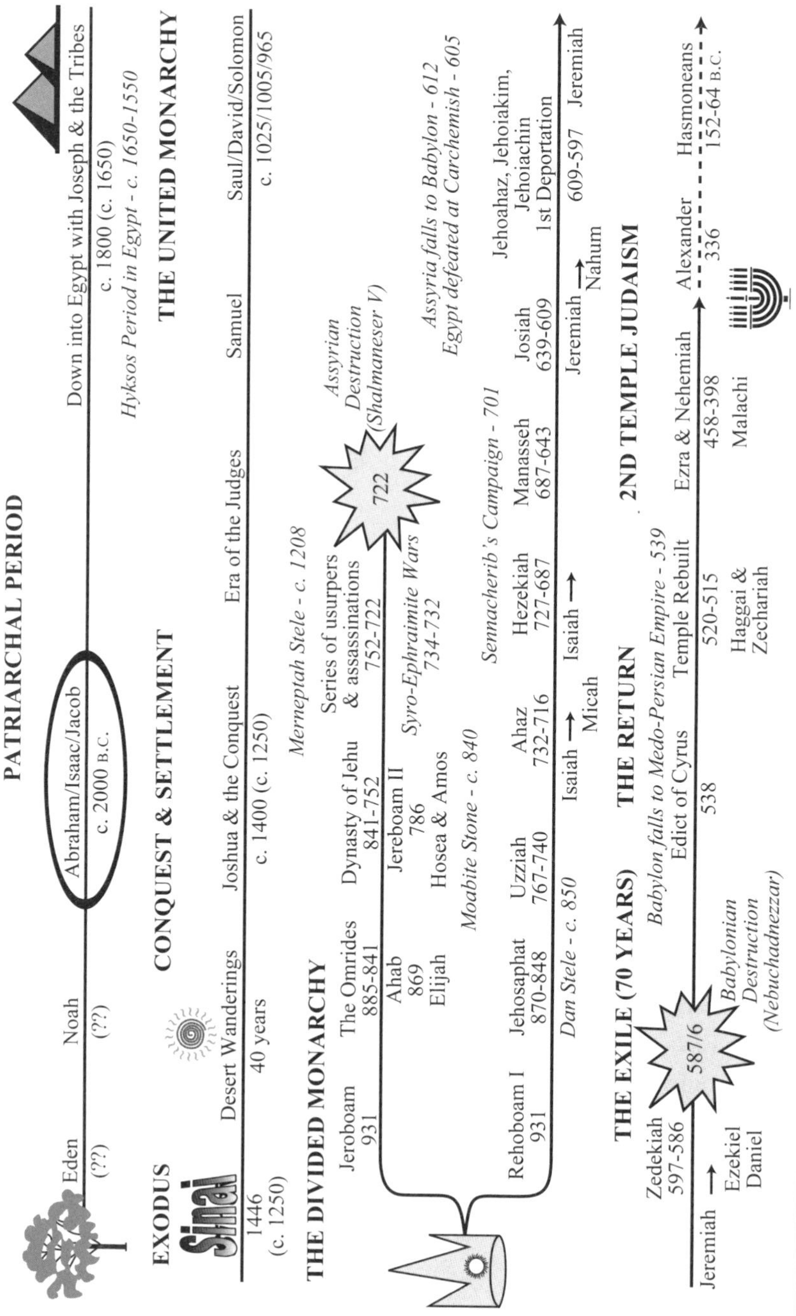

Figure 6.6. Abraham's real time

epigraphy, we can reconstruct the culture of Canaan during the Middle Bronze II period in which we anticipate he lived. We know that this period was a time of great change. A new culture was emerging, carried into Canaan by means of a people group known to the ancients as the *Amurru* or "Amorites." These people were Semites. They came from the north and eventually infiltrated (and transformed) all of Canaan and Mesopotamia.

This was a "dimorphic" society, meaning that it existed in two interdependent forms—urban and non-urban. The urban culture can be easily identified by the material remains of their cities. These were large (typically 25-50 acres), had a uniform layout, massive earthen fortifications (complete with what are known as two-chambered gate complexes and glacis) and innovative long-axis, tripartite temples.[32] This urban culture also shared secondary, group burials and the innovations of fast-wheel pottery and bronze metallurgy. This we know by means of archaeology.

Our window into the non-urban portion of this culture is epigraphic (i.e., written remains). One exceptionally important source is the recovered palace archives of a major Mesopotamian city-state named Mari.[33] Located in northwestern Mesopotamia, and booming during Abraham's era, the documents found in these archives describe an era in which mobile pastoralist communities were well-known and ranged across southwest Syria and Canaan. These communities were nomadic, tribal and Semitic. Their principal livestock were sheep and goats, and they did regular business with the urban centers betwixt and between which they found their seasonal pasturage.[34] Remembering our discussion in chapter two, it is obvious that this description of the Mari pastoralists in the Middle Bronze Age sounds a lot like the patriarchs. So similar is the profile of Middle Bronze Age Canaan to the culture described in the patriarchal naratives that Israeli archaeologist Amihai Mazar states unequivocally: "I find the similarities between the MB II culture and that illustrated in the Genesis stories too close to be ignored."[35] Me too.

So although we can't find archaeological or epigraphic evidence that speaks specifically of Abraham or his descendants, we can confidently state that what we know of the patriarchal era accurately reflects the cul-

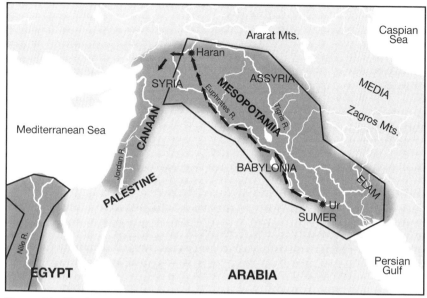

Figure 6.7. Abraham's migration

ture of the Middle Bronze II period. It is therefore reasonable to assume
that Abraham and his kin were somehow a part of this "Amorite" society
that moved into Canaan in the first half of the second millennium B.C.[36]

Abraham's real space. Having originally departed from southern Mesopotamia and the city of Ur, the first leg of Abraham's migration is complete when the family reaches Haran. Here they settle. But eventually
Terah dies, leaving his sons to begin their own family units, and it is at
this point that God speaks to Abram. His command? "Go forth." In other
words, leave everything and everyone that makes someone in a patriarchal
society secure and trust God for a new identity and a new place. Take
a moment to translate this into your current economic and social situation. Leave your house, your job, your friends, your church, your relatives,
abandon your inheritance, a 401K that will not transfer and maybe even
the equity in your home—and go somewhere where you don't speak the
language, you have no business contacts, friends or relatives . . . and trust
God to make a new place for you. This was a very tall order indeed. Especially in light of the fact that we have no evidence that there was any prior
relationship between Yahweh and Abram. I assure you that most folks in

the ancient world, and most folks today, would not have gone. But Abram believed in Yahweh's good word, and as it says in Genesis 15:6, "He [God] reckoned it to him as righteousness."

What was Yahweh's promise in response to Abram's reckless confidence in this as-of-yet unknown god? Yahweh promised to honor Abram with numerous offspring such that Abram would become the father of "a great nation" (Gen 12:2). Moreover, in covenantal language, Yahweh would become Abram's patron. Anyone who blessed Abram would be rewarded by his patron; anyone who cursed him would be penalized by the same (Gen 12:3).

Yahweh would also grant Abram fame. And through Abram, Yahweh promised to bless all the earth (Gen 12:3). These promises in Genesis 12:1-3 were not only monumental to a certain pastoral nomad in the Middle Bronze Age, they also laid the foundation for everything that would transpire between Yahweh and the patriarchs, and between Yahweh and the nation of Israel. In these promises we find a promised *people* ("a great nation") and a promised *place* ("a land which I will show you"). Abram accepts the stipulations of the covenant, obeys, and a great story begins.

Abraham's covenant. The sort of covenant *(bĕrît)* established between Yahweh and Abraham is a bit different from the suzerain/vassal agreement we studied in chapter three. Rather than an agreement between nations, this was a covenant sworn to by individuals involving a gift of land or continuing office, bestowed upon a servant who had distinguished himself by loyal service to his sovereign. It is identified in the literature as either a "covenant of grant" or a "royal grant," and it was given in perpetuity. Abram's gift of land and David's gift of dynasty are the biblical examples of this sort of covenant. As summarized in Genesis 12:1-3, because of his faithfulness in following Yahweh into an unknown future, Abraham is rewarded with land and heirs.[37] There will be two other great moments in Abram's life when this same covenant is reiterated to him, each moment having its own emphasis. The first is found in Genesis 15.

Genesis 15. Years have passed since Genesis 12. Abram is now a resident of Canaan. He has grown older, so has his wife, and his faith is wearing thin. In light of his childless state, Abram has done what any responsible man of substance would; he has chosen an heir from among his household. This was quite common in the ancient world; when no biological heir appeared, an adoptive one was selected. In Abram's case it was the faithful servant Eliezer of Damascus. Into this settled and comfortable state of affairs, Yahweh appears again.

> After these things the word of the LORD came to Abram in a vision, saying, "Do not fear, Abram, I am a shield to you; your reward shall be very great." Abram said, "O Lord GOD, what will You give me, since I am childless, and the heir of my house is Eliezer of Damascus?" And Abram said, "Since You have given no offspring to me, one born in my house is my heir." Then behold, the word of the LORD came to him, saying, "This man will not be your heir; but one who will come forth from your own body, he shall be your heir." And He took him outside and said, "Now look toward the heavens, and count the stars, if you are able to count them." And He said to him, "So shall your descendants be." Then he believed in the LORD; and He reckoned it to him as righteousness. (Gen 15:1-6)

So God reiterates and specifies his promise. The heir will not simply be a legal heir, he will be the offspring of Abram's own flesh (which of course is the heart cry of anyone from a tribal society). Moreover, through this child Abram's descendants will be as numerous as the stars of the night sky.

I first traveled to Israel in the winter of 1992. My entire experience from start to finish could be summarized in a line from an old John Denver song, "coming home to a place I'd never been before." I loved every hour of it. But the hour I loved the best was somewhere around 4:00 am, halfway up Mount Sinai. The goal of the hike was to reach the summit for sunrise. Being more than eager, I forged ahead of my group with a few friends. While trying to navigate a place where the path was particularly steep and narrow (and in the dark and ice a bit frightening), we stopped to look behind us. And what a sight we saw. There, high above the plain, without another human in sight or earshot, we saw the desert sky. I'd never been in a desert at 4:00 am before, so I didn't know that without streetlights and car lights the sky looks as though it is encrusted with diamonds. I didn't know that when you are perched on the side of a mountain it seems as though you can reach out and touch them. I didn't know. Now I can't read Genesis 15:5 without picturing that night sky in the southern reaches of the Sinai: "Count the stars, Abram, if you can . . . So shall your descendants be."

It is particularly interesting to us New Testament types that the narrator resolves the tension in Genesis 15 between Yahweh's promise and Abram's unbelief by the concluding phrase: "Then he [Abram] believed in the LORD; and He reckoned it to him as righteousness." Because when we turn our eyes to the New Testament we find that in Galatians 3:1-9 Paul states that what was asked of Abram is exactly what is asked of new covenant believers as well. Hmmm . . . maybe this old and new covenant thing is not as drastically different as I once thought.

The passage goes on to clarify God's covenantal promise regarding land, and for the first time Abram is made to understand that it is the land in which he has been living as an expatriate that will be his inheritance (Gen 15:7, 18). This man who has given up his homeland and his patrimony in order to follow God is now being promised more territory than he can imagine in the place he currently calls "home." But Abram asks the question that all of us would ask: "O Lord GOD, how may I know that I will possess it?" (Gen 15:8). Obviously, Abram is struggling to believe. Rather than abandoning him in his failure, God extends to Abram a confirmation that Abram will understand, one that will matter to him, one that will secure his faith.

> So He said to him, "Bring Me a three year old heifer, and a three year old female goat, and a three year old ram, and a turtledove, and a young pigeon." Then he brought all these to Him and cut them in two, and laid each half opposite the other; but he did not cut the birds. . . . Now when the sun was going down, a deep sleep fell upon Abram; and behold, terror and great darkness fell upon him. (Gen 15:9-12)

For me this is the most amazing episode in all of Abram's covenantal interactions with Yahweh. As we've already rehearsed in chapter three, these verses depict a ratification ceremony between a patron and his client ("The Concept of Covenant," pp. 77-78). Here Yahweh condescends to Abram's humanity by choosing a means of warranty that had currency in Abram's world. This in itself is amazing. But more amazing is that unlike every other patron/client or suzerain/vassal agreement we know of, in Genesis 15 it is the greater party (coming to Abram in the theophanic form of a smoking oven and a flaming torch) who takes the role of the lesser party by passing between the bloody pieces.

> It came about when the sun had set, that it was very dark, and behold, there appeared a smoking oven and a flaming torch which passed between these pieces. On that day the LORD made a covenant with Abram, saying, "To your descendants I have given this land, from the river of Egypt as far as the great river, the river Euphrates." (Gen 15:17-18)

God showed up. And on this day the Lord of the cosmos made a covenant with his servant Abram, which he sealed with the promise of his own blood.

Another important aspect of this interaction is the final clause of Genesis 15:1: "Do not fear Abram, I am a shield to you; your reward shall be very great." Hopefully your Bible offers you another translation in the margin, something like "*I am* your very great reward." In Hebrew, the sentence is ambiguous, and could be read either way. I lean toward the latter translation because it not only introduces the idea of the Presence into Abram's covenant, it also articulates what every seasoned believer knows—Yahweh himself will be Abram's reward.

Genesis 17. This chapter records the final covenant interaction between Yahweh and Abram. Abram is now an old man, and his beautiful wife, who was a fairly young woman when she answered Yahweh's call, is now "past childbearing." Thus the bright hopes of an earlier day have faded. And in the place of Sarai and Abram's long-awaited child, Hagar has borne Ishmael. This is another one of those biblical stories that leaves me amazed at the restraint of the narrator. If I pause for just a moment, I can feel Abram and Sarai's pain—their disappointment, their empty arms. I'm sure there are those reading these words who can feel their pain more acutely than I. And all this hurt in the midst of trying to honor a God who promised but has not delivered. But Yahweh does not seem at all embarrassed by this state of affairs. There is no child, but Genesis 17 opens with Yahweh's bold reaffirmation of the covenant we've come to know in Genesis 12 and Genesis 15.

> Now when Abram was ninety-nine years old, the LORD appeared to Abram

and said to him, "I am God Almighty; walk before Me, and be blameless. I will establish My covenant between Me and you, and I will multiply you exceedingly." Abram fell on his face, and God talked with him, saying, "As for Me, behold, My covenant is with you, and you will be the father of a multitude of nations." (Gen 17:1-4)

In the midst of this reaffirmation, Yahweh introduces a new element which is a bit confusing to us but carried great significance for Abram and Sarai—God changes their names. Here "Abram" coming from *ʾāb* ("father") and *rām* ("exalted") is transformed into something akin to *ʾāb hāmôn* ("multitude"). The one whose name had meant "exalted father" (referring either to Abram's lineage or to an unnamed deity his parents had chosen to honor upon his birth) becomes "father of a multitude." "Sarai" becomes "Sarah." These are dialectical variants of the same Semitic word meaning "princess" or "chieftainess."[38] With these changes of name God repeats and expands his promises of fertility and territory. Why the name change? In Abraham and Sarah's world, when a person was raised to a new position—a princeling to a throne, or a servant to an office— it was common for the patron to change that person's name in order to signify the new role. Thus, when Yahweh changes his clients' names, he formalizes their new roles as the parents of a new line of chosen people. Basically, what we have here is the designation of a new Adam and Eve.

Circumcision. There is another new element in Abraham's covenant in Genesis 17, the covenant sign of circumcision. Like so many things we find in Israel's religion, circumcision was not "new" with Abraham. Rather, we have good evidence that it was well known in Egypt quite early on. There are a few Old Kingdom tomb scenes showing circumcision being performed on adolescent boys. One Sixth Dynasty tomb depicts such an image with an accompanying inscription in which the priest assures his patient that it will not hurt.[39] In another inscription, a man states that he was circumcised along with 120 others. This suggests that whole groups were circumcised together as a rite of passage. The question remains, however, what sort of rite of passage? The Egyptian references above might indicate it was passage into puberty. Biblical references such as the story of Dinah and the prince of Shechem (Gen 34:14-17), as well as the odd story about Moses and Zipporah (Ex 4:24-31) may indicate it was a prenuptial rite. Many have postulated that in Egypt circumcision had to do with purity and was obligatory for men who were entering the priesthood.[40] Whatever this rite of passage had been in the broader ancient Near East, Israel is unique in that they circumcised babies. Thus circumcision became an important ethnic marker for Israel—setting them apart from their neighbors. More important, for the Israelite, circumcision was not practiced because of any sort of rite of passage, rather it was the mark of Yahweh's election of Abraham's offspring.

It is important to note that only the male members of Abraham's descendants could be marked as members of the covenant. Although I've found that this sometimes disturbs people, in a patriarchal society this should neither surprise nor trouble us. In this society, a woman's identity was defined by the men in her life. So if her father, her husband or her son were marked, essentially so was she. Note as well that circumcision is obviously a mark having to do with human reproduction. This makes sense since Abraham's covenant was also biological and reproductive:

> I will establish My covenant between Me and you and your descendants after you throughout their generations for an everlasting covenant, to be God to you and to your descendants after you. (Gen 17:7)

The promise here is to Abraham's descendants simply because they *are* Abraham's descendents. No decision of allegiance was anticipated or requested. Rather, by right of birth and bloodline, a child of Abraham was a child of the promise. Thus it was also wholly appropriate that the sign of this covenant be imposed upon an infant prior to his ability to make his own decisions.

As you may already have anticipated, members of the new covenant are marked as well. And the New Testament equivalent to circumcision is baptism. Just as the offspring of Abraham were marked as those belonging to Yahweh, so in the new covenant all those who confess with their mouth that Jesus Christ is lord and believe in their heart that God raised him from the dead are marked as those belonging to Jesus (Rom 10:9). Yet whereas Abraham's covenant was biological and reproductive, the new covenant, expressly, is not. Rather, the New Testament frequently repeats that membership in the new covenant requires a decision of allegiance—a decision that an infant is developmentally unable to make.[41]

CONCLUSIONS

As we close this chapter, we find that we have successfully navigated the first two stages of the great rescue plan. God has reestablished contact with fallen humanity through his covenant with Noah, and the *people* (the descendants of Abraham through Isaac), the *place* (the land of Canaan) and the *presence* ("I am . . . your very great reward," Gen 15:1 NIV) have been identified by means of Yahweh's covenant with Abraham. To our joy we also see that the plan is expanding. Whereas, in Eden every man, woman and child was welcomed into covenant relationship with Yahweh, with the Fall, all were excluded. But with Noah, one man and his immediate family are rescued and a bloodline identified, and with Abraham, one extended family is now permanently welcomed into covenant relationship. In the next chapter we will see that with the transition into the Mosaic covenant, this extended family will become a *nation*.

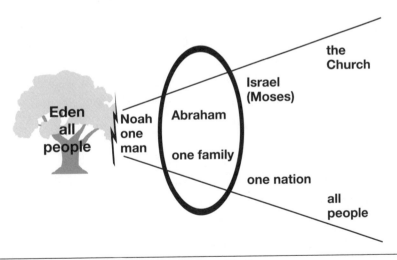

Figure 6.8. The people of redemptive history, Abraham

MOSES AND THE
TABERNACLE

With Moses we step into the next major juncture in redemptive history. Having reestablished contact with fallen humanity through his covenant with Noah, identified his *people* and *place* by means of his covenant with Abraham (and hinted at ʾĀdām's returned access to the *presence*), God now sets about to fulfill the promises to Abraham through the nation of Israel. This is the most detailed chapter in all of redemptive history, it is what your New Testament writers speak of as "the old covenant," and it lays the typological groundwork for the New Testament. Here we will also be introduced to the tabernacle—that first concrete step toward getting God and humanity back into the same space.

MOSES' REAL TIME

According to the internal dating of the Bible, we should be looking for the exodus somewhere in the middle of the second millennium b.c. According to 1 Kings 6:1, Solomon began to build the temple in his fourth regnal year, 480 years after the exodus. Since we know from the comparison of divided kingdom royal chronologies and those coming out of Mesopotamia that Solomon began his reign around 970 b.c., his fourth regnal year should be 966 b.c. Thus the exodus should be dated to 1447/6 b.c. This date is known as the "early date." But as you see on the timeline, I have offered you an alternative date as well, c. 1290 b.c. This "late date" emerges

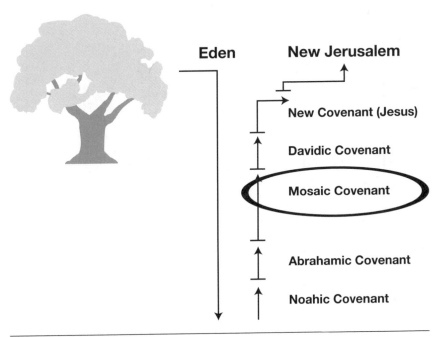

Figure 7.1. A synopsis of redemptive history, Moses

from the assessment of what we will call "external evidence"—evidence gathered from outside of the Bible. Although this late date is not derived from a specific biblical chronology, it actually attracts more adherents than the early date does. This is so partly because the archaeological and epigraphic evidence we currently have which supports an exodus points to this early thirteenth century date, and partly because the year record in Solomon's account is a little too "neat." What I mean by this is that the number 480 equals 40 x 12, and could easily have been intended as a stylized accounting of the generations between God's great deliverance in the exodus and the formalization of his presence among his people in Jerusalem by means of the temple. Twelve is, of course, the number of the tribes, and forty is the standard number offered for the length of a generation. Thus it is quite possible that 480 years was intended to communicate "twelve generations" or "the completion of generations" or some such message regarding this "perfect" period of time.[1] Even more suspect about this "480 years" is the fact that a survey of the chronological notices between the exodus and 1 Kings 6:1 produces a period longer than 480

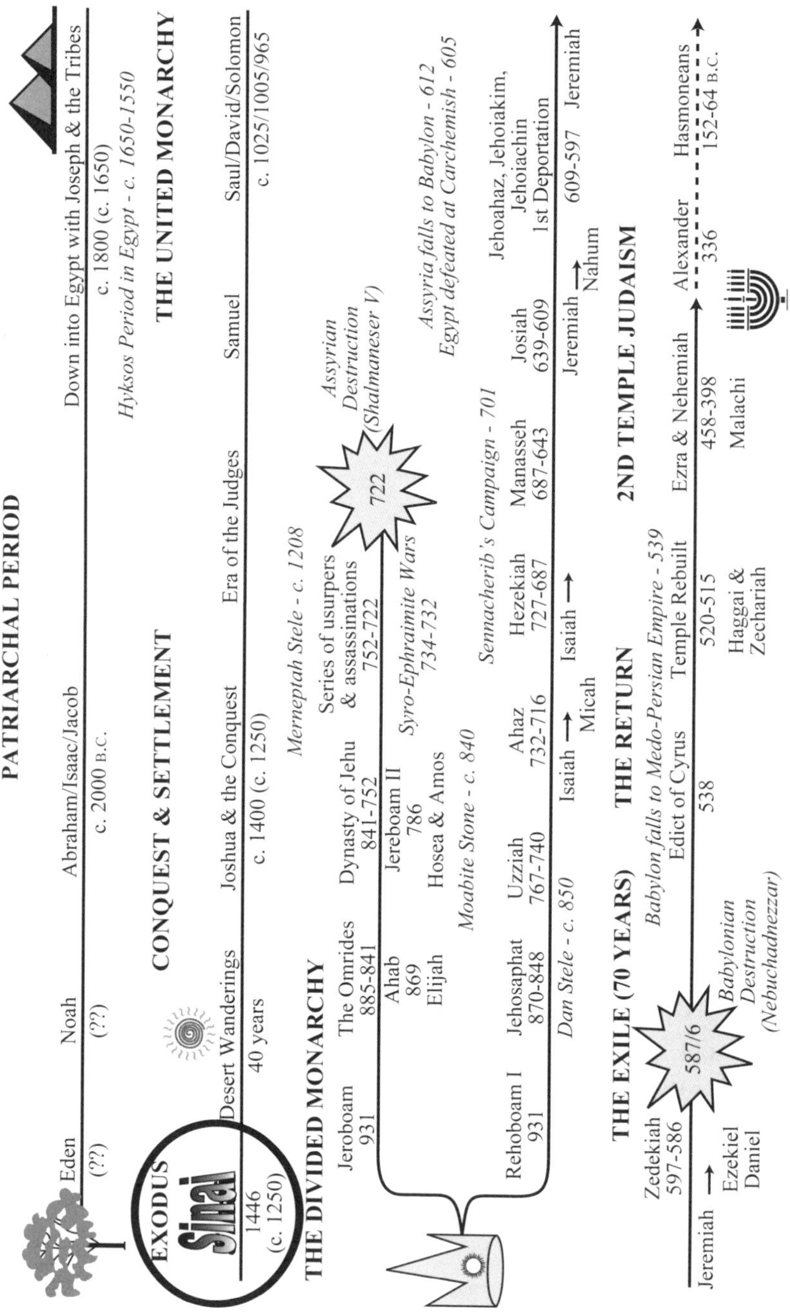

PATRIARCHAL PERIOD

Eden
(??)

Noah
(??)

Abraham/Isaac/Jacob
c. 2000 B.C.

Down into Egypt with Joseph & the Tribes
c. 1800 (c. 1650)
Hyksos Period in Egypt - c. 1650-1550

THE UNITED MONARCHY

CONQUEST & SETTLEMENT

Desert Wanderings
40 years

EXODUS
Sinai
1446
(c. 1250)

Joshua & the Conquest
c. 1400 (c. 1250)

Era of the Judges

Merneptah Stele - c. 1208

Samuel

Saul/David/Solomon
c. 1025/1005/965

THE DIVIDED MONARCHY

Jeroboam
931

The Omrides
885-841

Ahab
869

Elijah

Dynasty of Jehu
841-752

Jeroboam II
786

Hosea & Amos

Moabite Stone - c. 840

Series of usurpers
& assassinations
752-722

Syro-Ephraimite Wars
734-732

Assyrian
Destruction
(Shalmaneser V)

722

Assyria falls to Babylon - 612
Egypt defeated at Carchemish - 605

Rehoboam I
931

Jehosaphat
870-848

Dan Stele - c. 850

Uzziah
767-740

Isaiah →

Ahaz
732-716

Micah

Hezekiah
727-687

Isaiah →

Sennacherib's Campaign - 701

Manasseh
687-643

Josiah
639-609

Jehoahaz, Jehoiakim,
Jehoiachin
1st Deportation

Jeremiah
609-597

Jeremiah

2ND TEMPLE JUDAISM

Jeremiah →
Nahum

THE EXILE (70 YEARS)

Zedekiah
597-586

Jeremiah →

Ezekiel
Daniel

Babylonian
Destruction
(Nebuchadnezzar)

587/6

THE RETURN

Babylon falls to Medo-Persian Empire - 539
Edict of Cyrus
538

Temple Rebuilt
520-515

Haggai &
Zechariah

Ezra & Nehemiah
458-398

Malachi

Alexander
336

Hasmoneans
152-64 B.C.

Figure 7.2. Moses' real time

years.[2] This tells us that the Bible's chronological notices regarding this particular time span are either blatantly inconsistent or that individual biblical authors intended different messages by the numbers they named in their texts. So, let me repeat myself. Biblical dating is a tricky thing, and it is very possible that we do not yet know what the biblical writers meant by the dates they *seem* to be communicating. Thus it is best to hold this sort of thing loosely, and to never stake the authority of the Bible on what we *think* it is saying about dates.

MOSES' REAL SPACE

The story of Moses actually begins with Joseph. As we reviewed in chapter two, the Bible states that the young man is sold by his brothers to a caravan traveling through Dothan on its way to Egypt (Gen 37:17). "External" evidence lets us know that there was a well-traveled highway that led from Syria and Mesopotamia down the coast of Canaan into Egypt (the Via Maris), and there were several minor highways leading from the east to this same route.[3] Dothan was an important junction between the eastern routes and this coastal highway. Because of economic and legal

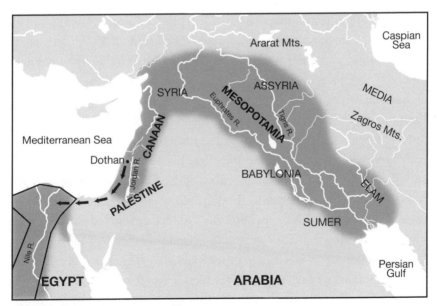

Figure 7.3. Joseph's journey into Egypt

records from surrounding countries, we also know that slave trade was a common and lucrative business in those days. In fact the price of a slave in the ancient Near East can actually be tracked with some confidence from approximately 2,000–400 B.C.[4] And the going price for a healthy slave in the eighteenth century was twenty silver shekels (Gen 37:28).[5] Thus external evidence lets us know that the Bible's tale of a caravan traveling from Gilead to Egypt through Dothan, trafficking in Semitic slaves and paying twenty silver shekels a head, is not only possible, it is probable.

In Egypt, Joseph is sold as a domestic servant.[6] He is unjustly incarcerated, miraculously released and, more miraculously, raised to a key position in the Egyptian government. If one ascribes to the late date, this promotion would have occurred during the Hyksos' era—that era in Egyptian history in which Semites were ruling Egypt.[7] Considering how unfavorably the indigenous Egyptians viewed the Semites (their standard designation was "vile Asiatic"!), this ethnic association between Joseph and the Hyksos might have made such a promotion more likely. Moreover, the details of Joseph's promotion—he is *shaved* before he is brought before Pharaoh (Gen 41:14), his promotion is marked by clothing him in *linen* and placing *the gold collar* around his neck (Gen 41:42), he is renamed with an Egyptian name and married to an Egyptian priestess (41:45)—are all details that can be substantiated by what we know of Egyptian society in this period and the promotion of other officials in Egypt's history.[8] Hence, either Joseph's promotion story contains real historical memory, or whoever wrote it was familiar enough with the inner workings of the Egyptian government in the second millennium to sprinkle the story with historically viable detail. Obviously, the former is more likely.

After Joseph is made prime minister, his family comes to Egypt in search of grain. Although we typically think of pyramids when we think of Egypt, it would be better to think in terms of the "breadbasket of the ancient Near East." This is because the Nile River flooded each year, every year, covering Egypt's fields with a wondrous layer of decomposing fish, fish poop, river weed, and other mucky stuff that would make any serious gardener's heart sing. (In the States you'll have to shop for this sort of mixture under the name "fish emulsion" as apparently "rotting fish parts" doesn't secure a significant clientele.) Not only did this annual inundation restore and enhance the fertility of the soil, it also brought to Egypt's fields that most precious resource in the ancient Near East, water. Between the inundation and a canal-irrigation system, the Nile Valley always produced, and Egypt *always* had food, specifically grain. So the idea that Jacob would send his sons to Egypt in time of famine is not far-fetched at all, rather, it is exactly what we know of ancient Egypt. In fact, Egyptian records testify that from its earliest days, Egypt found it necessary to defend itself from the forceful immigration of the less fortunate from Canaan who were brought near by drought and hunger.[9]

After Joseph's dramatic self-revelation to his brothers, Jacob and his clan migrate to Egypt and are settled in the eastern Nile delta, the region the Bible knows as Goshen. The reason given for settling them in Goshen is that "every shepherd is loathsome to the Egyptians" (Gen 46:34). This is not the first time a Semitic tribe had settled in the eastern Nile delta. Rather, throughout the Middle Bronze Age numbers of Semitic pastoralists from Canaan had settled in this same region. The Egyptian literature rails against this influx of the "vile Asiatic," citing the reason for their forceful immigration as the need for food and water.[10] The area showing the heaviest Semitic occupation during the Middle Bronze Period is the Wadi Tumilat.[11] This area is, you guessed it, in the eastern Nile delta.[12] Hence, Joseph settles his family among the other Semitic shepherds who have already colonized Egypt's eastern delta. Jacob and Joseph are thereby reunited. Jacob, then Joseph, dies (and is embalmed with the standard period of Egyptian mourning) and the book of Genesis ends.

THE EXODUS

As the story reads, years pass and a new pharaoh comes to Egypt's throne "who did not know Joseph" (Ex 1:8). Thus, rather than honoring the descendants of Joseph, this new pharaoh fears the prolific Semites and chooses to enslave them as a cheap work force for his building projects (Ex 1:9-14). But the race continues to multiply, and a federal form of birth control is mandated: all the male Hebrew children will be killed at birth. When that doesn't work, the Pharaoh commands that each male child be "cast into the Nile" (Ex 1:22). Every time I read this story I try to get my mind around what it would be like to be a midwife who assists a mother

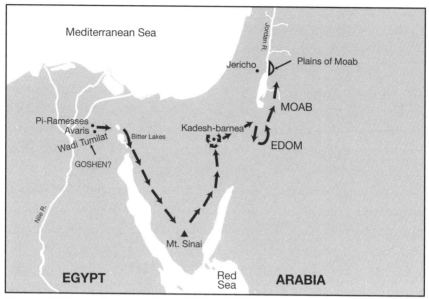

Figure 7.4. The exodus

all the way through a birth only to suffocate the newborn in her arms
. . . while the new mother lies there begging for her child's life. I wonder
what sort of Egyptian citizen would follow through on the Pharaoh's second order? And what sort of mayhem resulted when those citizens decided
it was time to ransack the Israelite villages, snatch the little ones from
their parents' arms and throw them into the river? Real people, real places
. . . real faith.

So what external evidence might we have for this oppression of the Israelites described in the Bible? Several times I have mentioned the Hyksos
period in Egypt. It lasted for only a hundred years, 1650–1550 B.C., but it
made a lasting impression upon the indigenous people of Egypt. Basically,
this hundred year period was the culmination of the ongoing migration
of Semites into Egypt during the Middle Bronze Age. Without any real
military initiative, the Hyksos took over Lower Egypt, built a capital city
(with all of the hallmarks of "Amorite" architecture),[13] adopted Egyptian
dress and culture, and ruled until the Egyptian patriots finally managed
to drive them out. Never again would the Egyptians allow a foreign people, particularly a Semitic people, to gain such an opportunity (cf. Ex 1:9-

10). After the Hyksos are driven out, there is a definite shift in Egyptian foreign and domestic policy. As regards foreign policy, the New Kingdom pharaohs (in particular Thutmosis III) campaigned regularly in Canaan, subjugating and controlling the entire region. As regards domestic policy, there was dramatic increase in slave labor for government-sponsored building projects.[14] Hence, although we cannot find any direct evidence of Abraham's kin in Egypt, we can find evidence that supports the Bible's general storyline: Semites migrate to Egypt and become influential toward the end of the Middle Bronze period; this era of influence ends suddenly when the Hyksos are driven out; and a new (and negative) view of the remaining Semitic population emerges.[15] If we ascribe to the late date, the pharaoh in question becomes Rameses II. Although the Bible never names the pharaoh of the exodus, Rameses II is a good candidate in that he is infamous for his massive building projects and equally massive ego. He is also responsible for what has been termed the largest single building project in the ancient world: Pi-Rameses (Ex 1:11).[16]

Into Israel's impossible situation comes a deliverer. Yahweh hears the cry of his people, remembers his covenant with Abraham and leads forth his people triumphant and loaded with spoil (Ex 12:35-36). In this tremendous act of deliverance Yahweh proves himself the Lord of the cosmos by defeating the greatest emperor of that era (and his gods) on their own turf. How does he do it? Through one man whose life had been directed by an unseen divine hand, who was prepared in ways that he could never have imagined were significant, and bringing that man to a point of conviction and belief. Think about it. The typical Israelite slave was illiterate, certainly had no military training and had never been allowed to organize into anything as sophisticated as a PTA. How would such a person organize and represent a nation? Write up a law code? Lead troops into battle? The typical Israelite slave could do none of these things. Moses, however, was not the typical Israelite slave. Rather, because of his "chance" adoption, Moses was trained *by the Egyptians* to read, write and administrate; he was at least bilingual, confident of his ability to interact with Egyptian royalty and trained in the arts of war and diplomacy.[17]

And so Moses confronts Pharaoh in the name of Yahweh. Over and over again in the narrative we hear Yahweh say, "let *My* people go" and Pharaoh responds, "why should I let *my* people go?" The ten plagues convince the Pharaoh (and the people of Egypt!)[18] that Yahweh means what he says, that Israel belongs to him and that he is more powerful than the Egyptian monarch. Yahweh secures victory and leads Israel out of bondage complete with the plunder due a conquering army (Ex 12:35-37). Thus Israel is rescued from a strong enemy against whom she had no defense. The people are delivered from slavery and poverty, returned to a place of security, given an identity, a future, a hope and an inheritance. Israel is *redeemed*.

This is the exodus. This is the single most important event in all Israelite history. Without the exodus, the children of Abraham were a forgotten race. Without the exodus, the promises of Abraham were nothing. Without the exodus, there would be no Mosaic covenant and no Israel. "I am Yahweh your God who brought you out of the land of Egypt, out of the house of slavery." You would be hard-pressed to read far in the Old Testament without bumping into this phrase or allusions to it, because this is the historical prologue of the Mosaic covenant—it furnishes the basis of the vassal's obligation. According to what we know about covenants, this is *why* Israel should serve Yahweh. Moreover, it is also how Yahweh has chosen to be known. For all of history our God has *chosen* to be identified by this singular event—the God who rescues slaves from their bondage and claims them as his own. As you and I would stand to our feet to speak of the day Jesus revealed himself to us, rescued us from our conflicted lives and sordid pasts and gave us a new start, the Israelite would stand to his or her feet to speak of the day Yahweh came to Egypt, delivered them from the slavery of their past and led them into freedom. Not just the freedom of freemen, but the freedom of the knowledge of the self-revelation of God. In fact, the Mishnah actually commands each Jew of every generation to "regard himself as if he came forth himself out of Egypt" (*Pesaḥ.* x.5). The ancient liturgies demand the same of the Christian. If we are to understand the God of our salvation, the faith of Israel and therefore our own faith, we *must* understand the exodus.

Sinai.

[T]he mountain of God is a beacon to the slaves of Egypt, a symbol of a new kind of master and a radically different relationship of people to state.

Sinai is not the final goal of the Exodus, but it does represent Yahweh's unchallengeable mastery over both.[19]

You yourselves have seen what I did to the Egyptians, and how I bore you on eagles' wings, and brought you to Myself. (Ex 19:4)

But you are A CHOSEN RACE, a royal PRIESTHOOD, A HOLY NATION, A PEOPLE FOR God's OWN POSSESSION, so that you may proclaim the excellencies of Him who has called you out of darkness into His marvelous light. For once you were NOT A PEOPLE, but now you are THE PEOPLE OF GOD; once you had NOT RECEIVED MERCY, but now you have RECEIVED MERCY. (1 Pet 2:9-10)

As we have already discussed in chapter two, God leads the people of Israel out of Egypt, through the Red Sea and south into no man's land. Utilizing a series of oases, this cumbersome group manages to sustain itself and its flocks until they reach their God-ordained destination: Mount Sinai.[20] Here Yahweh's great suzerain-vassal covenant is offered to Israel (see chapter three), and upon their acceptance the aggregate of kinsmen that Israel had been is transformed into a nation. The "flight plan" for this fledgling nation is summarized in Exodus 19–32 by means of a law, a calendar and a cultic system. The *law* creates and structures the nation by defining what Yahweh requires of them. The *calendar* organizes Israel's time (the sabbath ordinance, feasts and offerings). The *tabernacle* enthrones the suzerain in their midst. With this covenant and this blueprint for the nation, the kingdom of God is instituted on earth. The *people* of God are now dwelling with the *presence* of God housed amongst them and are on their way to claim the *place* of God.

Many Christians are surprised to hear the term "kingdom of God" applied to Israel in that they think this is a New Testament phrase. In our next section on typology, we'll explore how this is a both/and proposition. But Israel was indeed God's kingdom. It was a theocracy—a nation "ruled by God." (In case you're curious, *democracy,* that ultimate form of government to which my country subscribes, is a similar term. Except it means a nation "ruled by the mob.") As a theocracy, Yahweh was Israel's true king. With God as Israel's king, this means that Israel's territory was actually *God's* territory, Israel's enemies were *God's* enemies, and Israel's political interests were God's political interests. This is the nature of theocracy, and it is an extremely important piece of the theological puzzle when one attempts to understand the nature of the Mosaic covenant. Many of the perennially perplexing moral questions that this covenant engenders are answered by this one fact. More on this later.

How did God ordain that his theocratic nation be administrated? By three theocratic offices staffed by human representatives: the prophet, priest and king (see Deut 17–18). The job description of the priest was to speak for the people to God. The prophet was to speak for God to the people. And the king was a political leader, a representative of the nation whose job was to keep the nation on track in its adherence to the covenant. Folks normally assume that out of these three offices the king was the most powerful. But in Israel's government, this was not true. In Israel, the human king was only a steward of the true king, Yahweh. It was the prophet (whose job was to speak for the true king) who held the ultimate authority. This is dramatically illustrated in the infamous story of David, Bathsheba and the prophet Nathan.

The story runs like this. By the days of 2 Samuel 12, David was at the height of his career—successful, powerful and rich. His reputation was as one of the most effective military strategists in Israelite history. Remember that it was he who replaced the budding dynasty of Saul, claimed Israel's throne and secured her borders. Moreover David himself was someone you did not want to meet on the battlefield. Yet in the day of his sin with Bathsheba, one man dared to confront him. Picture the scene. David is elevated on a platform at the end of the long hall that is his throne room. He is dressed as a royal; his armed men line the walls. A man enters alone, unarmed: the prophet Nathan. Standing upon the floor, he recites the famous parable of the rich man and the poor man's ewe lamb (2 Sam 12:1-4). Then Nathan cuts loose, accusing the king of his crime (a crime any other royal would have considered his right) and even *detailing* David's offense in front of his subordinates. I assure you that in any other court in the ancient Near East, Nathan would have died where he stood. But in this court, it is David who bows the knee. Why? Because David understood that he was not the true king of Israel—he was a subordinate; he too must obey the law of the Great King. And although Nathan had apparently come alone and unarmed, he had also come as the messenger of Yahweh, and if David wanted to keep his throne, he would obey.

So the Mosaic covenant provides the blueprint for the nation of Israel as a suzerain/vassal relationship in which three human theocratic officers are commissioned to direct the nation according to the will of Yahweh. And

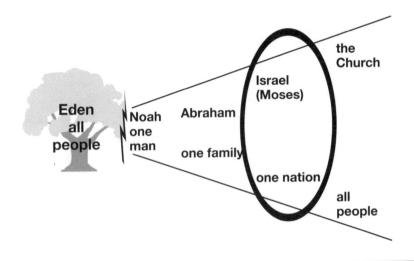

Figure 7.5. The people of redemptive history, Israel

within this covenant, we find that the Abrahamic promises have been fulfilled. Do you remember Genesis 12:1-3? Yahweh had promised to give Abraham numerous offspring, to make him the father of "a great nation," to give him the land of Canaan and to reward him with fame. According to Exodus 12:37, as many as two and a half million people walked out of Egypt that miraculous morning and conquered and inhabited Canaan. The embrace of redemptive history has widened, and now an entire nation is welcomed into relationship with God. Thus the promise of *people, place* and *presence* finds its first fulfillment here. Like the great hinge of redemptive history, the Mosaic covenant fulfills the Abrahamic covenant typologically and it foreshadows the new covenant typologically. But of course to understand this statement, we're going to need to understand the term "typological."

TYPOLOGY

The word *type* is about as plain vanilla a word as one can imagine. But in the field of biblical studies the word has a technical definition that makes it quite important. In the task of interpretation a *type* is an event or person in one era of redemptive history that has a specific parallel (an *antitype*) in another era of redemptive history. A type is not an allegory or a symbol, nor is the relationship between a type and its antitype(s) allegorical. As G. R. Osborne puts it: "A symbol is an abstract correspondence, while a type is an actual historical event or person . . . a specific parallel between two historical entities."[21] Typology (which has to do with interpreting the Bible through the lens of types) has to do with the principal of analogous fulfillment.

> Therefore, biblical typology involves an analogical correspondence in which earlier events, persons, and places in salvation history become patterns by which later events, persons, and places are interpreted. It is increasingly recognized that typology expresses the basic hermeneutic by which both OT and NT writers understood themselves and their predecessors.[22]

Let me offer an illustration. Do you remember the old 1965 movie *The Flight of the Phoenix?* I understand it has been recently redone with most everything from the original except the critical acclaim. In the original, Jimmy Stewart starred as the pilot of a downed plane in the Sahara desert. A mix of characters, including a hated German engineer, find themselves stranded with no hope of rescue or survival. As food and water begin to run out, the German reveals himself as an *aeronautical* engineer and proposes that the group pool their resources to build a plane out of the wreckage and fly themselves to safety. The plan sounds impossible, but it is their only hope. So the group gathers behind this man (whom they despise), brutally ration their food and water, and work themselves to the point of collapse to complete the patched-together machine before they all die. The night before the scheduled flight, in a rare moment of social conversation, Jimmy Stewart asks the German engineer what sorts of planes he designs. The engineer's response? *Model* aircraft. Can you imagine? This group has put every hope they have on the line to build an aircraft according to the design of a man who builds *model* airplanes! The despair of the exhausted men is palpable.

But the good news is that model airplanes operate upon the exact same principles as full-sized aircraft. The only real difference is how much cargo they can carry. A model airplane can carry very little cargo. A Boeing 747 aircraft, however, can carry more than four hundred people across a continent. This is the essence of a type. It is real. It works. It happened. But a type operates upon the principal of *limited* fulfillment. Thus, whereas the Mosaic covenant and all of its appurtenances were real and designed upon all of the same principles of atonement as the new covenant, it could carry no cargo. The new covenant, however, can carry as many souls as it must across the barrier from death into life and into eternity.

A few examples of types and antitypes we have already encountered in our study include:

- The "first Adam" as a type of the "Second Adam," Christ
- Noah's ark as a type of the salvation of the new covenant (cf. 1 Pet 3:21)
- Circumcision as a type of baptism

Probably the most important function of a type in God's redemptive plan is that it *teaches*. Like a cosmic flannelgraph, a type gives a concrete (and often simple) example of a more abstract (and often complex) concept so that we humans can get our minds around it. The Mosaic covenant is chock-full of such concrete examples. Let's consider one of the most significant, the tabernacle.

The tabernacle. Of all the types coming out of the Old Testament, few are as important as the tabernacle and its later embodiment, the temple. In fact, the New Testament writers constantly use the tabernacle (its functions, furniture, staff, decorations, floor plan, etc.) to explain our faith to us. So understanding the form and function of the tabernacle is vital to us "catching" the message of our New Testaments.

As we discussed in chapter four, we are first introduced to the tabernacle (Hebrew *miškān*, literally "the place of dwelling") when Yahweh says to Moses in Exodus 25:8: "Let them construct a sanctuary for Me, so that

I may dwell among them." The "so that" in this passage is critical because it lets us know that God's purpose in instituting the tabernacle was that he might live among his people. And do you see how Yahweh chooses to live as his people live? Since the Israelites dwell in tents, Yahweh will too. When Israel becomes a sedentary people, Yahweh shifts his residence to a

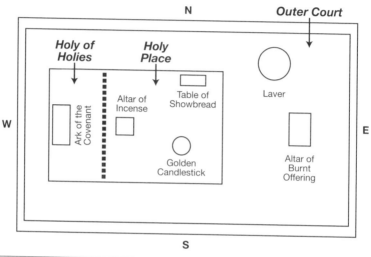

Figure 7.6. The footprint of the tabernacle

Figure 7.7. An artist's reconstruction of the tabernacle (copyright 2005 New Life Missions)

temple and becomes sedentary as well. Here we see the incarnation of the oft-repeated refrain: "I shall be their God and they shall be my people and I will dwell among them" (see Ex 29:45; Ezek 37:27, 48:35; Jn 14:23; 2 Cor 6:16; Rev 21:3). In the tabernacle the Presence *lives* on earth for the first time since Eden. This alone is a tremendous step forward in the plan of redemption. Even more important is the message that the design of this tabernacle, and the religious system associated with it, communicates.

Looking at figures 7.6 and 7.7 we see that the tabernacle was designed according to a tripartite plan. This means that it had three areas: an outer court, a holy place and the holy of holies. As one passed from the outer court through the holy place into the holy of holies, each area became increasingly restricted (sanctified). This increasing level of sanctification was due to the fact that Yahweh himself sat enthroned in the central-most area, above the cherubim of the Ark of the Covenant (see chapter four's section on the cherubim for more detail). The increasing holiness of these areas was communicated by each area's reduced size, the quality and value of its décor and the more limited number of individuals who might enter. Thus the tent-structure progressed from an open-air, linen-curtained courtyard, to an enclosed, purple-dyed and embroidered wool holy place, to the perfectly square and probably elevated holy of holies, which was hung with embroidered wool and ornamented with gold. Any clean, worshiping Israelite could enter the outer court, only priests could enter the holy place, and only the high priest could enter the holy of holies . . . and that only once per year on the Day of Atonement.[23] This was a day of profound anxiety for the one selected as high priest, and he went through *days* of ritual cleansing prior to entering God's presence. When he entered, he wore bells (Ex 28:31-35). Why? "The bells, which jingled as the high priest served in the tabernacle, assured all who listened that he had not died in the holy place and that he continued to minister on their behalf."[24] There's a job I want. A job where everyone I know is listening outside the veil to find out if God has found some impurity in me and struck me dead! Although more than a little intimidating, this aspect of the tabernacle cultus is actually just like everything else we've seen. The increasing sanctification of the three areas of the tabernacle, the restricted access, the elaborate measures taken for cleansing and atonement all communicate the same message: God lives here. And anyone who draws near must either be holy . . . or dead.

So the irony of the tabernacle is the agony of redemptive history. By its very form this structure communicates God's desire for *cohabitation*. But the increasing restriction of persons—and the elaborate systems of sacrifice and mediation even for those approved persons[25]—communicates the legacy of sin, *separation*. Yes, God lived among his people, but the common worshiper—even the average priest—would never stand in his presence. Only one man, once a year, entered the holy of holies, and he entered under threat of death (Lev 16:2). The double-edged sword of the tabernacle was the truth that God was once again with ʾĀdām, but ʾĀdām was still separated from God. Do you see how this type educated Israel as to what sin and forgiveness are all about? Here we see illustrated in the concrete realities of designated precincts, professional priests and animals slain in sacrifice, the real consequences of sin, the need for mediation and sacrifice, and the possibility of forgiveness. Also important as we think about the nature of types and typology is the fact that the tabernacle did provide some level of atonement for God's people (Lev 1:1-4; 4:35). It was real. It was effective. It was historical. But like all types, it provided *limited* atonement. If humanity was to fully reenter the Presence, the model airplane would not do—a Boeing 747 would be necessary.

And so the New Testament writers seize upon this type to explain the complex realities of the new covenant. Remembering the message of Exodus 25:8, "let them construct a sanctuary for Me, so that I may dwell among them," and keeping in mind the centrality of the tabernacle in Israel's understanding of their faith, hear how the apostle John introduces the gospel of Jesus Christ in John 1:14. "And the Word became flesh, and dwelt [or *tabernacled*] among us, and we saw His glory, the glory as of the only begotten from the Father, full of grace and truth."[26] Do you hear it? Every Israelite knew that the closest he would ever come to the Presence was standing in the outer court, every few months, *if* he was clean and whole and brought an appropriate sacrifice. These were the concrete realities of the tabernacle. But the paradigm-shattering news of the new covenant is that Jesus came in human form to bring the Presence to us. Pause over this for a moment. In the incarnation the veil is ripped in two, the holy of holies is thrown open, and the lost, the sick, the deformed, the disabled, even the ostracized foreigner who deserved her reputation as a loose woman, are invited to draw near. Romans says that "while we were still helpless . . . while we were yet sinners, Christ died for us" (Rom 5:6-8). In the incarnation we the exiled children of Adam and Eve are invited to see and touch the Presence.

The book of Hebrews cannot let these images alone. In an attempt to explain the gospel to his Jewish audience, the author repeatedly compares Jesus (the antitype) to the sacrifices (Heb 9:11-28), the priesthood (Heb 4:14–5:10; 7:1-28) and even the structure of the Old Testament tabernacle—the type. And over and over again the author declares Jesus "better than" what has come before. Jesus is the high priest who enters the holy of holies on our behalf and truly, finally, completely atones for our sin; Jesus is the sacrifice; Jesus himself is the veil, which he himself willingly tears asunder.

> Therefore, brethren, since we have confidence to enter the holy place by the blood of Jesus, by a new and living way which He inaugurated for us through the veil, that is, His flesh, and since we have a great priest over the house of God, let us draw near with a sincere heart in full assurance of faith, having our hearts sprinkled clean from an evil conscience and our bodies washed with pure water. Let us hold fast the confession of our hope without wavering, for He who promised is faithful. (Heb 10:19-23)

In sum, Jesus is the Boeing 747. And because of the model aircraft (the tabernacle), all humanity has been educated in the content of his mission: to be the final and ultimate means of sacrifice and mediation for the human race. And because of the tabernacle, we understand why the mission was necessary—so *that* God might dwell with us. So at the end of the story we should not be surprised to read,

> And I heard a loud voice from the throne, saying, "Behold, the tabernacle of God is among men, and He will dwell among them, and they shall be His people, and God Himself will be among them." (Rev 21:3)

Through the Mosaic covenant, for the first time since Eden, the tabernacle brings the Presence near. God dwells among his people. The cherubim still guard the entrance to God's throne room, but a means of entry has been established. Granted entry is only allotted to one man, once a year.

But the door is there, awaiting the One who will throw it wide for all the exiled children of ʾĀdām.

THE LAW

Whenever I teach on this material, and people realize (often for the first time) that the Mosaic covenant contains the foundations of the new covenant and (in its own way) announces the gospel, hands shoot up all over the auditorium with the same question: "What about the law?" Because of Paul's language throughout his epistles—and more importantly because of our inability to understand Paul's language throughout the epistles—Christians too often think that the law was a bad thing.[27] We tend to think of the law in terms of a cruel and evil taskmaster, the ultimate foil to the gospel of Jesus Christ. On the contrary, I need to declare with Paul that "the Law is holy, and the commandment is holy and righteous and good!" (Rom 7:12).

Think this through with me. In its place in redemptive history, the law served to sketch the profile of God to a fallen race who no longer had any idea who God was or what he defined as "good." Because of the Mosaic law, the Israelites learned that Yahweh (unlike the other "gods" of the ancient Near East) abhorred human sacrifice, self-mutilation and temple prostitution. They learned that Yahweh was immune to magic and competed with no one. They learned that unlike the deities of surrounding nations who were embedded in the created order, Yahweh was independent of his creation. He did not need humanity to feed or clothe him, nor was he impressed or swayed by the construction of fancy temples. Yahweh would not welcome the immolation of their children, nor would he speak to his people by means of the entrails of slaughtered beasts. This god was different, and what he expected of his people was different as well. This is what the Mosaic law brought into focus in Israel's world. It was a *very* good thing.

Now it is true that Jesus will "fine-tune" the law. The Sermon on the Mount (Matthew 5–7) is the most famous example of this fine-tuning. It is full of "You have heard that it was said to the ancients do thus and such, but I say to you do better than that."[28] The "better than" statements include commandments that address motive, emotion and relationship, not just behavior (Mt 5:17-48). But don't be fooled into thinking that the Mosaic law failed to address motive, emotion and relationship. It did.

But it was the rare old covenant believer that was able to actually *transform* motive, emotion and relationship in their own life, so ultimately their behavior didn't change too much either. As the book of Hebrews states: "The Law is only a shadow of the good things that are coming—not the realities themselves. For this reason it can never, by the same sacrifices repeated endlessly year after year, make perfect those who draw near to worship" (Heb 10:1 NIV). So Jesus' reiteration of the law was necessary partly to confront the Jews with the fact that their attempted adherence to the law wasn't working. And as both Jesus and Paul state repeatedly, adherence wasn't working because *hearts* were not changing. Thus a new covenant was needed—a new relationship between God and humanity in which the *people* could be transformed. How? By the impossible promise that the Presence would actually come to abide in the individual believer, making hearts of flesh out of hearts of stone, and writing God's expectations upon our hearts. All this to make compliance with the law not only possible, but probable. This transformation is the essence of the prophet Jeremiah's promise of the new covenant in Jeremiah 31:31-33:

> "Behold, days are coming," declares the LORD, "when I will make a new covenant with the house of Israel and with the house of Judah, not like the covenant which I made with their fathers in the day I took them by the hand to bring them out of the land of Egypt, my covenant which they broke, although I was a husband to them," declares the LORD. "But this is the covenant which I will make with the house of Israel after those days," declares the LORD, "I will put My law within them and on their heart I will write it; and I will be their God, and they shall be My people."

This is the new covenant. But keep in mind that even in his fine-tuning, Jesus does not do away with the Mosaic law. "For truly I say to you, until heaven and earth pass away, not the smallest letter or stroke shall pass away from the Law until all is accomplished" (Mt 5:18). Rather, Jesus and Paul make it clear that the law has served a critical role in redemptive history: "the Law has become our tutor to lead us to Christ" (Gal 3:24). Like an underage child, the law has served as our guardian until we might be of age and maturity to take possession of our inheritance. Like a flannelgraph, it has provided the concrete examples of truth, such that we might be prepared to receive the more abstract aspects of truth when they came. The law, which communicated the profile of the character of God, prepared humanity to recognize "the exact representation of his nature" when he came to tabernacle among us (cf. Heb 1:3). Therefore, as Paul says, "the law has become our tutor to lead us to Christ, so that we may be justified by faith. But now that faith has come, we are no longer under a tutor" (Gal 3:24-25). Scott Hafemann puts it this way:

> Rather than suggesting that the Law is somehow negated or done away with in the new covenant, Jeremiah 31:31-33 emphasizes just the opposite. According to Jeremiah 31:31-33 it is rather the ability to keep the Law, as a result of having a transformed nature, and thus to keep rather than perpetually break the covenant between God and his people, that distinguishes the new covenant from the covenant at Sinai. There is no indication in the text, or in Jeremiah as a whole, that the future eschatological restoration will entail the giving of a new Law or that the Law is now being thought about only in the abstract sense as a revelation of the general will of God. The Law written on the heart is the Sinai Law itself as the embodiment of the will of God. The contrast between the new and Sinai covenants is not a contrast between a covenant with and without an external Law; nor is it a contrast between two different kinds of Laws. Rather, the contrast between the two covenants is a contrast between the two different conditions of the people who are brought into these covenants and their correspondingly different responses to the same Law.[29]

Simply put, Hafemann is saying that the problem with the old covenant was not the law, it was the *people*. Thus the solution of the new covenant does not so much change the law, as it changes the people.[30] And this change will be enacted by the power of the Spirit. In the new covenant, God's people will be transformed—"born again"—such that they instinctively know the law, love the law, and are able to keep the law. In sum, it is not that the law is bad or that it has been eradicated in Christ; rather, the law was a partial, time-and-culture-bound revelation of the character of God. To use one of our previous metaphors, it is one of several transparency sheets that must be placed upon the overhead projector in order to project a complete image of who God is and what he intends for humanity. The law is good. And if you are interested in the follow-up question, "What role does the Law of Moses play in the Christian's life?" see the final section of this book: "Frequently Asked Questions."

THE FENCE AROUND THE LAW

One of the more confusing issues surrounding the New Testament discussion of Jewish religious practice is that it is difficult for us modern readers to determine when Jesus and the New Testament writers are speaking of the Mosaic law versus the rabbinic law. The core of the issue has to do with something known as "the fence around the law"—a body of once oral, now written, regulations designed to insure proper adherence to the Mosaic law.[a] This body of regulations was birthed in the post-exilic era when the Israelites returned to the land of Palestine from Babylonia as citizens of the Persian Empire. No longer having the luxury of national borders to distinguish them from their neighbors, they became very focused upon distinguishing themselves by means of social boundaries. Thus certain aspects of their religious practice that set them apart from their neighbors, which had not necessarily been central in the past, became very important in the post-exilic era. Examples include the keeping of the sabbath, the laws of kashrut (what may be eaten and drunk)[b] and marriage laws.

An example of how this "fence around the law" worked are the laws of the sabbath. The extent of the biblical witness is that the Israelites recognize the seventh day as belonging to Yahweh, and therefore no person or animal in the community is to work (Ex 20:10). Thus they were not to kindle a fire on the sabbath (Ex 35:3), nor buy or sell (Neh 10:31; 13:15-22). Yet, as they are

---

[a]The phrase itself comes from the first verse of a tractate in the Mishnah known as *Pirqe ʿābôt* ("The Sayings/Chapters of the Jewish Fathers"): "Moses received the Torah from Sinai, and handed it down to Joshua, and Joshua to the elders, and the elders to the prophets, and the prophets delivered it to the men of the Great Synagogue. They said three things, 'Be deliberate in judgment; raise up many disciples; and make a fence around the Law.'" Cf. Lev 18:30.
[b]In Ex 23:19 we read: "You are not to boil a kid in the milk of its mother." It has been postulated that the boiling of kids and lambs in their mother's milk was some sort of Canaanite fertility rite in which Yahweh forbade his people to participate. It has also been proposed that this law was originally intended simply as a guideline birthed of compassion: you shall not cook a baby in the milk of its own mother. Either way, this is a fairly narrow command that only affects one instance of practice: the boiling of nurslings from the flock. But the "fence around the law" evolved such that dairy products and meat were never to be consumed at the same meal, from the same dish or (eventually) even their plates and utensils washed in the same dishwasher. Thus with this "fence" no faithful Jew would ever accidentally consume cheese or milk with meat which may have been the nursing offspring of the animal that produced the dairy product.

currently recorded in the Mishnah,ᶜ there are thirty-six pages of sabbath regulations. These range from how a tailor ought to leave his needle on sabbath eve (Sabb. 1:3), to the point in time one's oven must be clear of certain foodstuffs prior to the sabbath (Sabb. 1:10), to what sort of material it is lawful to use for the wick of the sabbath lamp (Sabb. 2:3). These specifications of the biblical sabbath ordinance detail most conceivable situations in which a pious Jew might find himself and therefore "protect" the Mosaic law from violation. But as is obvious, these ordinances go far beyond the Mosaic law.

It is not difficult to imagine how this "fence around the law" engendered the sort of legalism that, for many, choked out the life-giving intentions of God's good word to the Israelites. Nor is it difficult to imagine why Jesus might condemn this sort of legalism (cf. Mark 7). I think in terms of Jesus' confrontation of the Jewish religious leaders in Jerusalem:

> *Woe to you, scribes and Pharisees, hypocrites! For you tithe mint and dill and cumin, and have neglected the weightier provisions of the law: justice and mercy and faithfulness. . . . You blind guides, who strain out a gnat and swallow a camel! . . . For you clean the outside of the cup and of the dish, but inside they are full of robbery and self-indulgence. (Mt 23:23-25)*

There is much more that could be said about this complex discussion. But it is important for us to realize that not every reference to religious law and practice in the New Testament addresses Mosaic law.

ᶜThe Mishnah is the written compilation of these once-oral legal traditions, codified by the end of the second century A.D., Jewish tradition is that these oral laws originated at Sinai. See Neusner, *Way of Torah,* pp. 47-53.

CONCLUSIONS

With the establishment of the Mosaic covenant, the kingdom of God may once again be found in 'Ādām's world. The theocracy of Israel is established with the *people* of God (Abraham's offspring), on their way to the *place* of God (Canaan), led by the *presence* of God (the tabernacle). God has fulfilled his good word to Abraham. And only one piece of the Old Testament puzzle remains to be put into place, the covenant of David.

DAVID AND
THE MONARCHY

THE COVENANT WITH DAVID IS THE LAST PIECE of the Old Testament puzzle. Your closet is almost finished! In the last chapter we learned that the Mosaic covenant established God's theocratic kingdom on earth and that this kingdom was designed to be administrated by three human officers: the prophet, the priest and the king. In this chapter we have to examine the job description of the last of these three officers, the king, and investigate the life and times of the paradigmatic king: David.

As we consider time and space, we see that the Mosaic covenant encompasses the bulk of Israelite history. Moses' covenant began at Sinai, and it ends either with the exile in 586 B.C. or with Jesus' ratification of the new covenant in the first century. I personally think this is a both/ and kind of thing. In some ways the Mosaic covenant does end in 586 B.C. when Israel is stripped of its nationhood and, for all intents and purposes, its land grant. But as you now know, God enables the Jews to return from exile and reestablish a community in and around Jerusalem which continued to practice temple worship and many of the forms and functions of the preexilic, Mosaic community.[1] Although Israel would never be a truly sovereign state again, this community will continue to exist and expand during the intertestamental period until it is dismantled by the Roman Empire in the first and second centuries A.D. So in many ways the Mosaic covenant continues to function into Jesus' day but not in true theocratic

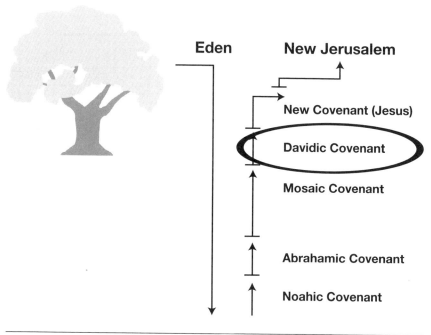

Figure 8.1. A synopsis of redemptive history, David

form. When Jesus comes and seals the new covenant with his own oath and blood, this is a clear and decisive ending point for the old. So we can speak of the Mosaic covenant as the umbrella which encompasses Israel's experience from Sinai to Jesus.

But this larger covenantal administration has a "subcovenant," David's royal grant. David's covenant does not change the identity of the *people, place* or *presence* of the Mosaic covenant, but it adds a critical new dimension—a royal, human representative who stands between Yahweh and his people. This is the last piece of the puzzle I spoke of above. As we discussed in the chapter on Abraham, a royal grant was a covenant-gift awarded to a servant who had distinguished himself by means of faithful service. Usually these gifts were some sort of permanent office or land grant. Abraham's gift was land, David's is permanent office, that is, dynasty. As detailed in 2 Samuel 7, Yahweh promises that there would always be a son of David on Israel's throne. But we are getting ahead of ourselves. Let's begin with David's real time and space.

FROM SINAI TO THE BIRTH OF THE MONARCHY

So how did we get from Sinai to the birth of the monarchy? The books of the Bible that detail this transition are the books of Joshua, Judges, Ruth and 1 Samuel. Here we read about Israel's conquest and ongoing struggle to control the land, their apportionment of the land into tribal territories, the era of the judges and, at last, the emergence of Saul as the first actual *king* in Israel's history. Politically speaking, this transition may be characterized as a transition from a "tribal league" into a "monarchy."[2]

The era of the judges. During the tribal league, the tribes lived very independent lives. The only activities that they regularly shared were their joint defense of the Promised Land and their united worship of Yahweh at the tabernacle (which was located primarily at Shiloh). Thus, outside of the three pilgrim festivals and the periodic (and typically regional) call to arms, the tribes did not see each other much. The tribal sheiks handled local problems; there was no centralized government, no taxation, no joint building projects and no standing army. And they liked it that way. They saw Yahweh as their king and their tribal elders as his local officials. The prophets and the judges were Yahweh's most influential representatives and, in combination with the priesthood housed at the tabernacle, his only national officers. The primary interest of each individual tribe was regional peace and prosperity and wrestling their allotted territory away from the Canaanites and Philistines.

In this early stage of Israel's history, Yahweh makes it very clear that national success would be dependent on adherence to the covenant. The promise was that when Israel kept covenant, they would experience prosperity and security. When they failed to keep covenant, the nation would be disciplined by means of some sort of national disaster—typically foreign oppression. Keep clearly in your mind that Israel was a *theocracy*, so the citizens of this nation were the people of God and the citizens of other nations were not. Moreover, the political and economic well-being of the nation was a direct indicator of whether or not God was pleased with his people. And as the people of God during this era of redemptive history were not terribly different from the people of God during our era of redemptive history, obedience to the covenant was not always a priority.

As a result, we see a repeating cycle throughout the book of Judges. This cycle is illustrated in figure 8.2.

The cycle begins with the people of Israel living in obedience and therefore experiencing national security and prosperity. The second stage results when the people take that security for granted and begin to violate the covenant. Covenant-breaking leads to stage three, foreign oppression. Stage four begins when the citizens realize their failure, repent and cry out to

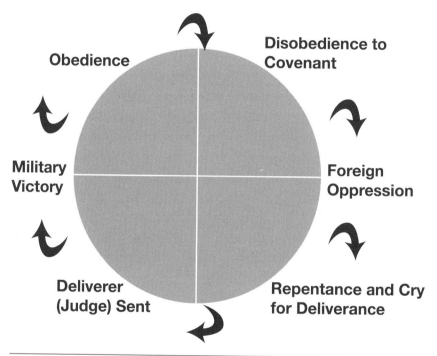

Figure 8.2. The era of the judges

Yahweh for deliverance. Yahweh responds by supernaturally empowering a leader of his choice to defeat the enemy and restore national well-being. We know these leaders as "judges." This title is a bit unfortunate, however, in that the word *judge* makes the modern reader think of someone with only a legal function. But a judge in Israel always began his or her career as a military leader—someone who, because of God's empowerment, was able to unify the tribes in battle and bring security and prosperity back to the nation. Typically, this same leader would then judge the nation for a period of years following. What we see in the book of Judges is that the people responded to this God-ordained leader with enthusiasm and gratitude . . . for a while. And then the cycle would begin again.

Thus the book of Judges offers us twelve different individuals who were raised up to confront military threats in various regions of the country and who ruled ("judged") the country for varying lengths of time after the initial military threat was resolved. (Some of these judges overlapped each other, with one judge ruling in the east, for example, while a second ruled at the same time in the west.) These twelve judges serve to organize the history of this period, and they also highlight the cycle above. Twelve times we see Israel pass through this same cycle of obedience > disobedience > foreign oppression > repentance > deliverance. And as we reach the twelfth repetition of this cycle, we notice that the movement is not merely horizontal, it is vertical as well. In other words, the covenant-faithfulness of God's people is also spiraling downward . . . a spiral which is shockingly illustrated by the jarring stories that conclude the book. Judges 19 is one of these stories. I have yet to read this narrative without it turning my stomach. Here an Israelite of reputation and substance is traveling through Israelite territory with his concubine (think "second wife"). When he reaches Gibeah he is welcomed into an elderly man's home, only to find himself harassed by the local rabble later in the evening. The demand is the same as the story of Lot and the angels in Genesis 19:1-11, "Bring out the man who came into your house so that we may have relations with him" (Judg 19:22). To protect himself and his host, this Israelite man drags his concubine outside and abandons her to these men. They rape and abuse her all night. When she is finally released at dawn, she stumbles to the home of her host and collapses on the threshold.

> When her master [possibly better translated "husband"] arose in the morning and opened the doors of the house and went out to go on his way, there was his concubine lying at the doorway of the house with her hands on the threshold. He said to her, "Get up and let us go," but there was no answer. Then he placed her on the donkey; and the man arose and went to his home. When he entered his house, he took a knife and laid hold of his concubine and cut her in twelve pieces, limb by limb, and sent her

throughout the territory of Israel. All who saw it said, "Nothing like this has ever happened or been seen from the day when the sons of Israel came up from the land of Egypt to this day. Consider it, take counsel and speak up!" (Judg 19:27-30)

This is the state of God's people by the end of the book of Judges. And as the narrator tells us in the final verse of the book, the reason was that "In those days there was no king in Israel; everyone did what was right in his own eyes" (Judg 21:25). In other words, rather than allowing the covenant to set the parameters of their behavior, these people (who claimed to belong to the covenant) were creating their own morality. And their self-centered lifestyles (influenced by the ideals of their culture) were resulting in a "people of God" who looked and acted just like (and in the case above, worse than) the Canaanites. Sound familiar? Interestingly, from the perspective of the Israelites, the problem was foreign oppression. They thought that what they needed was a better army. What they did not see was that the role of foreign oppression in their covenant was disciplinary—its purpose was to bring Israel back into right relationship with Yahweh. Hence, the *solution* to the problem of foreign oppression was not a more effective military; it was adherence to the covenant.

Samuel. The bright spot in this mess is Samuel. Dedicated as a child by his godly mother Hannah, raised by the priests, called of God to be a prophet and empowered as a judge, Samuel leads Israel all his life (see 1 Sam 1–8). Samuel is one of my favorite characters in the Old Testament. Not only does he stand for God in the midst of a society that has forgotten how, he is tough as nails. Yes, he was wise and holy, compassionate and kind, but he also knew what to do with a sword—and he was not to be "messed with." Samuel becomes the transition figure who moves Israel from confederation to kingdom. He is Israel's last judge, he leads for a lifetime, and he anoints Israel's first king.

THE EMERGENCE OF THE MONARCHY

As Samuel's career draws to a close, the elders of Israel approach him asking for a king. The anthropologists would tell us that this sort of evolution from tribal confederacy to monarchy is fairly typical and predictable and that it is often fraught with ambivalence and conflict.[3] In Israel's case, previous conflict over this question is resolved when God grants the request by instructing his representative, Samuel, to identify and appoint Saul as Israel's first king. But we can still hear some of the ambivalence spoken of above.

The pro-voice may be heard in Deuteronomy 17:14-20. Keep in mind that Deuteronomy is a detailed reiteration of the Sinai covenant—the "Constitution" of ancient Israel. And in this cornerstone political document, God announces that he intends Israel to have a king some day. He also specifies what the characteristics of a good king would be: (1) someone chosen by Yahweh; (2) a native Israelite; (3) one who doesn't spend his ambition multiplying horses, wives or money; (4) and one who will "write for himself a copy of this law on a scroll in the presence of the Levitical priests" and read it every day of his life (Deut 17:18-19). What is the significance of multiplying horses, wives, and money? These are all archetypical designations of international influence in the ancient world. Horses have to do with chariotry—a military innovation that belonged to Egypt and the Canaanites. Wives were taken to form international alliances. Money is money. Ultimately what Deuteronomy is describing is an individual whose reliance was not upon the standard instruments of kingly power (a strong military, substantial foreign alliances and a voluminous national treasury) but upon Yahweh. To succeed, this human king of Israel must be the faithful steward of the *true* king of Israel and, therefore, must be fully versed in Yahweh's expectations (the law). As the covenant with David will detail, if this vassal keeps the covenant, his suzerain will do what suzerains do—defend him from internal and external threat. But if this human king failed to keep covenant, he would be disciplined and/or replaced. So we see that in Deuteronomy the monarchy was clearly *God's* idea.

But when we come to 1 Samuel 8, we get a very different picture of the monarchy. Yahweh actually states that by choosing a king, the people have rejected him from being king over them (1 Sam 8:7). He warns them of the consequences of their choice and, seemingly, reluctantly concedes to appoint a king. But haven't we just read in Deuteronomy that a king was part of Yahweh's plan? The key to this apparent contradiction is found in asking *why* the people of Israel want a king. First Samuel 8:19-21 tells us that the people want a king so "that we also may be like all the nations, that our king may judge us and go out before us and fight our battles." In other words, these folks wanted a king who would conscript a professional army and thereby resolve their ongoing problem with foreign oppression. But what had Yahweh told them about foreign oppression? It was Yahweh's disciplinary response to covenant unfaithfulness. Thus the solution to the problem at hand was not a king and his professional army, but adherence to the covenant. Ultimately, a king would be no more able to solve their problem with foreign oppression than had the judges before him if the people refused to live within the confines of the covenant. So what seems to be a contradictory report in Scripture regarding the idea of kingship is more an issue of the right question asked for the wrong reasons. A king had always been a part of God's plan, but Israel's request for a king was inspired for all the wrong reasons. This issue becomes very clear in the career of Saul.

Saul.

Now there was a man of Benjamin whose name was Kish. . . . He had a son whose name was Saul, a choice and handsome man, there was not a more handsome person than he among the sons of Israel; from his shoulders and up he was taller than any of the people. (1 Sam 9:1-2)

With this statement our biblical narrator lets us know that Saul was a socially and culturally appropriate choice for king. Being physically intimidating he seemed a good choice for a military leader. And his good looks would help ease a transition that everyone knew was going to be bumpy. So God instructs Samuel to anoint Saul. Anointing was the standard public declaration of a new leader in Israel. The Hebrew verb for "anoint" is *māsah,* and the idea was that the oil symbolized the outpouring of God's Spirit in empowerment for the new office. This verb is the source for the Hebrew noun *māsîah* which we know in English as "messiah." In other words, the word "messiah" means the one who was anointed—and therefore chosen and empowered to lead.[4] Thus Saul is announced as God's choice who would "deliver My people from the hand of the Philistines" (1 Sam 9:16). Note that there is nothing in this call narrative that intimates that Saul is anything less than chosen, or that he would be anything less than successful. Well, actually, there is one little clue that Saul is going to have trouble. Hear the words of God regarding Saul: "And the LORD said to Samuel, 'Listen to *their* voice and appoint *them* a king'" (1 Sam 8:22). But of David we read: "I will send you to Jesse the Bethlehemite for *I* have selected a king for *Myself* among his sons" (1 Sam 16:1). The point is subtle but substantial—Saul is the choice of the people; David is the choice of God.[5]

So Saul, from the northern tribe of Benjamin, is welcomed as king.[6] His mission is to create a centralized government, complete with a standing army, and mobilize that army against the current threat to national security in Israel, the Philistines. Looking at figure 8.3, note that Israel's early settlement was primarily in the central hill country. This is largely because the Canaanites (a significant and advanced civilization at the time of Israel's settlement in c. 1200 B.C.) were already settled in the agriculturally favorable low country. Thus the central hill country became the backbone of Israelite settlement; the heartland of the country. From this beachhead, Israel slowly expanded until they managed to control and occupy most of the land of Canaan.

But there was another migration taking place in c. 1200 B.C. as well. The Mycenaean civilization of Greece was collapsing, and as a result, lots and lots of regular citizens of this seafaring land found themselves with no place to go. So they took to the sea. And the coasts of Canaan, Egypt and Anatolia were flooded with refugees.[7] Armed and desperate, this group claimed much of the coast of the Levant and began to press toward the interior. The locals spoke of these immigrants as "the Sea Peoples"—one of which was the "Philistines." Do you see the problem? In the early stages of their settlement, the Philistines are pushing into the hill country of Canaan from the coast, and the Israelites are pushing toward the coast from the hill country. Both are fighting for their lives, and it is not at all clear who will win.

Enter Saul. Tall, dark and handsome, and empowered by God to lead, Saul immediately organizes a campaign against the Philistines. But as we proceed through 1 Samuel, we find that Saul is not faring well. Not only is he failing militarily (a very bad sign in Israel's theocratic covenant), but the narrator clues us in to his ultimate demise with two troubling stories:

1 Samuel 13:5-14 and 1 Samuel 15:1-35. Here we find that Saul is letting his insecurities get the best of him. And as 1 Samuel 15:24-31 makes crystal clear, this first king of Israel is allowing *his* career and *his* success to become more important than that of the kingdom of God. Saul forgot who he worked for and became confused as to whose kingdom it was.

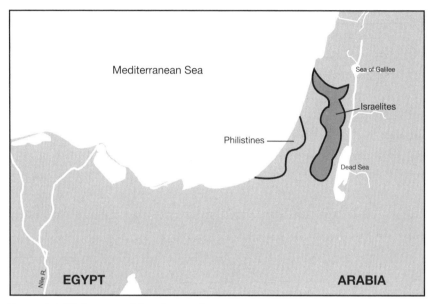

Figure 8.3. Philistine and Israelite settlements

So Saul's story ends in 1 Samuel 31. Here the Israelites are once again duking it out with the Philistines. But this time Israel flees before their enemy. The Philistines overtake Saul and his sons. Saul's sons are slain, "and [Saul] was badly wounded by the archers" (1 Sam 31:1-3). Saul, knowing that he would die—knowing that the Philistines would find him wounded and unable to defend himself—"took his sword and fell on it." And so the chosen man of God, called by the prophet and anointed before the people, the one commissioned to lead the kingdom of God, fell by his own hand before the enemies of the kingdom. And the people of God were left leaderless and scattered because Saul could not rise to his calling.

David. After it becomes clear that Saul is more interested in his kingdom than in God's, God calls David as his replacement. First Samuel actually reports three different call narratives for David. The first is 1 Samuel 16:1-13, in which David the youngest of eight is called in from the fields and anointed by Samuel (the same prophet who anointed Saul). Remembering our discussion of patriarchal culture in chapter one, David is obviously not a culturally appropriate choice. Not only should each of his seven brothers have had a crack at the job before him, he is so young he is still not even draft-age. But "God sees not as man sees, for man looks at the outward appearance, but the LORD looks at the heart" (1 Sam 16:7). So David's first call narrative illustrates a critical aspect of David's kingship: he is chosen by God and this because of the content of his heart. The second call narrative follows close behind in 1 Samuel 16:14-23. Here we learn that at some point in David's youth he was hired to play soothing music for Saul in order to quiet his fits of rage. These fits were apparently connected with the departure of God's anointing upon him (1 Sam 16:14), and many have surmised that Saul was battling either depression or some other mental illness. What is significant in this story is that David was a man of music and worship. And as David is closely associated with the book of Psalms, this is significant.[8] The third call narrative is one you have probably heard many times in many mediums—the story of David and the giant in 1 Samuel 17.

Once again Israel is facing the Philistines. Once again the security of God's kingdom is in peril. Here the narrator explains to us that although three of David's older brothers had answered the call to arms, David was not old enough to go. So his father kept him home to tend the sheep and to serve as a courier of news and supplies between Jesse and his sons on the frontline. You know the story. The Philistines and the Israelites face off in the "Valley of Blood" (you have to wonder how a valley gets a name like that). This is in the region of the Shephelah—the low hill country that stood between the Philistine territory on the coast and the Israelite territory in the high country (see figure 8.3). Tension is running high in both camps when the Philistines' *îš-habbēnayim* ("the man from between") steps forward to challenge the Israelites to a one-on-one contest for sovereignty over the region.[9] "Send me down your champion," says Goliath. "If he prevails over me, we will become Saul's servants; but if I prevail over him, you will become our servants."[10]

Goliath is huge—nine-and-a-half feet tall according to the Hebrew text, a little shorter according to the Greek[11]—and he's decked out with more armor and weaponry than Hebrew has words for. The Israelites are absolutely terrified. No one will accept his challenge. Rather, Goliath spends forty days mocking Israel *and their God*. Because no one will step forward to either trust God for the victory or die for Yahweh's reputation, the kingdom of God was being discredited. Let's ponder this situation for a moment. Who was the tallest person in Israel's camp? Who do you think owned the most sophisticated weaponry? Who *should* step forward to answer the challenge of this Philistine? Of course the answer to these questions is "Saul." But instead of the anointed leader, a boy who was too young to answer the draft steps up to the plate. Where would a boy find that sort of courage? From his past experiences of God's provision.

> But David said to Saul, "Your servant was tending his father's sheep. When a lion or a bear came and took a lamb from the flock, I went out after him and attacked him, and rescued it from his mouth; and when he rose up against me, I seized him by his beard and struck him and killed him. Your servant has killed both the lion and the bear; and this uncircumcised Philistine will be like one of them, since he has taunted the armies of the living God." (1 Sam 17:34-36)

Hear David's emphasis: "the LORD who delivered me from the paw of the lion and from the paw of the bear, *He* will deliver me from the hand of this Philistine" (1 Sam 17:37). David was very clear on one fact—it was Yahweh who had rescued him in the past, and it was Yahweh who would rescue him in the future. The adversary really made no difference at all. Moreover, David had practiced being faithful. With his confidence in God, David had challenged the bear and the lion and God had helped him. That's why he was confident he could challenge Goliath. Just think, if David hadn't taken on the bear and lion, where would he have been when the giant came calling? The same place Saul was. Hiding in his tent.

So our young hero steps forward. Without a sword, armor, javelin or shield he confronts the seasoned warrior. "You come to me with a sword, a spear, and a javelin, but I come to you in the name of the LORD of hosts, the God of the armies of Israel, whom you have taunted. This day the LORD will deliver you up into my hands" (1 Sam 17:45-46). And the giant mocks him. For good cause. But with his sling and his stone, the one who did not look like a king, who was still too young to be king, felled the biggest Philistine anyone had ever seen.[12] And he did it by the hand of God. Why? So that "all this assembly may know that the LORD does not deliver by sword or by spear; for the battle is the LORD's and He will give you into our hands" (1 Sam 17:47).

Thus, although David (unlike Saul) is introduced with less than "regal" stature, it is evident that David (unlike Saul) knows where his confidence and loyalty must lie. Moreover, unlike Saul who was the people's choice, David is God's choice. In fact, the famous passage that describes David as "a man after God's own heart" (1 Sam 13:14) actually communicates just this. Although most interpret this phrase to mean that David had a particularly keen affection for Yahweh or that David had bent his will after Yahweh's, in reality, this text reflects an Akkadian idiom that has to do with the *choice* of a suzerain.[13] Yahweh says that he has rejected Saul and chosen David because David is (in Hebrew) *îš kilēbābô*, "a man according to his heart." In other words, David is, "a king of God's choosing"—a new vassal of whose loyalty God was sure. David was God's choice because Yahweh was sure of his loyalty. There is much to be learned from these narratives as regards the qualifications of a successful leader in God's kingdom.

THE DAVIDIC COVENANT: 2 SAMUEL 7

It would be years before David would receive his kingdom. For more than a decade David is chased and harassed by Saul's forces. But in God's time, David is at last crowned king—first over the southern region of the country at Hebron and then over all Israel. David's first royal act is to wrest Jerusalem from the Jebusites in order to establish it as Israel's united, national capital. His second royal act is to transport the tabernacle (the throne room of the true king of Israel) into that capital city. Over the course of his career, David succeeds where Saul failed. He drives back the Philistines, hemming them into their coastal territory, and subdues the Moabites, Ammonites and Edomites. David is the one who finally brings the national boundaries promised to Abraham out of the realm of hope, into the realm of reality.

And so in 2 Samuel 7, when Yahweh "had given him rest on every side from all of his enemies," David inquires of the Lord as to whether or not he may build a temple (a permanent house of worship) for Yahweh's honor in Jerusalem. In this complex exchange, David is rebuked for his presumptuousness in proposing the building plan, but David's real concern (his longevity on Israel's throne) is addressed in Yahweh's response. These themes are masterfully communicated by a clever play upon the Hebrew word for "house" *(bayit)*. This word can mean the structure in which a person lives ("house"), the structure in which the deity lives ("temple"), or a person's "household." When one is a king, one's household is a "dynasty." Thus, whereas David asked if he could build a "house" (temple) for Yahweh, and Yahweh says "no," Yahweh goes on to say that he will build a "house" (dynasty) for David. This is David's covenant of grant.[14]

> The LORD also declares to you that the LORD will make a house [i.e., "dynasty"] for you. When your days are complete and you lie down with your fathers, I will raise up your descendant after you, who will come forth from

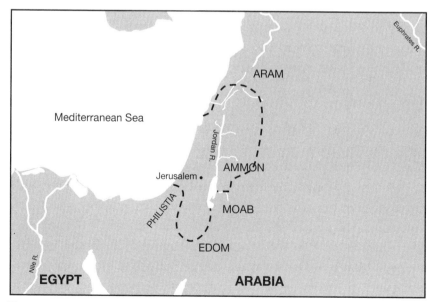

Figure 8.4. David's kingdom

you, and I will establish his kingdom. He shall build a house [i.e., "temple"]
for My name, and I will establish the throne of his kingdom forever. I will
be a father to him and he will be a son to Me; when he commits iniquity,
I will correct him with the rod of men and the strokes of the sons of men,
but My lovingkindness [i.e., "covenant faithfulness"] shall not depart from
him, as I took it away from Saul, whom I removed from before you. Your
house and your kingdom shall endure before Me forever; your throne shall
be established forever. (2 Sam 7:11-16)

In sum, our fledgling king is awarded an *eternal* dynasty for his outstand-
ing record of personal service to his suzerain. Pay special attention to
2 Samuel 7:14-16. These verses are the very taproot of the messianic hope.
Any attentive reader must stumble over the word "forever" in 2 Samuel
7:16. Obviously such a promise reaches beyond David, his children and
the nationhood of Israel itself. How could Yahweh fulfill such a tall order?
The answer, of course, will be by means of a child of David who reaches
beyond David and Israel and is himself eternal. When we recall that the
legitimate kings of Israel were publicly identified by means of anointing,
we see how it is that the Jewish hope for "the Messiah" was actually the
hope for the return of the kings of Israel. It is the one chosen of God and
empowered to lead, the Anointed One (Hebrew *māšiah*), upon whom
Israel pegs its future and its hope.[15]

There is one last detail of 2 Samuel 7 that is critical to the theology of
Israel's theocratic covenant. Note the words of verse 14. In speaking of the
kings who will follow in David's steps, Yahweh says: "I will be a father to
him and he will be a son to Me; when he commits iniquity, I will correct
him with the rod of men and the strokes of the sons of men." What we
find here is that Yahweh's response to covenant disloyalty remains un-
changed. When David's descendants fail to rule according to the dictates
of Deuteronomy 17, they will be disciplined by means of foreign oppression. So although the people of Israel demanded a king to resolve their
ongoing problem with foreign oppression (1 Sam 8), under the monarchy
they are in the exact same position they were previously. The solution to
the problem will not be a king and his professional army any more than
it was a judge and his volunteer army. The solution to Israel's ongoing
problem is still adherence to Yahweh's covenant.

FROM DAVID TO THE NEW COVENANT

David passes his kingdom on to his son Solomon, who is a very successful political figure.[16] Maintaining David's successes, Solomon adds substantial international alliances, a booming economy and several enormous building projects to his father's accomplishments. He fortifies key cities, expands and professionalizes the government and establishes one of the few periods in Israelite history in which Israel was recognized as a world power. He is most famous for one particular building project, the Temple Mount in Jerusalem. In this twenty-year enterprise, Solomon more than doubles the footprint of Jerusalem and constructs a palace and temple complex that rivaled the most elaborate of his day.[17] But eventually Solomon was consumed by his own power, wealth and influence. And as 1 Kings 10:14–11:8 details, Solomon broke all the rules of conduct laid out in Deuteronomy 17. He greatly multiplied his silver and gold, foreign wives, and horses and chariots. As a result, Yahweh says to Solomon, "Because you have done this, and you have not kept My covenant and My statutes, which I have commanded you, I will surely tear the kingdom from you, and will give it to your servant" (1 Kings 11:11). Thus the majority of David's kingdom (the territory of the ten northern tribes) is promised to another, Jeroboam I (1 Kings 11:26-40). And upon Solomon's death a civil war erupts that splits the country evermore.

> What portion do we have in David?
> We have no inheritance in the son of Jesse.
> To your tents, O Israel!
> Now look after your own house, David! (1 Kings 12:16)

"To your tents, O Israel" has been characterized as a summons to political separatism, which it surely is.[18] But I would go so far as to say that it is a rallying cry against monarchy and for tribal authority. As a result, "Israel has been in rebellion against the house of David to his day" (1 Kings 12:19), and no dynasty would ever succeed in completely monopolizing the throne of that kingdom.

Thus begins the divided monarchy. One critically important development of this new divided kingdom is the illegitimate "alternate" religion that Jeroboam I establishes in the north (1 Kings 12:25-33). Although

TO YOUR TENTS, O ISRAEL!

A significant catalyst for Israel's civil war was Solomon's preferential actions toward his own southern tribe, Judah, and his discriminatory actions against the northern tribes.^a Just as Samuel had warned a generation prior, Solomon's success as an entrepreneur, builder and international figure took a significant amount of funding (1 Sam 8:9-18). And, of course, the way governments make money is taxation . . . and, in Solomon's day, corvée labor. But throughout his reign, the bulk of Solomon's taxation and corvée demands were placed upon the north. He had even gone so far as to give twenty cities from the north in payment to the Phoenician king, Hiram, who had assisted him in his building projects in Jerusalem (1 Kings 9:11). This inequity set the stage for the revolt under Rehoboam, Solomon's heir. Thus in 1 Kings 12:1-21 we read of how the tribal elders from the north approached Rehoboam at his inauguration asking for relief from this hard service. Rehoboam sought the advice of his father's counselors, who confirmed the northern complaint and advised Rehoboam to lighten up and thereby win the enduring allegiance of the north (1 Kings 12:6-7). But then Rehoboam consulted his young friends (think "frat brothers" or "pub mates"), who advised him instead to prove to the north that he was twice the man his father was by increasing their burden. "My little finger is thicker than my father's loins! Whereas my father loaded you with a heavy yoke, I will add to your yoke; my father disciplined you with whips, but I will discipline you with scorpions" (1 Kings 12:10-11). Guess whose advice Rehoboam chose to follow? Refusing the request of the northern tribal leaders, Rehoboam's unwise decision triggered an immediate revolt against the house of David.

---

^aSee n. 3 in this chapter.

Yahweh had sanctioned a political division in Israel, he did not sanction a religious division. But because of Jeroboam's insecurities,

> Jeroboam said in his heart, . . . "If this people go up to offer sacrifices in the house of the LORD at Jerusalem, then the heart of this people will return to their lord, even to Rehoboam king of Judah; and they will kill me

and return to Rehoboam king of Judah." So the king consulted, and made two golden calves, and he said to them, "It is too much for you to go up to Jerusalem; behold your gods, O Israel, that brought you up from the land of Egypt." He set one in Bethel, and the other he put in Dan. (1 Kings 12:26-29)

Big mistake! Do you hear the language of verse 28? "Behold your gods, O Israel, that brought you up from the land of Egypt." This is a direct quotation of Aaron's words during the unfortunate golden calf incident at the foot of Mount Sinai in Exodus 32. So the narrator is letting us know right off the bat that Jeroboam is in big trouble. An important detail here is that the indigenous deity of northern Canaan was Baal, and his cult symbol was a *calf*.[19] In other words, Jeroboam's cult was not only "alternate," it was an intentional, syncretistic blending of Yahwism and Baalism.[20] And not only does Jeroboam choose the symbols of Baal for Yahweh's worship center, but he attributes the historical prologue of the Sinai covenant to this pretender: "Behold your gods, O Israel, *that brought you up from the land of Egypt.*" Yahweh and his prophets are outraged by this act of treason, and the northern kingdom is condemned on the spot (cf. 1 Kings 13:34). From this point onward it is simply a matter of time before the north is swept away.

As the timeline indicates, it is best to work on this section of Israelite history with a few benchmarks. In the north the benchmarks are the three major dynasties: that of Jeroboam, Omri and Jehu. Although several of these dynasties produce impressive leaders, in the end the "sin of Jeroboam" prevails. The northern kingdom is subjected to the covenant curse, and is ransacked and exiled in 722 B.C. by the Assyrian Empire (2 Kings 17). These are the "ten lost tribes" of Israel. Outside of the refugees that escape over the border into the south, these citizens of Israel are lost to the pages of history—they never come home. In the south, the Davidic dynasty endures. But the cycle of the book of Judges reemerges: sin and rebellion followed by foreign oppression and deliverance. This cycle begins with Rehoboam, is interrupted by two major revivals (those of Hezekiah and Josiah) and finally culminates in the 586 B.C. destruction of Jerusalem at the hands of the Babylonian Empire (2 Kings 24–25).

Throughout this era, every king of Israel will be compared (for good or for ill) to David. David is the paradigm, his covenant-loyalty the standard. And as the years go by and the storm clouds continue to gather on the horizon, the same question begins to form itself in the heart of every faithful Israelite: "Is there a son of David out there somewhere who can clean up the mess we've made, stand against our enemies and speak up for the voiceless?" But the sons of David continue to disappoint. And after years of warnings and second chances, the covenant curse is at last enacted, and Judah is swept away. The land grant is recalled, the temple is razed, and the proud children of Abraham are slaughtered and dragged off into exile in Babylonia. A broken covenant, a broken dream, a broken people.

Yet even in the silence of exile, the promise of the prophets continues to echo.

> The people who walk in darkness, will see a great light. . . . For a child will be born to us, a son will be given to us, and the government will rest on His shoulders; and His name will be called Wonderful Counselor, Mighty God, Eternal Father, Prince of Peace. There will be no end to the increase of His government or of peace, on the throne of David and over his kingdom . . . from then on and forevermore. (Is 9:2, 6-7; cf. Ezek 37:21-28)

CONCLUSIONS

The Davidic covenant may be understood as the covenant of the monarchy and the last piece in the Old Testament typological puzzle. At this point in redemptive history we have recovered a *people* (the offspring of Abraham), a *place* (the borders promised to Abraham), and the *presence* (the dwelling of Yahweh now located in the capital city of Jerusalem). Thus the people, place and presence of the Mosaic covenant have not changed, but the Davidic covenant adds to this picture the typological figure who will play such a major role in the fulfillment of the promised new covenant: a king for God's kingdom, a shepherd for his people. This figure takes on the responsibility of representing God's people, leading them in obedience to the covenant, defending their inheritance and defeating their enemies. Thus, not only does the Davidic covenant carry us through the monarchic period of Israel's history—illustrating the distinctions between the faith*less*ness of Saul and Jeroboam I and the faith*ful*ness of David—it also sets us up for Messiah. It is David's reputation as a man who served God with a whole heart, and his resultant political success, that establishes in the mind of the Israelite nation that their only true hope is the return of one from "the stem of Jesse." And so as our heroes wait in exile in the land of Babylon, grieving their profound losses (and fully aware that these are the earned consequences of their national and individual sin), the heart of every faithful Israelite turns toward this singular hope. If only God could forgive us. If only he would send us a champion, a king born of the line of David, a just and righteous leader, perhaps this broken people could regain their lost inheritance and find peace.

THE NEW COVENANT AND THE RETURN OF THE KING

ON OCTOBER 30, 539 B.C., Cyrus the Great of Persia entered the city of Babylon, claiming it as his own and thereby ending the Babylonian Empire (see fig. 9.1). In an unprecedented act of imperial generosity (and political savvy), Cyrus told the Jewish captives that if they wished, they could go home.[1] And so just as Isaiah (Is 40:1-11; 45:1-7), Jeremiah (Jer 25:11-13) and Ezekiel (Ezek 37:1-14) had prophesied, the exile (impossibly and unbelievably) ended.

> When the LORD brought back the captive ones of Zion, we were like those who dream. Then our mouth was filled with laughter and our tongue with joyful shouting; then they said among the nations, "The LORD has done great things for them." The LORD has done great things for us; we are glad. (Ps 126:1-3)

Under the capable leadership of Zerubbabel, then Ezra and then Nehemiah, three different corps of exiles chose to believe God and make the difficult trip home. Upon their return they began the long and seemingly impossible task of rebuilding their community—in particular their temple—in the devastated Judean territory. It is important to realize that only a tiny remnant of the population of the once-great nation of Judah chose to make the return.[2] And even with their best efforts, the city and temple that they were able to reconstruct were only shadows of their former glory. Ezra tells us that when the foundation of the second temple was laid, the

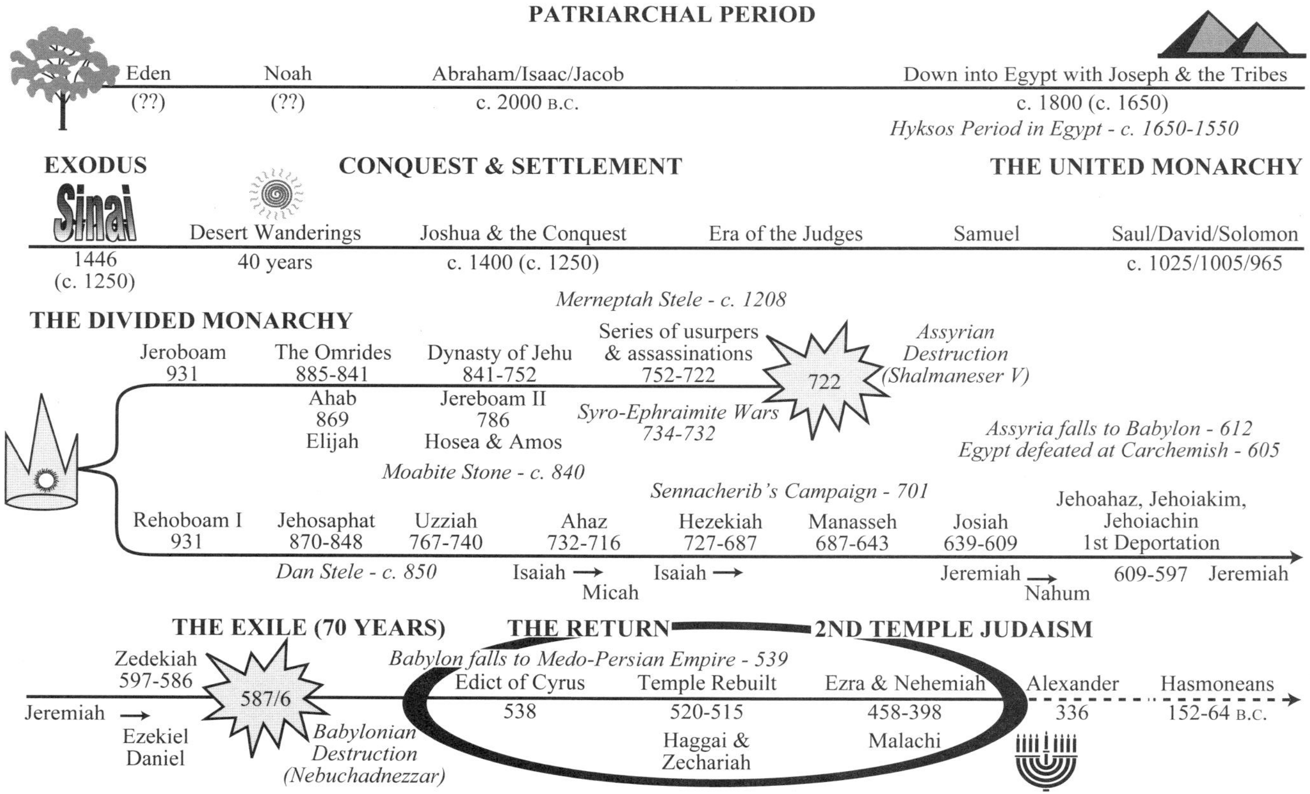

PATRIARCHAL PERIOD

Eden   Noah   Abraham/Isaac/Jacob   Down into Egypt with Joseph & the Tribes
(??)   (??)   c. 2000 B.C.   c. 1800 (c. 1650)

Hyksos Period in Egypt - c. 1650-1550

EXODUS   CONQUEST & SETTLEMENT   THE UNITED MONARCHY

Desert Wanderings   Joshua & the Conquest   Era of the Judges   Samuel   Saul/David/Solomon
1446   40 years   c. 1400 (c. 1250)   c. 1025/1005/965
(c. 1250)

Merneptah Stele - c. 1208

THE DIVIDED MONARCHY   Series of usurpers
                                         & assassinations   Assyrian
Jeroboam   The Omrides   Dynasty of Jehu   752-722   Destruction
931   885-841   841-752   (Shalmaneser V)
              Ahab   Jereboam II   Syro-Ephraimite Wars   722
              869   786   734-732
              Elijah   Hosea & Amos   Sennacherib's Campaign - 701

                      Moabite Stone - c. 840
Rehoboam I   Jehosaphat   Uzziah   Ahaz   Hezekiah   Manasseh   Josiah
931   870-848   767-740   732-716   727-687   687-643   639-609

         Dan Stele - c. 850   Isaiah   Isaiah
                                 Micah

                                         Assyria falls to Babylon - 612
                                         Egypt defeated at Carchemish - 605

Jehoahaz, Jehoiakim,
Jehoiachin
1st Deportation

Jeremiah   609-597   Jeremiah
        Nahum

THE EXILE (70 YEARS)   THE RETURN   2ND TEMPLE JUDAISM
                        Babylon falls to Medo-Persian Empire - 539
Zedekiah   Edict of Cyrus   Temple Rebuilt   Ezra & Nehemiah   Alexander   Hasmoneans
597-586   520-515   458-398   336   152-64 B.C.
                         538   Haggai &   Malachi
Jeremiah   Babylonian   Zechariah
        Ezekiel   Destruction
        Daniel   (Nebuchadnezzar)
                  587/6

Figure 9.1. Timeline of the new covenant

elderly among the group, who had seen the first temple in all its glory, actually wept (Ezra 3:10-13).

Most important to our story is the fact that the Israelites who returned to Palestine after the exile came back as the citizens of another nation. From this point onward Israel would remain a subject people.[3] First a Persian province, then Greek, then Roman, this proud nation was stripped of its former independence. The Davidic dynasty and the national boundaries first promised to Abraham and the Solomonic temple were faded and distant memories. And Israel was greatly changed. The most obvious changes were that the Israelites were now known as "Jews," and they spoke Aramaic as opposed to Hebrew.[4] Having been without a temple for nearly two generations, Torah-centered synagogue worship had begun to evolve and now stood alongside the sacrifice-centered religion of the temple. As discussed in the last chapter, the lack of national boundaries encouraged the development of *social* boundaries such that much more emphasis was laid upon endogamy (marrying Jews only), the keeping of the dietary laws and the observance of the sabbath. Rabbinic leadership with its "fence around the law" was emerging and pre-exilic Yahwism was being transformed into the religion we now know as Judaism. And as the kings were gone, the priesthood now served as Israel's national leaders.[5]

THE RETURN OF THE KING

In spite of (and for many because of) all these changes, the faithful in Israel lived with the hope of a promise—the return of the Davidic dynasty. Isaiah had promised that in God's time "a shoot will spring from the stem of Jesse," and in that day "the nations will resort to the root of Jesse, who will stand as a signal for the peoples" (Is 11:1, 10). The prophet had said that one day a child would be given to the nation, "and there will be no end to the increase of His government or of peace, on the throne of David or over his kingdom" (Is 9:6-7). Predictably, the Jews understood these promises to mean that this coming child of David would throw off their foreign overlords, restore their national sovereignty, reunite north and south and bring back the golden days of independence and prosperity as they remembered them under David. And so the citizens of Judah watched and waited for their deliverer.

But how after all these years would the chosen king be identified and confirmed by the populace? He would be identified as had all the legitimate kings of Israel—by genealogy and the confirmation of the prophet. And so the Gospel of Matthew opens, "The record of the genealogy of Jesus the Messiah, the son of David, the son of Abraham" (Mt 1:1). I know that if we were being honest, many of us would admit that opening the New Testament with a genealogy seems to be a less-than-effective literary strategy. How often have brand new believers sat down with a brand new Bible, eager to speed through the story of Jesus, only to find themselves shipwrecked in the first few paragraphs of "begats" . . . only God knows. But hopefully now that you know something about God's larger redemptive plan, this literary strategy does not seem as obscure as it once did. By opening with a genealogy, Matthew is opening his gospel with a list of Jesus' most essential credentials. Every Jew knew that God's promise was a son of David; and every Jew knew that the target of his deliverance must be the children of Abraham. Although the (apparent) offspring of a common, blue-collar laborer and an unknown village maiden, Jesus bore these credentials. Jesus was the one.

A few years ago I was prepping to teach the Christmas story to my daughter's "Toddler Church" class. Although I've read the story of Jesus' birth hundreds of times (and was fully equipped with a flannelgraph and nonbreakable nativity figurines), being the compulsive person I am, I felt the need to reread all of the gospel accounts prior to my presentation. And I'm glad I did. Because I noticed for the first time an innocuous little line tucked into the angel's announcement to Joseph in Matthew 1:20-21:

> Joseph, son of David, do not be afraid to take Mary as your wife; for the Child who has been conceived in her is of the Holy Spirit. She will bear a Son; and you shall call His name Jesus, for He will save His people from their sins.

Can you imagine how these words stunned this simple man? The appearance of an (enormous, brilliant, supernatural) angel would be enough to render most anyone speechless. And then there is the Mary part. Apparently the very thing that was keeping Joseph up at night was no longer an issue. And this woman he had committed himself to had *not* been unfaithful; there wasn't someone else; they did still have a future together. And of course there is that little detail about a child conceived by the Holy Spirit! How this message must have impacted this man as a Jew, a man living with the realities of Israel's failures. In this announcement Joseph hears that Israel has not been forgotten, that the desperate longings of this people had not been cast aside. The Messiah *is* coming. God has forgiven and he *will* save his people from their sins. You can almost hear the ice crack as one heart dares to hope again.

And now for the previously unnoticed phrase: "Joseph, *son of David*." As we rehearsed in the last chapter, David was the greatest king and warrior of Israel's history. He was their greatest legacy, and his promised child was their greatest hope. Had anyone *ever* addressed Joseph—a humble laborer living far from the circles of power in Jerusalem—by the titles of his ancient lineage? Who would think to speak to this common man in the language of a distant ancestry long past and long forgotten? I guess God would. And by identifying Joseph as a child of kings, he also identifies Joseph's calling: to parent the promised heir of David who would rule a new Israel and at last bring that people back into relationship with their God. So why did all this strike me? Because it was Christmas. And I was thinking about this same God, who has born so many disappointments from the children of Adam, who with the coming of the Christ calls out to each of us *again* saying, "Son of Adam, daughter of Eve, I see you, I know who you were meant to be, I know where you are . . . come home."

Thus the child of Joseph, the son of David, is identified by his genealogy as the one who could be the promised one of 2 Samuel 7. But how can we be sure? Just as throughout Israel's history the final word was that of the prophet, so too with Jesus. Hence, each of the four gospels introduces the ministry of Jesus with the same figure, John the Baptist, the last prophet of the Mosaic covenant.

Now in those days John the Baptist came, preaching in the wilderness of Judea, saying, "Repent, for the kingdom of heaven is at hand." For this is the one referred to by Isaiah the prophet when he said, "THE VOICE OF ONE CRYING IN THE WILDERNESS, 'MAKE READY THE WAY OF THE LORD, MAKE HIS PATHS STRAIGHT!'" (Mt 3:1-3)

In the Old Testament, if there were some doubt or controversy over who should be king, the chosen one was identified by public anointing. (Do you remember the verb *māšaḥ* and its relationship to the word Messiah?[6]) In this ritual, the oil was a symbol that the Holy Spirit had come upon the one chosen in order to empower him to serve as God's steward over the kingdom. Thus in Matthew 3 we read,

> Then Jesus arrived from Galilee at the Jordan coming to John, to be baptized by him. But John tried to prevent Him, saying, "I have need to be baptized by You, and do You come to me?" But Jesus answering said to him, "Permit it at this time; for in this way it is fitting for us to fulfill all righteousness." Then he permitted Him. After being baptized, Jesus came up immediately from the water; and behold, the heavens were opened, and he saw the Spirit of God descending as a dove and lighting on Him, and behold, a voice out of the heavens said, "This is My beloved Son, in whom I am well-pleased." (Mt 3:13-17)

I think of this event as new wine in old wineskins. Because here symbols of the old and new covenants are juxtaposed upon the other such that there is a cacophony of announcement, and the symbols of the old simply cannot hold themselves together as the realities of the new are brought upon the scene. Here the last prophet of the Mosaic order *baptizes* the newly identified king (a sign of the new covenant) while the heavens open, and the reality of which the oil of the old covenant was merely a symbol (the Holy Spirit) visibly descends upon the Chosen One, and the voice of God himself (as opposed to merely the voice of the prophet) announces in the words of the coronation psalm of David and his sons (Ps 2:7) that *this is the One.*[7] This identification of the king embraces the tension of the institutions of the old covenant and the innovations of the new covenant, and by all lists of qualifiers, Jesus the Nazarene is identified as *the* chosen one of Israel. Add to Matthew's account the words of John the Baptist in the Gospel of John, "Behold, the Lamb of God who takes away the sin of the world" (Jn 1:29), and there simply is no doubt. This is the long-awaited child of David upon whose shoulders the kingdom will rest.

PRINCE OF PEACE

Probably the most famous prophecy regarding the Son of David is Isaiah
9:6: "For a child will be born to us, a son will be given to us; and the gov-
ernment will rest on His shoulders; and His name will be called Wonderful
Counselor, Mighty God, Eternal Father, Prince of Peace." Not long ago,
one of my students made me notice Isaiah's word choice for "government"
in this passage (Hebrew miśrâ*). The word occurs in the Hebrew Bible only*
here (Is 9:5-6), which, considering how often the Bible addresses the idea
of government, is noteworthy. The distinctive nature of this vocabulary
is furthered when we realize that the word probably derives from an As-
syrian loan word having to do with governmental officials, particularly
the vassal underlings of the Assyrian monarch (Akkadian šarru *> Hebrew*
śār; cf. Is 10:8; Hos 8:10). The root is repeated at the end of the verse in the
Messiah's coronation title: "Prince of Peace." If you're up on your Isaianic
studies, you know that the oracle of Isaiah 9 was originally spoken during
a horrifically war-torn period in Israel's history—a time in which God's
people had been brutally subjugated by the most powerful political force of
the age, the Assyrian Empire.[a] *The population had been decimated, vil-*
lages burned, women brutalized, children slaughtered. Yet in this prophecy
a word of hope is offered to this weary and injured land. And the core of
that hope is a new leader, a child of the line of David, whose destiny was to
reclaim control of Israel's territory, to extend his authority to every border,
and to thereby bring peace. And as Isaiah makes very clear by his choice
of Assyrian vocabulary, this promise is to be heard in juxtaposition to the
cruelty and oppression of the Assyrian Empire. In other words, whereas
the legacy of Assyria was violence, fear and loss, the legacy of this leader
would be peace.[b] *How appropriate for the Christ child. The legacy of our*
sin is violence, fear and loss; the legacy of this child will be peace.

---

[a]As discussed in chapter three, "The Concept of Covenant," the Assyrians had a well-
deserved reputation for brutality.
[b]See H. Niehr, "שׂר *śar*" *TDOT*, 14:190-215.

The plan of redemption dovetails here. The type of the Davidic king is fulfilled with the coming of the man Jesus, a descendant of the line of David on both his mother and legal father's side. But the one promised in 2 Samuel 7, who will sit on David's eternal throne, is now revealed to be more than just a man. As Matthew 1:23 tells us, he is Immanuel (Hebrew ʿimmanû-ʾēl) "God with us." He is the Word become flesh; the Presence come to "tabernacle among us" (Jn 1:1, 14).[8] Behold the miracle of God's redemptive plan: the fully human Last Adam (who is the offspring of Abraham and the legitimate heir of David) is also the fully divine son of God. In the flesh of Jesus, Adam will pay the penalty for his crime, but rather than being consumed by the great enemy Death, this Last Adam will rise from the grave and give birth to a new lineage, a new people of God, and thereby fulfill the impossible rescue plan first hinted at in Genesis 3:15.[9]

> He is the image of the invisible God, the firstborn of all creation. For by Him all things were created, both in the heavens and on earth, visible and invisible, whether thrones or dominions or rulers or authorities—all things have been created through Him and for Him. He is before all things, and in Him all things hold together. He is also head of the body, the church; and He is the beginning, the firstborn from the dead, so that He Himself will come to have first place in everything. For it was the Father's good pleasure for all the fullness to dwell in Him, and through Him to reconcile all things to Himself, having made peace through the blood of His cross; through Him, I say, whether things on earth or things in heaven. (Col 1:15-20)

> For those whom He foreknew, He also predestined to become conformed to the image of His Son, so that He would be the firstborn among many brethren. (Rom 8:29)

This is the objective of the incarnation. The God-man Jesus Christ has died for humanity, so that we the offspring of Adam and Eve might be born again to a second chance at life.

JESUS THE ULTIMATE COVENANT MEDIATOR

Thus the long plan of redemption comes to its first climax. As the book of Hebrews states, Jesus is prophet, priest and king. He is the Last Adam who defeats Eden's curse; the second Noah commissioned to save God's people from the coming flood of his wrath; the seed of Abraham; the new lawgiver who stands upon the mountain and amazes his audience by the authority with which he speaks; and he is the heir of David. Indeed,

> God, after He spoke long ago to the fathers in the prophets in many por-
> tions and in many ways, in these last days has spoken to us in His Son,
> whom He appointed heir of all things, through whom also He made the
> world. (Heb 1:1-2)

And as the fulfillment of all the covenantal actions that have come before, the man Christ Jesus is now the "one mediator between God and men" (1 Tim 2:5). Even more amazing to the Jews of Jesus' day was the realiza-tion that their Messiah actually intended to mediate God's covenant to *all* humanity—"For God so loved the world, that He gave His only begot-ten Son, that whoever believes in Him shall not perish, but have eternal life" (Jn 3:16). Although the prophets had hinted at the breadth of God's redemptive plan, this kingdom-come was much bigger and broader than anyone could have imagined!

SO WHERE IS THE KINGDOM OF GOD?

With Jesus we step into the new covenant. But immediately we are con-fronted with a problem. If Jesus' purpose was to establish the kingdom of God, where is the kingdom? Should not this son of David free Abraham's descendants from Roman oppression? Shouldn't he be enthroned in Jeru-salem? And what of the Abrahamic boundaries? This apparent conflict was very confusing to the disciples; it is no surprise that it still confuses believers today. Take a look at Matthew 13.

The scene begins as a public one. Jesus is teaching the masses about the nature of the kingdom of heaven, but they don't understand. So Jesus' dis-ciples come to him privately, asking him to explain. The essence of their questions? "Where is the kingdom?" I always picture this scene as similar to a locker room dialogue between a coach and his high-school football team. The players are full of passion; their coach has all the answers and they'll follow him anywhere. So decked out in all their gear, they lean forward with eager anticipation to hear their coach impart the secret strategies of the coming playoffs. So too the disciples. Young, impressionable, passionate, these men believed that they were following Jesus to Jerusalem to unseat the bad guys and restore the kingdom. They were pumped! "Tell us about the kingdom," they beg. So locking their eyes and lowering his voice, the coach begins:

> The kingdom of heaven is like a man who sowed good seed in his field. But while everyone was sleeping, his enemy came and sowed weeds among the wheat, and went away. When the wheat sprouted and formed heads, then the weeds also appeared.
>
> The owner's servants came to him and said, "Sir, didn't you sow good seed in your field? Where then did the weeds come from?"
>
> "An enemy did this," he replied.
>
> The servants asked him, "Do you want us to go and pull them up?"
>
> "No," he answered, "because while you are pulling the weeds, you may root up the wheat with them. Let both grow together until the harvest. At that time I will tell the harvesters: First collect the weeds and tie them in bundles to be burned; then gather the wheat and bring it into my barn." (Mt 13:24-30 niv)

Can you picture the disciples' response? "Okay . . . can you try that again?"

> He told them another parable: "The kingdom of heaven is like a mustard seed, which a man took and planted in his field. Though it is the smallest of all your seeds, yet when it grows, it is the largest of garden plants and becomes a tree, so that the birds of the air come and perch in its branches." (Mt 13:31-32 niv)

In my mind's eye I see James and John (the "sons of thunder") and impulsive Peter, "the kingdom of God is like a *mustard seed?*" So they ask again.

> He spoke another parable to them, "The kingdom of heaven is like leaven, which a woman took and hid in three pecks of flour until it was all leavened." (Mt 13:33)

Imagine the disciples' reaction. They lean back, the look of incredulity all over their faces. "*What?* The kingdom of God is like *women* making *bread?* This is NOT what I signed up for!"

So what is Jesus talking about? In Matthew 13:36-52 of the same chapter, Jesus goes on to explain what theologians have come to call the "already . . . not yet" principle of New Testament theology. The idea is that with Jesus' entry into our world, the kingdom is *already* here. The new covenant has begun. God has invaded our exile, and every man, woman and child of Adam's race has been extended the invitation to come home. Death is defeated, Heaven is ours. Satan knows it is just a matter of time. Yet we still await the kingdom's consummation, the *not yet*. The plan is not complete until the New Jerusalem arrives. It is with Jesus' second coming that all is restored. This is the end of the story. Consider the account of Jesus' second coming in Revelation 19–22. Here at the end of all things Jesus returns to earth as a conquering king, he defeats all who oppose him, and he reestablishes his kingdom on earth. It is with the New Jerusalem that Eden is restored and the people of God return to the place of God with full access to the presence of God. What we live right now is the "already," but the hope of our lives is the "not yet." The mark of the "already" in our lives is that we have been born again (1 Pet 1:23). Our hearts have been sealed with the promise of the Holy Spirit (2 Cor 1:22), we are right now being conformed to his image (Rom 8:29), and we have begun to live the quality of life known in the Bible as "eternal life" (Jn 5:24). But we await the resurrection of our bodies when the fleshly aspect of us is also "born again," rejoined to our already born-again immaterial selves and placed into his eternal kingdom (Rom 8:23). So although right now the wheat must grow side by side with the tares, and many will not be able to see the difference until the day of harvest, although right now the kingdom and its strategy for conquest look absurdly weak like the tiniest of the seeds of the garden, and although right now the leaven is almost indiscernible within the lump of dough, just wait. Because as "regular" as kingdom citizens might appear *now*, as foolish as the kingdom strategy might sound, and as indiscernible as the presence of his presence might seem in this fallen world, a day is coming when the kingdoms of this world will become the kingdom of our Lord and of his Christ, and he will reign forever and ever (Rev 11:15). And whereas the wheat will be brought into the barn, the tares will be consumed in fire. And even though the mustard seed is tiny now, it will grow larger than all the other plants of the garden. And although the leaven seems to have been lost in the flour, it will transform the entire lump of dough. Glory to God.

The "already." Let's put some flesh on this. With the new covenant the *people* of God are no longer defined as the biological offspring of Abraham but as anyone who calls upon the name of the Lord and endures to the end (Rom 10:9-13; Gal 3:26-29; 2 Tim 2:11-13). The embrace of redemptive history has been expanded to include all humanity as it once did in Eden (see fig. 9.3).

The *place* of God is also redefined. Rather than being the land of national Israel as in the days of David, the promised place is the New Jerusalem—the restored and recreated earth (Rev 21:1–22:5). But in this "already" era the earth is "not yet" restored. So we the redeemed of this new covenant dwell on this present planet as Abraham lived in Canaan.

> By faith Abraham, when called to go to a place he would later receive as his inheritance, obeyed and went, even though he did not know where he was going. By faith he made his home in the promised land like a stranger in a foreign country; he lived in tents, as did Isaac and Jacob, who were heirs

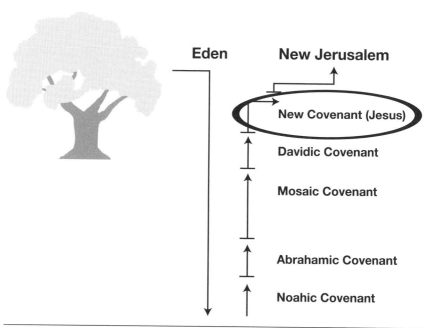

Figure 9.2. A synopsis of redemptive history, new covenant

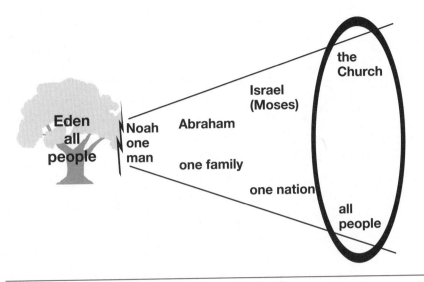

Figure 9.3. The people of redemptive history, the church

with him of the same promise. For he was looking forward to the city with foundations, whose architect and builder is God. (Heb 11:8-10 NIV)

Like Abraham, we are sojourners in the land of promise. One day all the earth will be ours, but right now we are citizens of another kingdom, awaiting the time of the consummation. Once we realize this, perhaps we will not feel as compelled to build enormous houses and more enormous careers in this land which is not yet our own.

And what of the *presence?* This may be the most amazing aspect of Jesus' new covenant with us. For in the new covenant the Presence is set free from its temple restraints. As we have already seen, according to John 1:14 the Presence has come to "tabernacle among us" in Jesus. In fact, in John 2:21 Jesus refers to his body as the new temple. And in Acts 2, where we read of the dramatic inauguration of the ministry of the church, we find that Jesus has entrusted this task of housing the Presence to his church.

Suddenly a sound like the blowing of a violent wind came from heaven and filled the whole house where they were sitting. They saw what seemed to be tongues of fire that separated and came to rest on each of them. All of them were filled with the Holy Spirit and began to speak in other tongues as the Spirit enabled them. (Acts 2:2-4 NIV)

Do you recognize this imagery? In Exodus 40 and 1 Kings 8, the tabernacle and the temple were also inaugurated with cloud and fire and wind. These were the hallmarks of Yahweh's indwelling, his acceptance and approval of the habitation fashioned for him by his people. The book of Acts rehearses these same hallmarks in order to communicate that the living church has now replaced the tabernacle/temple of old. Just as those structures had been set apart ("sanctified") to house the Presence, so now the church is being set apart for the same. This idea is furthered in 1 Corinthians 3:16: "Do you not know that you are a temple of God and that the Spirit of God dwells in you?" The individual believer has *become the temple* (cf. 1 Cor 6:19). Second Corinthians 6:16 takes the message a step further, "For we are the temple of the living God; just as God said, 'I WILL DWELL IN THEM AND WALK AMONG THEM; AND I WILL BE THEIR GOD, AND THEY SHALL BE MY PEOPLE'"—we as individuals and as a community are now the New Testament equivalent to the Old Testament temple (cf. Eph 2:19; 1 Pet 2:5). The Presence from which Adam and Eve were driven, that rested upon Mount Sinai with thunder and storm, that sat enthroned above the cherubim, now resides in *you*. It is nearly too much to apprehend. And just as the old covenant temple housed the Presence in order to make God available to saint and sinner alike and stood as a testimony to the nations that Yahweh dwelt among his people, so too the church. You and I, and we as the church, are designed to be that place to which believer and unbeliever can come and find God. Moreover, our restored lives are God's testimony to the nations that he lives and dwells among us. And whereas the temple was one building that could only be in one place, the church is an ever-expanding community that is slowly, steadily bringing the Presence to the farthest reaches of this world.

The "not yet." And what of the "not yet"? The identity of the *people* of God does not change in this final stage of the rescue plan. All those who have chosen Christ and endured to the end in the "already" will be the citizens of God's kingdom. The great distinction between the "not yet" and the "already" is that those who have rejected Christ will have no part in his final kingdom. The tares of Jesus' parable in Matthew 13, those who practice "abomination and lying," shall never enter, "but only those whose names are written in the Lamb's book of life" (Rev 21:27). And because of this, there will be no danger (or potential of danger) in the New Jerusalem. Rather, we read that "its gates shall never be closed" (Rev. 21:25). Those who have endured through the trials, suffering and peril of this current world will finally find rest, peace and completion in the New Jerusalem.

The *place* of this consummation is Eden restored—the "new heaven and new earth" of Revelation 21:1. Here the children of Adam and Eve will finally fulfill their destiny as the just and obedient stewards of God's

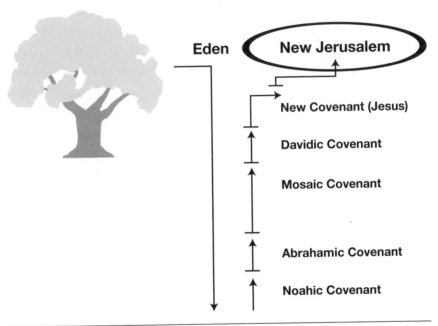

Figure 9.4. A synopsis of redemptive history, New Jerusalem

good earth. I find it almost too magnificent to believe that one day the lands and creatures we have wantonly destroyed in our greed will be recreated and returned to the perfect balance of their intended state. My heart longs for that day.

And what of the *presence?*

Behold, the tabernacle of God is among men, and He will dwell among

them, and they shall be His people, and God Himself shall be among
them . . . I saw no temple in it [the New Jerusalem], for the Lord God the
Almighty and the Lamb are its temple. And the city has no need of the sun
or of the moon to shine on it, for the glory of God has illumined it, and its
lamp is the Lamb. (Rev 21:3, 22-23)

As the prophet foretold, in the New Jerusalem "they will not hurt or destroy in all My holy mountain, for the earth will be full of the knowledge
of the LORD as the waters cover the sea." (Is 11:9). At the end of all things,
God is once again with his people. Access to the Presence is restored.
ʾĀdām has returned to the garden. Redemption has been accomplished.

CONCLUSIONS

So we have come full circle. What began in Eden, ends in Eden. God's
original intent to offer kingdom citizenship to every man, woman and
child has been reaccomplished in Christ. God's original plan that the
children of ʾĀdām might build their city in the midst of his kingdom is
recreated in the new earth. His driving desire to be with us is fulfilled as
the Presence that walked in the garden now illuminates the New Jerusalem. As the final chapters of the New Testament declare, the great rescue
has been accomplished, ʾĀdām is safely home.

I trust that as you read these final lines, the Old Testament has become
your story, that you have crossed the great barrier, and that the God of Israel now seems anything but strange. Moreover, my hope is that you now
have a fully functioning closet in which to store the treasures of your Old
Testament heritage. In closing, my prayer for you is this:

*May the God of Abraham, Isaac and Jacob, who delivered the children of
Abraham from the slavery of Egypt and the exiles of Eden from the curse of
death, live in your hearts and bring you home.*

FREQUENTLY ASKED
QUESTIONS

What Role Does the Law of Moses Play in the Christian's Life?

I find that when I teach this material people always want to learn more about the relationship between the Christian and the law of Moses. In chapter seven, "Moses and the Tabernacle," we began a discussion regarding the nature of the Mosaic law. And I argued long and loud that contrary to what many of us have been taught, the law was a *good* thing. I argued that the law served to sketch the profile of God to a fallen race, and it directed the steps of Israel toward righteousness. I also argued that with the new covenant it was not so much the law of Israel that changed, it was us.[1] So now for the follow-up question. If the law is good and has an eternal place in redemptive history, what role does it play in the new covenant believer's life?

This is a huge topic, for which I have yet to hear a completely satisfactory answer. Most everyone recognizes that simply abolishing the entire Mosaic law contradicts the New Testament (what do you do with the Ten Commandments?). Most equally recognize that imposing the law in its entirety on the Christian also contradicts the New Testament (what of God's instructions to Peter in Acts 10 to embrace unclean foods as clean?). So most have concluded that there must be a middle-of-the-road position. The most enduring approach to defining this middle-of-the-road position has been the attempt to somehow delineate the law according to "moral" versus "civil" (or "ethical" versus "ritual") categories.[2] The claim is typically that the moral/ethical features of the law are still in force for the Christian, but the civil/ritual features are obsolete and can be put safely aside. For example, some would claim that the Ten Commandments can be cataloged as "moral" and are therefore still binding, but the law requiring tassels on the four corners of a person's garment is to be catalogued as "civil/ritual" and is not (Num 15:38-39). The problem with this sort of delineation, however, is that in Israel's world, there was no distinction between the civil/ritual and moral/ethical aspects of the law. All of these laws were deemed as the imperatives of God's divine will. Moreover, to "honor your father and your mother" (Ex 20:12) was both a moral expectation and the civil requirement of a patriarchal society to provide for the elderly of one's clan. And proper worship in a theocracy was an expression of both a moral/ethical and civil/ritual expectation. So what to do? In the end, most assume that the Mosaic law is generally annulled as regards the Christian but hold onto those aspects of the law that are either reiterated by Christ (a good idea) or those that generally just seem "right" (obviously not a satisfactory response to the question). Although I cannot offer a complete solution to the conundrum, let me at least contribute to an answer.

First, it is important to realize that as covenantal administrations change, so do the stipulations of those covenants. So, yes, the rules can and do change.[3] And they change according to the will of the suzerain. Hence, the first question we want to ask is, how does Jesus (our suzerain and mediator) change the rules with the new covenant? We find the answer to that question as we read through the Gospels. Here Jesus regularly calls his audience back to the *intent* of the Mosaic law. Was the sabbath created for man, or man for the sabbath (Mt 12:10)? Is adultery the problem, or unbridled lust (Mt 7:27)? Is it more important that a person keep themselves ritually clean, or serve a neighbor in need (Lk 10:30-37)? So one thing Jesus tells his audience is to look beyond a legalistic adherence to particulars and see the *goal* of the law. This is clearly articulated in interactions like Matthew 22:36-40:

> "Teacher, which is the great commandment in the Law?" And He said to him, "'You SHALL LOVE THE LORD YOUR GOD WITH ALL YOUR HEART, AND WITH ALL YOUR SOUL, AND WITH ALL YOUR MIND.' This is the great

and foremost commandment. The second is like it, 'YOU SHALL LOVE YOUR NEIGHBOR AS YOURSELF.' On these two commandments depend the whole Law and the Prophets."

Galatians 5:14 says the same: "For the whole Law is fulfilled in one word, in the statement, 'YOU SHALL LOVE YOUR NEIGHBOR AS YOURSELF.'" Thus, whereas the detailed message of the Mosaic law embodied the love of neighbor and God in concrete, time- and culture-bound expressions, Jesus finds a way to articulate the transcultural and all-embracing message of that same law to a new audience. Moreover, he makes it clear that this message is still binding upon us new covenant adherents as well.

We also read that Jesus redefines the major institutions of Israel's theocracy: the temple and the theocratic government. The temple is first redefined as Jesus' own body, and then as the individual believer and the church (Jn 2:19-21; Eph 2:19-22). Jesus is identified as the *final* sacrifice (Heb 9:24-26) and as the church's new high priest (Heb 2:17). Thus, with the new covenant we learn that Israel's temple cultus is obsolete. And if this theocratic institution is obsolete, I believe it is safe to conclude that the complex processes dictated by the Mosaic law that directed the function of this institution (e.g. the design and décor of the building, the cleanness of priest and worshipper, sacrifice, mediation and the calendar of cultic celebration) are now obsolete as well. This means that in the new covenant the specific Mosaic regulations regarding these issues are annulled: our buildings of worship are no longer dictated by a certain architectural model, the believer is no longer required to bring sacrifice, the laws of "clean and unclean" are abrogated, the mediation of human priests is unnecessary, and the holidays of Israel's cult have become "a mere shadow of what is to come" (Col 2:16-17).

And what of Israel's theocratic government? Keep clearly in your mind that Israel was a nation that was directly ruled by God.[4] Yahweh sat enthroned in the temple in Jerusalem, "between the cherubim," and carried out his ordinances by means of his officers, the prophet, priest and king. Israel was a political entity with national territory. Its citizenry were, exclusively, the people of God. Foreign oppression, drought and famine were God's communiqués that his people had somehow broken covenant; national prosperity was the sign that they had kept covenant. Thus the nation of Israel could justly go to war in the name of Yahweh, slaying Ammonites, Moabites and Edomites to defend the national boundaries of God's kingdom. But Jesus makes it clear that his only throne will be in heaven (Mk 16:19; Heb 8:1; etc.). And as we've seen, the new citizenry of his kingdom will come from every tongue, tribe and nation. As opposed to the land of Canaan being the Promised Land, now all of the recreated earth is. Thus, in the new covenant there is no longer any single nation that can lay claim to being "the people of God" nor any single piece of real estate that is promised to them. There are new officers for this new kingdom too. Even a cursory glance at Ephesians 4:11; 1 Corinthians 12:28 or 1 Timothy 3 lets us know that apostles, prophets, evangelists, pastors, deacons and teachers have replaced the prophet, priest and king of the Mosaic covenant. The only title that survives into the new covenant is that of "prophet," but even this office is substantially transformed.[5] Thus the very literal political realities of Israel's theocracy are abrogated by the new covenant, and I believe we can safely say that the complex lists of laws and regulations that governed the theocracy are abrogated as well.

Then, of course, there are those aspects of the Mosaic law that the writers of the New Testament specifically address as being changed or terminated. A few examples would be the necessity of circumcision (1 Cor 7:19), the regulations of *kashrut* (Acts 10:15), the rabbinic restrictions regarding the sabbath (Mt 12:1-9) and even divorce (Mt 19:3-9).

In sum, I think we can identify at least three categories of Mosaic law which, in their specific expectations, no longer apply to the Christian: those involving the regulation of Israel's government, those involving the regulation of Israel's temple, and those laws that the New Testament specifically repeals or changes. I would still argue that the values that shaped these regulations express the character of God and therefore must be attended to by the Christian, but the specifics of their application are no longer our responsibility. Thus my contribution to the conundrum named above is that rather than attempting to delineate the law of Moses based on categories foreign to that law itself ("moral/ethical" and "civil/ritual"), perhaps we should address the question through a lens that is more native to both Old and New Testaments—Jesus' redefinition of certain major institutions of the Mosaic covenant. And for all the Mosaic law, be it superseded or not, we need to recognize that we can (and must) still learn a great deal about the character of God through these laws, even if we can no longer directly apply them to ourselves in this new covenant. So rather than thinking in terms of the Mosaic law being obsolete *except* for what Jesus maintains (as has been the predominant view), perhaps we should begin to think in terms of the law being in force except for what Jesus repeals.

What About Modern-Day Israel?

In light of all we've learned regarding the trajectory of redemptive history, how each of the covenantal administrations gives way to the next, and how the picture is only complete when the New Jerusalem is firmly in place, a last and frequently asked question has to do with the modern nation of Israel and its place in the new covenant. I tremble to address this as I know so many of us have been taught that this topic is a litmus test for true faith. Is the modern land of Israel and the modern nation of Israel still the locus of God's promises to his people? For most that I teach, this issue forms itself into two questions: Can I apply the promises given to Israel to my country (I call this "Christian nationalism"), and can I apply the promises given to Mosaic Israel to modern day Israel (this may be labeled "Christian Zionism")? A thorny set of questions indeed!

I believe the first step to a biblical perspective on these issues is to remind ourselves of the definition of "theocracy."[6] As a theocracy, Israel's true king was Yahweh. This meant that Israel's territory was actually *God's* territory, Israel's enemies were *God's* enemies, and Israel's political interests were *God's* political interests. We've reviewed the upshot of these realities a number of times: national prosperity was a mark of covenant obedience; national crisis was the mark of covenant disobedience; war was a means by which to expand or defend the kingdom, etc. But Jesus makes it very clear that with the inauguration of the new covenant, the theocracy that was Israel is over. The kingdom of God has been redefined. In the new covenant, God's *people* are no longer limited to the offspring of Abraham, God's *presence* is no longer confined to the temple, and God's *place* is no longer limited to that hilly patch of real estate along the eastern Mediterranean Sea. Jesus now rules from heaven a kingdom whose citizenry is drawn from every nation of the earth. And the "promised land" of this new kingdom is the new heaven and new earth of Revelation 21:1. God has "blown the doors off" the limitations of Israel's covenant with the ushering in of the new.

Thus, different from Mosaic Israel, the influence of the church in this "already" stage of the new covenant is that of the leaven in the lump, the wheat among the tares (see pp. 218-19). And Jesus' kingdom will not be expanded by means of conquest. In fact the New Testament writers are careful to redefine the concept and implements of war for the church. The "weapons of our warfare" are no longer swords and shields, but the word of God and the gospel of peace (2 Cor 10:4; Eph 6:15-17). As soldiers of the cross, we are no longer called to win new territory by overpowering our adversaries in physical battle, but to win lost souls by convincing them of the truth. And the enemies we defeat are no longer the Philistines and the Assyrians but the "world forces of this darkness." Paul says it best:

> Finally, be strong in the Lord and in the strength of His might. Put on the full armor of God, so that you will be able to stand firm against the schemes of the devil. For our struggle is not against flesh and blood, but against the rulers, against the powers, against the world forces of this darkness, against the spiritual forces of wickedness in the heavenly places. Therefore, take up the full armor of God, so that you will be able to resist in the evil day, and having done everything, to stand firm. Stand firm therefore, HAVING GIRDED YOUR LOINS WITH TRUTH, and HAVING PUT ON THE BREASTPLATE OF RIGHTEOUSNESS, and having shod YOUR FEET WITH THE PREPARATION OF THE GOSPEL OF PEACE; in addition to all, taking up the shield of faith with which you will be able to extinguish all the flaming arrows of the evil one. And take THE HELMET OF SALVATION, and the sword of the Spirit, which is the word of God. With all prayer and petition pray at all times in the Spirit, and with this in view, be on the alert with all perseverance and petition for all the saints, and pray on my behalf, that utterance may be given to me in the opening of my mouth, to make known with boldness the mystery of the gospel, for which I am an ambassador in chains; that in proclaiming it I may speak boldly, as I ought to speak. (Eph 6:10-19)

The New Testament teaches us that the church will not see the kingdom of God legitimately take up arms again until the second coming. Here

Jesus will return to this earth as a conquering king and, like Joshua in the conquest of Canaan, lead the people of God in battle to win back the territory of the King which has been held illegitimately by those who have rejected his rule (Rev 19:11-21).

What are some of the contemporary implications of Jesus' reinterpretation of the kingdom? One involves the assumption of many Christians that when one's country experiences prosperity or crisis, these are signs of God's pleasure or displeasure with one's country. Although God can do what he likes, and therefore he may choose to bless, limit or destroy a particular human organization in order to accomplish his plans, as a blanket statement, this assumption simply cannot be true in the new covenant. This is true primarily because the new covenant doesn't offer this set of criteria—God is no longer in the business of theocracy. Although I am a citizen of the kingdom, unlike Mosaic Israel, God no longer rules my country, nor are all the citizens of my country God's people. So to strike a little closer to (my) home, it would be difficult to argue that the wealth of the United States is the result of God's pleasure with this country or that the disaster of September 11 is the mark of his displeasure. Similarly, the conflicts in the Middle East say little about God's attitude toward Israelis or Palestinians. Both countries have Christian citizenry, and both countries have unbelieving citizenry. And none of these governments is "sponsored" by the Most High.

Another implication is that in this new covenant it is theologically indefensible to take up arms to spread the gospel. Please hear me, I am not a pacifist. And I think in the arena of international law, there are times when war is just and necessary. But that sort of war does not have as its objective the expansion of God's kingdom. How could an act of war by my country, whose army and government are a mixture of believer and unbeliever, be an act of evangelism toward another country—whose government and army are also a mixture of believer and unbeliever? I think of the account of the Christmas Truce of 1914. It was Christmas Eve on the western front of Germany. The story goes that without administrative permission, the soldiers of both armies spontaneously ceased fire in honor of the import of the night. And in the peculiar silence, wafting over the demolished, body-strewn strip of earth that had come to be known as "No

Man's Land," the German soldiers heard the strains of a familiar melody, albeit sung in a foreign tongue—"Silent Night." A moment of ironic and pregnant silence was followed by an answering chorus, quiet at first, but building as it came: "Stille Nacht, heilige Nacht, Alles schläft; einsam wacht . . ." I remember the first time I heard this story, my heart broke for the eighteen-year-old boys who were far from their families and far too close to their own mortality that bitterly cold night. I won't propose any political commentary here. But do we actually think that God was *for* the death and defeat of his people on one side or the other? My country is a mixed bag of believers and unbelievers as is yours. So when your country attacks mine, or visa versa, which side is God on? In Mosaic Israel the answer was easy, "the side of his people." Under the new covenant the response is the same—but now his people live in both nations. So the side God is on is that of the kingdom. And this new covenant kingdom does not expand by means of political conquest.

With the new covenant, a radical new allegiance has been announced. One that supersedes everything the human race has embraced in the past. With Christ my first allegiance is no longer to my country, my race, my tribe or even my family—my allegiance is to the One who gave his life for me and for the people birthed of that sacrifice. Thus, regardless of nationality, race or language, the Christian is now my brother, my compatriot and my ally.

> For you are all sons of God through faith in Christ Jesus. For all of you who were baptized into Christ have clothed yourselves with Christ. There is neither Jew nor Greek, there is neither slave nor free man, there is neither male nor female; for you are all one in Christ Jesus. And if you belong to Christ, then you are Abraham's descendants, heirs according to promise. (Gal 3:26-29)

Bringing this all back to the question of modern-day Israel, we must conclude that this country has the same status as any other political entity in this new covenant era. Certainly the citizens of Israel, like the citizens of the United States, are a mixed bag of believer and unbeliever. Those who are believers deserve my allegiance and will share my inheritance. Those who are not believers will not share my inheritance. And according to the New Testament, even the citizens of modern day Israel who have identified themselves with Christ look to the restored heaven and earth as their inheritance—not that hilly patch of real estate on the eastern edge of the Mediterranean Sea.[7]

NOTES

Chapter 1: The Bible as the Story of Redemption

[1]Darrell L. Whiteman, ed., *An Introduction to Melanesian Cultures: A Handbook for Church Workers*, Point Series 5 (Goroka, Papua New Guinea: The Melanesian Institute, 1984), p. 23.

[2]The 1820s were the decade of American mission to Hawaii. See Kenneth Scott Latourette, *A History of Christianity: Reformation to the Present* (New York: Harper & Row, 1975), pp. 1298-1300; Stephen Neill, *A History of Christian Missions* (New York: Penguin Books, 1964), pp. 300-301, 473; cf. James A. Michener's historical fiction *Hawaii* (New York: Random House, 1959).

[3]See Marshall D. Sahlins, *Tribesmen* (Englewood Cliffs, N.J.: Prentice Hall, 1968), and Max Weber, "Bureaucracy" and "Patriarchalism and Patrimonialism," in *Economy and Society: An Outline of Interpretive Sociology*, 2 vols., ed. Guenther Roth and Claus Wittich (Berkeley: University of California Press, 1978), pp. 956-1069. See as well Roland de Vaux's older but still very valuable discussion of the family and segments of Israelite society in *Ancient Israel: Its Life and Institutions* (Grand Rapids: Eerdmans, 1997), pp. 3-79; and Robert D. Miller's recent discussion of Israel's societal structure as a "Complex Chiefdom Model" (*Chieftains of the Highland Clans: A History of Israel in the 12th and 11th Centuries B.C.E.* [Grand Rapids: Eerdmans, 2005], pp. 6-28).

[4]"The conical clan . . . the main strategy of chiefdom organization . . . is a ranked and segmented common descent group. Genealogical seniority is the first rule of rank, and it holds throughout the clan: individuals of the same lineage are graded by their respective distance from the lineage founder; equivalent lineage-branches are likewise ranked according to the position of their respective founders in the clan genealogy. Priority goes to the first-born son of first-born sons, and a different rank is ascribable to every member of the clan, precisely in proportion to his genealogical distance from the senior line" (Sahlins, *Tribesmen,* p. 49; cf. p. 24).

[5]Sahlins, *Tribesmen,* p. 15; cf. Miller, *Chieftains,* pp. 6-28.

[6]Although the term "clan" is more familiar, Sahlins clarifies that this layer is better described as "local lineages" which are gathered into village communities (Sahlins, *Tribesmen,* p. 15). Carol Meyers opts for the term "residential kinship group" ("The Family in Early Israel," in *Families in Ancient Israel,* ed. Leo G. Perdue et al., The Family, Religion, and Culture Series [Louisville, Ky.: Westminster John Knox, 1997], p. 13).

[7]Lawrence E. Stager, "Archaeology of the Family in Ancient Israel," *BASOR* 260 (1985): 20-22. This societal structure is reflected throughout the Old Testament, but it is particularly visible in the account of Josh 7:14-15 in which Joshua is instructed to identify the individual who has violated the ban in the battle of Ai. Here the lot is used to identify first the tribe, then the clan, then the household and then the individual who is guilty (ibid., p. 22; cf. Philip J. King and Lawrence

E. Stager, *Life in Biblical Israel* [Louisville, Ky.: Westminster John Knox, 2001], pp. 36-38).

[8]Stager, "Archaeology of the Family," p. 20; cf. King and Stager, *Life in Biblical Israel*, pp. 39-40.

[9]King and Stager, *Life in Biblical Israel*, pp. 1-19.

[10]Carol Meyers comments that the shared living of extended families creates relational dynamics that are difficult enough that "extended families are actually not all that common" in the history of human civilization. Rather, these family configurations tend to form "in situations in which labor requirements are so demanding that a residential group cannot survive at subsistence level without the productive labor of more than a conjugal pair and their children" (Meyers, "Family in Early Israel," p. 18). These "demanding" conditions would certainly be true of the settlement period of Israel's history (the Iron I period, 1200-1000 b.c.), during which time Israel's tribal coalition was attempting to carve out an agrarian existence in the heretofore unsettled, mountainous, forested, rocky central hill country of the "promised land."

[11]If the *paterfamilias* was unable to resolve a legal situation within the family, the village elders (hence, the patriarchs of the clan[s] living in the village) would be expected to bring order and to carry out justice. An example of this is the law of the rebellious son in Deut 21:19. See Sahlins, *Tribesmen*, p. 17; and Oded Borowski, *Daily Life in Biblical Times* (Atlanta: Society of Biblical Literature, 2003), pp. 221-22.

[12]See the similar story of Jacob and Esau in Gen 36:6-8.

[13]See King and Stager, *Life in Biblical Israel*, pp. 47-48; de Vaux, *Ancient Israel*, pp. 41-42; and Jon D. Levenson, *The Death and Resurrection of the Beloved Son: The Transformation of Child Sacrifice in Judaism and Christianity* (New Haven, Conn.: Yale University Press, 1993), pp. 55-68.

[14]For further reading see King and Stager, *Life in Biblical Israel*, pp. 53-57.

[15]Carol Meyers speaks of the Israelite farmers as "smallholders: 'rural cultivators practicing intensive, permanent, diversified agriculture on relatively small farms'" ("Family in Early Israel," p. 3). Because of the typical Israelite family's subsistence approach to farming, agricultural production ran year round. The planting of cereal grains occurred in the fall, legumes in the winter and the care and pruning of vineyards and orchards throughout the year. The barley harvest began with the spring equinox, wheat in late April. Grapes and other fruits were harvested during the summer months, with the olive crop gathered from late August to late October. For further reading see Borowski, *Daily Life in Biblical Times*, pp. 13-42; and "Day in Micah's Household," pp. 12-19, in King and Stager's, *Life in Biblical Israel*.

[16]Interestingly, there is no epigraphical evidence (inscriptions) for the sale or purchase of real estate in Israel. Even though there is a great deal of such evidence from Israel's neighbors (Christopher J. H. Wright, *God's People in God's Land: Family, Land, and Property in the Old Testament* [Grand Rapids: Eerdmans, 1990], pp. 55-58; cf. pp. 119-41).

[17]For further reading see Wright, *God's People;* Meyers, "Family in Early Israel," pp. 19-21; Joseph Blenkinsopp, "The Family in First Temple Israel," in *Families in Ancient Israel*, ed. Leo G. Perdue et al., The Family, Religion, and Culture Series (Louisville, Ky.: Westminster John Knox, 1997), pp. 54-56; and Borowski, *Daily Life*, pp. 26-27.

[18]Lawrence Stager has done seminal work on this topic in his ethnoarchaeological study "The Archaeology of the Family in Ancient Israel," 1-35. See his updated discussion of the topic (complete with wonderful images) in *Life in Biblical Israel*, pp. 21-35. His student, J. David Schloen, has significantly expanded our understanding of the family compound in *The House of the Father as Fact and Symbol: Patrimonialism in Ugarit and the Ancient Near East* (Cambridge, Mass.: Harvard Semitic Museum, 2001).

[19]For further discussion see Stager, "Archaeology of the Family," p. 19; *Life in Biblical Israel*, p. 11; Amihai Mazar, *Archaeology of the Land of the Bible: 10,000-586 b.c.e.* (New York: Doubleday,

1990), pp. 338-45, 485-88; cf. J. David Schloen, *The House of the Father;* and Israel Finkelstein, *The Archaeology of Israelite Settlement* (Jerusalem: Israel Exploration Society, 1988), pp. 254-60.

[20]Larry G. Herr and Douglas R. Clark, "Excavating the Tribe of Reuben," *BAR* 27, no. 2 (March/April 2001).

[21]Note that the number of rooms delineated by the pillars is somewhat fluid; one, two or three rooms have been excavated.

[22]Douglas Clark offers an engaging summary of what would go into the construction of one of these houses in "Excavating the Tribe of Reuben," *BAR* 27, no. 2 (March/April 2001).

[23]Stager, "Archaeology of the Family," p. 15.

[24]Stager, *Life in Biblical Israel,* p. 35.

[25]Stager, "Archaeology of the Family," p. 15; cf. King and Stager, *Life in Biblical Israel,* p. 29 for an image.

[26]For further reading see King and Stager, *Life in Biblical Israel,* pp. 363-72; de Vaux, *Ancient Israel,* pp. 56-61; Borowski, *Daily Life in Biblical Times,* pp. 83-85; and Elizabeth Block-Smith, *Judahite Burial Practices and Beliefs About the Dead* (Sheffield, U.K.: Sheffield Academic Press, 1992).

[27]King and Stager, *Life in Biblical Israel,* p. 365.

[28]μοναι, μονή = "a place to stay, a mansion" (Henry George Liddell and Robert Scott, *Greek-English Lexicon,* abridged from the 9th ed. [Oxford: Clarendon Press, 1996], p. 451).

[29]The term used here is the unusual "mother's house" *(bêt ʾēm)* as opposed to "father's house." Other occurrences include Gen 24:28 and Song 3:4; 8:2. Carol Meyers points out that these are "all apparently" generated by female experience" and open a window into the centrality and autonomy of women in the day-to-day operation of the Israelite household ("Family in Early Israel," p. 34). In this particular case the phrase may also indicate that Naomi recognizes Elimelech's household as the girls' legal affiliation and their households of origin as something else.

[30]The modifier used to describe Gomer is Hebrew *zĕnûnîm,* meaning the "status and practice of the *zônâ*"; *zônâ* means "women occassionally or professionally committing fornication" (*HALOT* s.v. "זְנוּן" and "זְנוּנִים" p. 275). Thus, Gomer's exact status is unclear. Is she a woman with a reputation for promiscuous behavior, or is she a woman professionally employed as a prostitute? Are the food, water, wool, linen, oil and wine her lovers have given her "wages" or simply gifts (Hos 2:5, 12)? Both interpretations are credible; neither alters her ultimate fate as a woman being sold into slavery (Hos 3:2).

[31]It is the price that Hosea offers for Gomer that encourages the conclusion that the transaction being carried out is the sale of a slave (Hos 3:2). The *homer* contained ten ephahs (Ezek 45:11), which means that Hosea is offering fifteen ephahs of barley along with his silver money. According to 2 Kings 7:1, 16, 18 this amount of barley equates to fifteen silver shekels. Thus, Hosea's payment, although half in grain and half in silver, was equivalent to thirty shekels. According to Lev 27:4, the going price for a female slave was thirty shekels in silver (cf. Ex 21:32). Why the mixed medium? Perhaps Hosea was offering all the silver he had and making up the rest in grain. As barley was the common man's grain, it is quite possible that he is offering the contents of his larder for his wife's freedom (see C. F. Keil and F. Delitzsch, *Commentary on the Old Testament: Minor Prophets,* trans. James Martin [Peabody, Mass.: Hendrickson, 1989], 10:68-69; and Frances I. Andersen and David Noel Freedman, *Hosea,* AB 24 [Garden City, N.Y.: Doubleday, 1980], pp. 298-301).

[32]See Lev 25:47-55 for the kinsman's responsibility to "redeem" an enslaved relative.

Chapter 2: The Bible in Real Time and Space

[1]I encourage the reader to purchase an affordable atlas such as the paperback version of the *Harper-*

Collins Atlas of Bible History, ed. James B. Pritchard and Nick Page (San Francisco: HarperCollins, 2008). An atlas is an important companion for Old Testament study as it summarizes critical social and historical information and makes it easily accessible for Bible study. I have found that the HarperCollins atlas is very helpful to my students at whatever level of expertise they find themselves.

[2]See James Barr's excellent discussion of early attempts to date Old Testament events in "Why the World was Created in 4004 B.C.: Archbishop Ussher and Biblical Chronology," *BJRL* 67, no. 2 (1985): 575-608. As Barr reports, there is a long tradition of an approximately 4000 B.C. creation date. The Talmud reports, "The world is to exist 6000 years. The first 2000 years are to be void [Hebrew *tohu*]; the next 2000 years are the period of the Torah; and the following 2000 years are the period of the Messiah" (ibid., p. 581; cf. *b. 'Abod. Zar. 9a*). This schematized chronology of the world was the Jewish tradition and was still embraced at the time of the Reformation. The distinction between this classic Jewish chronology and that of Bishop Ussher is that the Jewish dating of the world is exclusively based on the biblical data, whereas Ussher nuanced the biblical scheme by synchronizing biblical dates with those known from secular history. One change, for example, was Ussher expanding the biblical chronology according to the real dates of the Persian Empire. Because the biblical writers were not terribly interested in the Persian Empire, they provided very little data regarding it. Thus, the medieval Jewish chronographers assigned periods such as fifty-two or even thirty-two years to the entire Persian Empire, "which had in fact lasted just over two centuries" (ibid., p. 580).

[3]In addition to James Barr's piece named above, see his "Chronology 1. Israelite Chronology," in *Oxford Companion to the Bible,* ed. Bruce M. Metzger and Michael D. Coogan (New York: Oxford University Press, 1993), pp. 117-19.

[4]An example of the social function of genealogy may be found in the book of Numbers (Num 2:2-4, 17; 3:40-51; 7:11-89; 10:1-28). Here the camp itself, battle lines, taxes and offerings are all organized according to genealogy. There are a number of good dictionary articles that summarize the social, political and religious functions of genealogies in kinship-based societies. See R. K. Harrison, "Genealogy," *ISBE,* pp. 424-28; Robert Wilson, "Genealogy, Genealogies," *ABD,* 2:930-32; J. W. Wright, "Genealogies," *DOTP,* pp. 345-50. For a technical introduction with extensive bibliography, see Kenton L. Sparks, *Ancient Texts for the Study of the Hebrew Bible: A Guide to the Background Literature* (Peabody, Mass.: Hendrickson, 2005), pp. 344-60.

[5]Wilson, "Genealogy, Genealogies," 2:931.

[6]Harrison, "Genealogy," 2:427.

[7]It is significant that Israel's focus on genealogy in Genesis and Exodus is somewhat unique in the ancient world. Genealogies appear rarely in ancient Near Eastern literature, being "attested primarily in Mesopotamian king lists and in second millennium texts dealing with the political organization and history of the Amorites" (Wilson, "Genealogy, Genealogies," p. 930). This parallel with the second-millennium Amorites is particularly interesting because the Amorites were also a kinship-based society of Semitic origin, and they quite possibly shared ancestry with the Israelites. Thus it is probable that, like the Amorites, the biblical genealogies emerge from the most ancient records of Israel's premonarchic identity.

[8]This same pattern of the seventh ancestor of the antediluvian generations being somehow special to the gods has been identified in later versions of the ancient Sumerian King's List. Here King Enmeduranki (the most frequent occupier of the seventh slot), was the first to be taken up to the heavenly assembly to receive the secrets of omen and astrological lore. See the chapter "Genealogies, King Lists, and Related Texts," in Kenton L. Sparks, *Ancient Texts for the Study of the Hebrew Bible,* pp. 346-47.

[9]The scripts and systems by which the ancients represented numbers created relationships between

those numbers that are not readily apparent to the modern reader. This is due in part to the fact that in the ancient Near East numbers served as literary tools (therefore certain numbers were understood to represent certain qualities) and partly because the same symbol could be used to represent a number *or* a sound. Thus, when symbols were reversed or somehow manipulated, dual meanings could be created which added another layer of meaning to a narrative. A good example of this is an inscription from an eighth-century-B.C. Assyrian king, Sargon II. In Sargon's inscription memorializing the building of his city Dur Sharrukin (Khorsabad), he speaks of constructing a city wall measuring four (units of 3,600), three (units of 600), one (unit of 60), three (units of 6), and two cubits and states that this number is "the numeral of my name" (cf. *ARAB* II §108, p. 57). When these numbers are passed through the sexagesimal number system native to Mesopotamia and shifted to their alphabetic (actually syllabic) meaning, they are seen to be symbols communicating the king's name (*sarru-kīnu* = Sargon) as well as the dimensions listed above (cf. Jöran Friberg, "Numbers and Counting," *ABD*, 4:1144). Thus, the king has embedded his name into the building dimensions of his architectural accomplishment. So are these numbers truly the dimensions of the wall at Dur Sharrukin? Or have they been "massaged" to communicate a dual meaning? I think the latter must be concluded. More important, if this sort of record keeping is acceptable in a monumental text in Mesopotamia, it is likely that it was acceptable in Israel as well.

[10]One of the challenges facing Ussher was the still unformed understanding of calendration in the ancient world. For example, he was not aware of the distinctions between solar and lunar systems for reckoning time. Egypt was known to have used a solar calendar, pastoralists like the early Israelites and the Amorites made use of a lunar calendar, Mesopotamia harmonized lunar and solar by means of intercalation, and later Jews made use of what James Barr calls a "luni-solar" system ("Why the World Was Created in 4004 B.C.," p. 599). These differing systems of calendration obviously produced differing results as to dates, months and even years. And when these ancient dates are plugged into the modern solar calendar without nuance, confusion reigns!

[11]Harrison, "Genealogy," p. 428.

[12]See *HarperCollins Concise Atlas*, pp. 16-17. For a technical discussion see David A. Dorsey, *The Roads and Highways of Ancient Israel* (Baltimore: Johns Hopkins University Press, 1991), pp. 117-46. Paul Wright of Jerusalem University College clarifies that both these titles are modern conventions; we do not know what this route was called in ancient times. But as with others like it, the route was probably known by its point of destination. In other words, if the traveler were in Jerusalem and going to Bethel, he might call it the Bethel Route (or, "the Way to Bethel"); conversely, the Jerusalem Route (or "the Way to Jerusalem") if the traveler lived in Bethel (cf. Judge 21:19; Paul Wright, written communication July 20, 2007).

[13]See James Hoffmeier, *Israel in Egypt: The Evidence for the Authenticity of the Exodus Tradition* (New York: Oxford University Press, 1996), pp. 183-85.

[14]The Hebrew version of the Old Testament speaks of the sea through which the Israelites passed either as "the sea" (*yām;* cf. Ex 14:2) or the *yam sûp*, meaning "sea of reeds" (cf. Ex 13:18). It is now nearly certain that *sûp* is related to the Egyptian term *ṭwf(y)*. Like Hebrew *sûp*, Egyptian *ṭwf(y)* means "plants that grow in marshy waters." The common translation of Hebrew *yam sûp* "Red Sea," which is found in most English Bibles, comes from the third-century-B.C. Greek translation of the Hebrew text (the Septuagint). Scholars hypothesize that this "Red Sea" translation of Hebrew *yam sûp* was based either on the assumption that the coastline of the Red Sea reached further north in ancient times and therefore the Red Sea was attached to the lakes that dotted the eastern border of ancient Egypt, that it was an error on the part of these later translators, or that the translation emerged from some other as of yet unknown tradition involving the exodus. For a thorough (but technical) discussion see Hoffmeier, *Israel in Egypt*, pp. 199-222.

Chapter 3: The Concept of Covenant

[1]Although the socio-historical information that would define and inform the concept of covenant would not become available until the 1950s, it had long been understood that this concept was central to biblical theology. One illustration of this is Walther Eichrodt's enormous (and enormously important) *Theology of the Old Testament* written in the 1930s. Each of the ten major divisions of this book has the term *covenant* in its title. For example, "The Covenant Relationship," "The Covenant Statutes," "The Name of the Covenant God," etc. Another giant of Old Testament theology, Gerhard von Rad, also wrote before we could define *covenant* in the terms in which the Old Testament writers understood it. But he pointed out that the form itself must somehow reflect the literary mores of the ancient Near East. Weinfeld describes von Rad's conclusions as follows: "He correctly observes that such a strange combination of elements could not be an invention of scribes, but must have had its roots in a certain reality" (Weinfeld, "בְּרִית *bĕrît*," *TDOT*, 2:265; cf. Gerhard von Rad, "The Form-Critical Problem of the Hexateuch," in *The Problem of the Hexateuch and Other Essays*, trans. E. W. Trueman Dicken [New York: McGraw-Hill, 1966], pp. 1-78).

[2]The use of the term *testament* to refer to the two divisions within the Bible is in some ways an accident of translation history. When the Bible was translated into Latin early on in the history of the church, Greek *diathēkē*, which can mean either "covenant" or "will," was translated according to only one of these meanings, "will," into Latin *testamentum*. In this fashion, the idea of covenant was lost to the titles of the Old and New in Latin, and eventually in English as well. As this is now the normative English designation for the Bible, I would not suggest changing it, but it is important to realize that the term "testament" is not actually a correct representation of the language of the biblical writers. For Old and New (outside of some double entendre in Heb 9:15-22) the biblical writers were speaking of "covenant" not "testament."

[3]Jon Levenson, *Sinai and Zion: An Entry into the Jewish Bible* (San Francisco: HarperSanFrancisco, 1985), p. 36.

[4]George Mendenhall and Gary A. Herion, "Covenant," *ABD*, 1:1178.

[5]Frank Moore Cross, *From Epic to Canon: History and Literature in Ancient Israel* (Baltimore: Johns Hopkins University Press, 1998), p. 7.

[6]See Weinfeld, "בְּרִית *bĕrît*," 2:267; and Gary Beckman, *Hittite Diplomatic Texts*, 2nd ed., SBL Writings from the Ancient World Series 7 (Atlanta: Scholars Press, 1995), no. 18B, §§2-4.

[7]Bill T. Arnold and Bryan E. Beyer, eds., *Readings from the Ancient Near East: Primary Sources for Old Testament Study* (Grand Rapids: Baker Academic, 2002), p. 98; cf. James B. Pritchard, ed., *Ancient Near Eastern Texts Relating to the Old Testament*, 3rd ed. (Princeton, N.J.: Princeton University Press, 1969), p. 203.

[8]See again the treaty between the Hittite king Mursilis and Duppi-Teshub, which dedicates several paragraphs to detailing the sort of military assistance expected from Duppi-Teshub (ibid.).

[9]Arnold and Beyer, *Readings from the Ancient Near East*, p. 99; cf. *ANET*, p. 204.

[10]Ibid., p. 100; cf. *ANET*, p. 205.

[11]Cross, *From Epic to Canon*, p. 5; Katharine D. Sakenfeld, *The Meaning of Hesed in the Hebrew Bible: A New Inquiry*, HSM 17 (Missoula, Mont.: Scholars Press, 1978); cf. *HALOT*, s.v. "חֶסֶד," pp. 336-37.

[12]For further reading on the concept of covenant and examples of these international documents, see "Covenants and Treaties," in Arnold and Beyer, *Readings from the Ancient Near East*, pp. 96-103; *ANET*, pp. 199-206, 659-61; G. E. Mendenhall, "Covenant Forms in Israelite Tradition," *BA* 17 (1954): 50-76; Dennis J. McCarthy, *Treaty and Covenant: A Study in Form in the Ancient Oriental Documents and in the Old Testament*, Analecta Biblica 21 (Rome: Pontifical Biblical Institute, 1963); Delbert Hillers *Covenant: The History of a Biblical Idea* (Baltimore: Johns Hopkins Univer-

sity Press, 1969); and Weinfeld's article, "בְּרִית *běrit*," 2:253-79.

[13]For a technical summary of the excavations and the documents discovered see Philo H. J. Houwink Ten Cate, "Hittite History," *ABD*, 3:220-21. For the initial literary study of this collection see V. Karošec, *Hethitische Staatsverträge*, Leipziger Rechtswissenschaftliche Studien 60 (Leipzig, 1931).

[14]These promissory oaths called for the vassals' future loyalty to Esarhaddon's heir, Ashurbanipal. See *ANET*, pp. 534-41. For a more technical introduction see D. J. Wiseman, *The Vassal Treaties of Esarhaddon* (London: British School of Archaeology in Iraq, 1958).

[15]For an easily accessible introduction to the Amarna Letters, see James B. Pritchard, *The Harper-Collins Concise Atlas of the Bible* (New York: HarperSanFrancisco, 1991), pp. 24-25; for samples of these letters see Arnold and Beyer, *Readings from the Ancient Near East*, pp. 166-68 and *ANET*, pp. 483-90.

[16]See n. 13 as well as George Mendenhall and Gary Herion, "Covenant," *ABD*, 1:1179-1202.

[17]Because in Mari the ritually appropriate animal for confirming a covenant was a donkey foal, the idiom in Mari was "to kill a donkey foal." See Moshe Held, "Philological Notes on the Mari Covenant Rituals," *BASOR* 200 (1970): 33; cf. *ANET*, p. 482 and Arnold and Beyer, *Readings from the Ancient Near East*, p. 96.

[18]Arnold and Beyer, *Readings from the Ancient Near East*, p. 101; *ANET*, pp. 532-33.

[19]William Moran wrote an important article on this topic: "The Ancient Near Eastern Background of the Love of God in Deuteronomy," *CBQ* 25 (1963): 77-85. Here Moran demonstrated that the word *love* in ancient Near East treaty documents (and by extrapolation in the book of Deuteronomy) was political terminology having to do with covenant loyalty—not any sort of sentimental or emotional posture toward the covenant partner. In light of this, consider Rom 9:13: "Jacob I loved, but Esau I hated." Gallons of ink have been spilt over this passage! Could the resolution to this difficult language perhaps be found in covenant terminology? In other words, rather than this passage communicating that God has *despised* Esau and his offspring, perhaps "love" and "hate" were intended to communicate something akin to: "Jacob I have chosen as Isaac's heir and therefore heir to Abraham's covenant; Esau I have not chosen as heir."

[20]Over half the treaties now known from the ancient Near East are from the Hittite archives (Beckman, *Hittite Diplomatic Texts*, p. 1). The format of these treaties was first distilled through the study of second-millennium-B.C. Hittite treaties published in 1923 by E. F. Weidner (*Politische Dokumente aus Kleinasien* [*Boghazköi Studien* 8 and 9], 1923) and 1931 by V. Korošec, *Hethitische Staatsverträge*. As Sparks states: "Although there is some variation, the many preserved texts allow us to describe the basic form of the Hittite treaty genre. The much-discussed pattern includes six components presented in a standard order" (Kenton L. Sparks, *Ancient Texts for the Study of the Hebrew Bible*, p. 438).

[21]Arnold and Beyer, *Readings from the Ancient Near East*, p. 98; *ANET*, p. 203.

[22]See McCarthy, *Treaty and Covenant*, p. 96 and *Old Testament Covenant: A Survey of Current Opinions*, Growing Points in Theology (Atlanta: John Knox Press, 1972), p. 26.

[23]Arnold and Beyer, *Readings from the Ancient Near East*, pp. 97-98; *ANET*, pp. 205-6; cf. Delbert Hillers, *Covenant: The History of a Biblical Idea*, pp. 36-37.

[24]Arnold and Beyer, *Readings from the Ancient Near East*, p. 97; *ANET*, p. 205.

[25]George E. Mendenhall, "Covenant Forms in Israelite Tradition," pp. 50-76. In the Bible, the "Book of the Covenant" is the first recitation of the Mosaic covenant (Ex 19:1–23:19). Deuteronomy, as its name indicates (Greek *deuteros* + *nomos* meaning "second law"), is the second. In other words, Deuteronomy is the reiteration and reapplication of the contents of the Book of the Covenant to the post-wilderness generation of Israel.

[26]Sometimes my students assume that the ancients worked with something akin to eight-by-eleven-inch prefab clay tablets which were exchanged when space ran out. This is not the case. Rather, if it was at all possible, a text was placed in its entirety on a single tablet. Hence, the tablets we have from the ancient world come in a range of sizes, from an inch or two square, to twelve inches and more.

[27]The official copies of the Hittite treaties were typically inscribed on silver, with clay copies kept in the archives of both countries (Sparks, *Ancient Texts*, p. 439; cf. Beckman, *Hittite Diplomatic Texts*, p. 3). In light of this, it is interesting that Ex 32:16 speaks of the writing on Moses' tablets as "engraved" (Hebrew *ḥrt*). This particular verb is derived from Hebrew *ḥrš* and appears in the Old Testament only here; it is related to the craft of engraving on metal, stone or wood, not clay (*HALOT*, s.v. "*ḥrš*," p. 358). Moreover, it has been suggested that *ḥrt* is a loan word from the *lingua franca* of Israel's world, Aramaic (ibid., s.v. "*ḥrt*," p. 359). This loan hypothesis further substantiates the idea that Israel's covenant tradition represented a participation in an international practice and genre.

[28]Beckman, *Hittite Diplomatic Texts*, p. 91.

[29]See Kenneth A. Kitchen, "Patriarchal Age: Myth or History?" *BAR* 21, no. 2 (1995): 48-58, 88; cf. *Ancient Orient and Old Testament*, 1st ed. (Chicago: InterVarsity Press, 1966), pp. 90-102, for a helpful chart that compares these literary forms.

[30]D. J. McCarthy has attempted to argue that the historical prologue is not characteristic of the second-millennium Hittite treaties, but less than successfully (*Old Testament Covenant*, pp. 26-28, n. 29).

[31]Know, however, that the dating of the Sinai covenant as extrapolated from the literary form of secular covenants remains a matter of significant debate. Weinfeld, for example, argues that Deuteronomy must be a first-millennium document and leaves the dating of the Book of the Covenant in Exodus open ("בְּרִית *běrit*" 2:253-79). His argument is not based on the form of Deuteronomy, he agrees that the form parallels the second-millennium Hittite treaties. Rather his argument is based on the content of Deuteronomy's curse list in chapter 28. These curses parallel the curses of Assyrian king Esarhaddon's treaties from the seventh century B.C. It is certainly true that Deuteronomy 28 echoes the words of Esarhaddon too closely to be mere coincidence. Some means of transmission must have brought this list to Israel. One possibility is that it came to Israel during Esarhaddon's era, making Deuteronomy a first-millennium document. But it is more probable that the curses of Esarhaddon's treaty are not new with that particular Assyrian king but are themselves an echo of a set of stock phrases that were employed throughout the generations of the highly conservative literary typology of the monumental tradition of Mesopotamia. Hence, both Esarhaddon and Deuteronomy could be echoing phraseology that is significantly older than either text. It is also entirely possible that the curse list of Deuteronomy 28 contains later additions to what had been the original core of the book (note that the curse list comprises the final *two thirds* of the chapter as opposed to the *half* we would anticipate, and it repeats the curse section of Deuteronomy 27). As many would argue that Deuteronomy through 2 Kings was collected into a national history in the seventh century by an historian sponsored by King Josiah (cf. 2 Kings 22 and Josiah's seventh-century-B.C. discovery of the "book of the law"), it is quite possible that this first-millennium curse language found its way into Deuteronomy's *běrit* well after the book's initial composition.

[32]Another significant theological concept introduced through the *běrit* is that of canon. Meredith Kline, the man to whom this book is dedicated, first introduced me to this idea (cf. *The Structure of Biblical Authority*, 2nd ed. [Grand Rapids: Eerdmans, 1989], pp. 27-44). As a suzerain demanded that his authoritative words be written, preserved and never altered so that future generations

might know and obey, so Yahweh demands that his authoritative words be preserved in similar fashion. Kline argues, therefore, that *bĕrît* is the seedbed of the idea of canon.

[33]It is important to note that although the covenantal theology of the Bible has often been utilized as an argument for the unconditional and irresistible grace of the Reformed theological paradigm, more recent research has demonstrated that it is impossible to remove mutuality from the covenant concepts of the ancient world. As Frank M. Cross summarizes, "From the time of Wellhausen there has been the tendency to strip the term *bĕrît* 'covenant,' of any element of mutuality, or of any legal overtones, at least in its use in early contexts. . . . The covenants of Abraham and David thus are claimed to be covenants of grace, the Sinaitic covenant a covenant of law" (Cross, *From Epic to Canon*, p. 15). But the anthropological roots of this social mechanism make it obvious that mutuality is inherent: "Tribal covenants structured by kinship-in-law . . . were mutual covenants. Even the international treaties of the Hittites and the suzerainty or parity treaties of north Syrian Semites in the 2nd millennium were mutual, at least in form and language, obligations being undertaken by both parties" (ibid., p. 16). Gary Knoppers makes a similar point in "Covenant of Grant" in "Ancient Near Eastern Royal Grants and the Davidic Covenant: A Parallel?" *Journal of the American Oriental Society* 116, no. 4 (1996): 670-97 (cf. Weinfeld, "בְּרִית *bĕrît*," 270-72, and "The Covenant of Grant in the Old Testament and in the ANE," *JAOS* 90 [1970]: 184-203).

Chapter 4: God's Original Intent

[1]Jordan S. Penkower, "Verse Divisions in the Hebrew Bible," *VT* 50, no. 3 (2000): 381; cf. G. F. Moore, "The Vulgate Chapters and Numbered Verses in the Hebrew Bible," *JBL* 12, no. 1 (1893): 73.

[2]Note how Jn 1:1-18 intentionally echoes Gen 1 and serves the same literary function for the Gospel of John as does Gen 1 for the Pentateuch. Whereas Gen 1 provides a sweeping introduction to who Yahweh is, Jn 1 provides an equally magnificent introduction to the person of Christ. Both begin at the beginning and introduce their subjects by speaking in terms of their mighty acts on behalf of humanity.

[3]There is a myriad of information available regarding the debate over the earth's origins and that debate's relationship to Christian faith. This material can be found on the Internet with very little effort. But for a theological discussion of the same, my favorite is an older book by Henri Blocher, *In the Beginning: The Opening Chapters of Genesis* (Downers Grove, Ill.: InterVarsity Press, 1984).

[4]For exposure to the major creation stories of the ancient Near East, see Bill T. Arnold and Bryan E. Beyer, eds., *Readings from the Ancient Near East: Primary Sources for Old Testament Study* (Grand Rapids: Baker Academic, 2002), pp. 13-70; *ANET* 3-10, 60-100; cf. Hess and Tsumura, *I Studied Inscriptions from Before the Flood* (Winona Lake, Ind.: Eisenbrauns, 1994).

[5]See Blocher, *In the Beginning*, p.39.

[6]There are reams of material written on the interpretive theories for Gen 1. Any commentary on Genesis will offer some of this material. Two books that summarize various views, however, and are easily accessible are Blocher's *In the Beginning*, pp. 39-59, and J. P. Moreland and John Mark Reynolds, eds., *Three Views on Creation and Evolution* (Grand Rapids: Zondervan, 1999). The former has more to do with the interpretation of Genesis, the latter has more to do with coordinating that interpretation with science.

[7]In the 1917 revised version of this influential study Bible, the commentary on Gen 1:2 reads as follows: "Jeremiah 4:23-27; Isaiah 24:1; 45:18 clearly indicate that the earth had undergone a cataclysmic change as the result of divine judgment. The face of the earth bears everywhere the marks of such a catastrophe. There are not wanting intimations which connect it with a previous

testing and fall of angels. See Ezekiel 28:12-15; Isaiah 14:9-14 which certainly go beyond the kings of Tyre and Babylon."

[8]See Bruce K. Waltke, "Genesis 1," *BSac* 132 (1975): 25-36, 136-44, 216-28, 327-42, 133 (1976): 28-42.

[9]A sample bibliography on this topic includes Weston W. Fields, *Unformed and Unfilled* (Nutley, N.J.: Presbyterian & Reformed, 1976); Duane T. Gish, *Evolution: The Fossils Say No* (San Diego: ICR, 1973); Walter E. Lammerts, ed., *Scientific Studies in Special Creation* (Nutley, N.J.: Presbyterian & Reformed, 1971); Henry M. Morris, *Biblical Cosmology and Modern Science* (Nutley, N.J.: Craig, 1972); *The Remarkable Birth of Planet Earth* (San Diego: ICR, 1973); *Scientific Creationism* (San Diego: Creation Life, 1974); Edward J. Young, *Studies in Genesis One* (Grand Rapids: Baker, 1964); and Paul A. Zimmerman, ed., *Creation, Evolution and God's Word* (St. Louis: Concordia, 1972).

[10]Many would identify this theory under the category of "Progressive Creationism." See Robert C. Newman, "Progressive Creationism," in *Three Views on Creation and Evolution*, pp. 105-58.

[11]E.g., Gen 2:4 ; 35:3; Ex 6:28; Num 3:1; Ps 90:4. See *HALOT*, s.v. "תּוֹלֵדוֹת" meanings 3, 4, 7, 10 (pp. 400-401).

[12]See Blocher, *In the Beginning*, p. 45.

[13]Meredith G. Kline, *Kingdom Prologue I* (Meredith G. Kline, 1986), p. 30.

[14]*HALOT*, s.v. "שָׁבַת" (p. 1407).

[15]Blocher, *In the Beginning*, p. 57.

[16]Don Francisco, "Adam, Where Are You?" *He's Alive* (Newport Beach, Calif.: Ministry Music, 1997).

[17]Although Genesis makes it clear that we are to associate Eve (Hebrew *hawwâ*) with "all the living" (cf. Hebrew *hayyâ*), like the etymologies of many of the biblical names, the exact linguistic connection is uncertain. See *HALOT* s.v. "חַוָּה" (p. 296) and "חַי" (p. 307).

[18]Daniel Fleming, "By the Sweat of your Brow: Adam, Anat, Athirat and Ashurbanipal," *Ugarit and the Bible: Proceedings of the International Symposium on Ugarit and the Bible Manchester, September 1992* (Munster: Ugarit-Verlag, 1994).

[19]C. S. Lewis, *The Great Divorce* (New York: Macmillan, 1952), p. 73.

Chapter 5: God's Final Intent

[1]Othmar Keel, *The Symbolism of the Biblical World*, trans. Timothy J. Hallett (Winona Lake, Ind.: Eisenbrauns, 1997), pp. 170-71. There is still debate as to whether or not the biblical cherubim should be broadly associated with other such composite creatures in the ancient Near East. See Freedman and O'Conner, "כְּרוּב *kĕrûb*," *TDOT*, 7:314-19.

[2]For images see Elie Borowski, "Cherubim: God's Throne?" *BAR* 21, no. 4 (July/August 1995) or James B. Pritchard, *The Ancient Near East Vol. 2: An Anthology of Texts and Pictures* (Princeton, N.J.: Princeton University Press, 1958), plates 163, 165, 166. See as well the websites for the Oriental Institute of the University of Chicago (April 30, 2008) <http://oi.uchicago.edu/museum/highlights/assyria.html>, and the British Museum (April 30, 2008) <http://www.thebritishmuseum.ac.uk/explore/galleries/middle_east/room_10c_assyria_khorsabad.aspx>.

[3]Keel, *Symbolism of the Biblical World*, p. 123.

[4]Ibid., pp. 168-71.

[5]To see an image of Ahiram's sarcophagus and explore the archaeological background of this piece, see the Beirut National Museum website at <http://www.beirutnationalmuseum.com/e-collection-bronze.htm>. Ironically, an even better image of this sarcophagus, in which Ahiram's cherubim throne is fully visible, is available at Wikipedia at <http://en.wikipedia.org/wiki/Ahiram> (April 30, 2008).

[6]Keel, *Symbolism of the Biblical World*, pp. 168-71; H. Seyrig, "Trônes phéniciens flanqués de sphinx," *Syria* 36 (1959), and de Vaux, "Les chérubins et l'arche d'alliance, les sphinx gardiens et les trônes divins dans l'ancien Orient," *Melanges de l'Université St. Joseph* 37 (1960/1961), pp. 91-124, 245-52.

[7]For a discussion of the decorative themes of Solomon's temple in light of ancient Near East archaeology as well as illustrations, see Victor Hurowitz, "Inside Solomon's Temple," *BR* 10, no. 2 (April 1994): 24-37. For a more technical presentation, see Keel, *Symbolism of the Biblical World*, pp. 163-70.

[8]Ezekiel was a priest in Jerusalem taken into exile during the first deportation in 598 B.C. Thus, he was taken captive before the fall of Jerusalem and the razing of the temple. But his ministry as a prophet and a community leader in Babylon extended through these horrific events, during which he was closely tied to the Jerusalem community. In Ezek 24:25-27 he speaks of the fall of the city, and in Ezek 11:22-25, by prophetic vision, he witnesses the unimaginable—Yahweh departing from his ruined temple.

[9]As we continue through this chapter we find the biblical author describing the New Jerusalem with every hyperbolic modifier that he can generate. John speaks of this city as having foundations made of precious jewels, streets of gold and gates of pearl. Moreover, just like the holy of holies, just like Ezekiel's temple, John's city is perfectly square (Rev 21:16-17).

Chapter 6: Noah and Abraham

[1]See the discussion in chapter two, "Adam."

[2]Flooding was due in part to the annual early spring snowmelt in the mountains of eastern Turkey where both rivers originate, and in part to the low-lying alluvial plain between the rivers. This plain between the Tigris and Euphrates offers almost no resistance to flooding. In fact, this plain was formed in part by flooding and might be better described as a "double-delta." But the rich soil and availability of water for irrigation made this area extremely attractive for early settlement and agriculture. This is confirmed by the scores of ancient settlements on the plain and the fact that it is riddled with equally ancient canal systems and levees. Currently, flooding in this region is controlled by heavy (and controversial) damming (see "The Tigris-Euphrates River Dispute," ICE Case Studies [April 30, 2008] <http://www.american.edu/ted/ice/tigris.htm>).

[3]See James Sauer, "The River Runs Dry," *BAR* 22, no. 4 (July/August 1996): 56, for a sidebar on Wooley's excavation at Ur.

[4]The Gilgamesh Epic was first discovered in 1872 by George Smith among the tablets of Ashurbanipal's library stored in the British Museum. Smith's tablet dates from the seventh century B.C., but the story itself probably dates back to 2600 B.C. See Bill T. Arnold and Bryan E. Beyer, eds., *Readings from the Ancient Near East: Primary Sources for Old Testament Study* (Grand Rapids: Baker Academic, 2002), pp. 66-70; cf. James B. Pritchard, ed., *Ancient Near Eastern Texts Relating to the Old Testament*, 3rd ed. (Princeton, N.J.: Princeton University Press, 1969), pp. 93-97.

[5]The most complete version we have of the Epic of Atrahasis is an Old Babylonian copy dating from c. 1650 B.C. See Arnold and Beyer, *Readings from the Ancient Near East*, pp. 21-31; cf. *ANET*, pp. 104-6.

[6]The tablet containing Ziusudra's story was discovered at Nippur and first published in 1914. See *ANET*, pp. 42-44.

[7]As the Epic of Atrahasis illustrates, the Mesopotamian belief was that humanity had been created as a slave race—to do the manual labor that the lesser gods did not want to do. One of these tasks was food preparation. In the worldview of the ancient Near East, sacrifice was done to feed the deity. Thus, for the Mesopotamians, wiping out humanity meant no food for the gods. In the

Epics of Atrahasis and Gilgamesh the narrator details how the gods had not thought through this aspect of their plan. So when the hero offered sacrifice after exiting the boat "[the gods sniffed] the smell, they gathered [like flies] over the offering" (Arnold and Beyer, *Readings from the Ancient Near East*, pp. 21, 30; cf. p. 69). Full bellies resulted in softened attitudes. The gods decided to let humanity live and to control their population by means of infant mortality instead of future floods (ibid., p. 31).

[8]Cf. Gen 8:6-12 and Arnold and Beyer, *Readings from the Ancient Near East*, p. 69.

[9]The original version of this list probably dates to 2100 B.C., the early part of the III Dynasty of Ur (Michael Roaf, *Cultural Atlas of Mesopotamia* [Oxford: Equinox, 1990], p. 82). See *ANET*, pp. 265-66; Arnold and Beyer, *Readings from the Ancient Near East*, pp. 150-51 (for the antediluvian section of this list).

[10]*ANET*, p. 265.

[11]Arnold and Beyer, *Readings from the Ancient Near East*, p. 69. The clay imagery here is significant because in Mesopotamia nearly all architecture was constructed of mud brick. There were very few trees in the region, and less stone. Moreover, one did not fire mud brick (it would take forever to amass enough building supplies for the most humble structure); rather, bricks were simply dried in the sun. Thus most everything in Mesopotamia was built of (clay) mud. And when exposed to excessive amounts of water (i.e., a flood), most everything would return to mud. As Ut-napishtim looks out on his world once the waters had receded he states: "The landscape was as level as a flat roof" (ibid.). Comparing these images to what we know of the creation of humanity in Gen 2, it would seem that just as a mud brick building would sink back into the mud of the field after a flood, so humanity sinks back into the clay of its creation after this judgment. The post-flood world was "washed clean," showing no evidence that humanity had ever been.

[12]A number of people have attempted to connect Noah's flood with an ancient worldwide disaster that may be identified by means of the fossil record. Probably the most technical is Walt Brown's hydroplate theory. See *In the Beginning: Compelling Evidence for Creation and the Flood* (Phoenix: Center for Scientific Creation, 1995). His website is <http://www.creationscience.com/online-book/IntheBeginningTOC.html> (April 30, 2008).

[13]See Arnold and Beyer, *Readings from the Ancient Near East*, p. 42.

[14]The same theme reappears in the Canaanite epic of Baal. In his youth, Baal had to defeat the sea-god Yam in order to preserve life on the earth (Arnold and Beyer, *Readings from the Ancient Near East*, pp. 50-62).

[15]See chapter four, "God's Original Intent," and the sidebar "The Image of God."

[16]John Sailhamer offers a brief but thoughtful literary assessment of this difficult pericope in *The Pentateuch as Narrative* (Grand Rapids: Zondervan, 1992), pp. 129-30.

[17]*HALOT*, s.v. "II פתה," p. 985.

[18]*HALOT*, s.v. "בנע," pp. 484-85

[19]See James B. Pritchard, ed., *The HarperCollins Concise Atlas of the Bible* (New York: HarperSanFrancisco, 1991), pp. 58-59.

[20]Jude 1:6 reads: "And angels who did not keep their own domain, but abandoned their proper abode, He has kept in eternal bonds under darkness for the judgment of the great day." As "sons of God" is a title applied to non-angels as well as angels, and Jude 1:6 does not actually speak of the fallen angels copulating with human women, the source of the interpretation above might seem a bit obscure. But the source of this idea is clarified when one considers the pseudepigraphical book of Enoch in which a major theme is the evil brought to our earth by fallen angels ("sons of God") who were coupling with the daughters of men in Gen 6. Although an important source of information on the intertestamental era, the documents belonging to

the Pseudepigrapha lie outside the canon. They are "pseudepigraphic" in that they are writings attributed to someone who did not write them. These documents are typically understood as works written in honor of and/or inspired by Old Testament heroes. First Enoch was written around the second century B.C., and claims to have been written by Noah's great-grandfather Enoch (George Eldon Ladd "Apocalyptic Literature," *ISBE*, 1:156; George Eldon Ladd, "Pseudepigrapha," *ISBE*, 3:1040).

[21]See John Sailhamer, "Genesis," *The Expositor's Bible Commentary*, Frank E. Gaebelein, ed. (Grand Rapids: Zondervan, 1990), 2:76; cf. *Pentateuch as Narrative*, p. 120 n. 43.

[22]Whereas "Seth cherished the pure and lawful worship of God, from which the rest had fallen," for the line of Seth to mix with the line of Cain was 'the most extreme disorder' and resulted in Seth's line becoming 'degenerate'" (John Calvin, *Genesis*, trans. John King [1847; reprint, Edinburgh: Banner of Truth Trust, 1984], pp. 237-39; cf. Sailhamer, *Pentateuch as Narrative*, p. 120 n. 45). Calvin's view was propagated in the Scofield Bible and is still broadly held today.

[23]See Sailhamer, *Pentateuch as Narrative*, pp. 120-22.

[24]Ibid., p. 121.

[25]If this noun and its spelling are indeed native to biblical Hebrew, then its *qātil* form indicates that it must be a resultative noun indicating one's "(having) fallen." Thus, a "fallen" angel, a morally "fallen" individual, or a warrior who will "be fallen" in battle some day. If it is a phonemically adapted loanword that did not originate as a *qātil*, or if it is a term "for officials and other terms for individuals in legal or cultic contexts," then the term might have to do with "those who cause to fall," which, considering its application to warriors and heroes, is worth pursuing (see John Huehnergard, "*qātil* and *qetil* Nouns in Biblical Hebrew," in Moshe Bar-Asher Festschrift, ed. Steven E. Fassberg and Aharon Maman [Jerusalem: Magnes, forthcoming]).

[26]We actually have no evidence that angels have either male or female body parts (and therefore the capacity to have intercourse). Moreover, this interpretation of Gen 6:1-4 has much more in common with the cavorting capers of the Greek gods and goddesses than it does with the monotheistic witness of the biblical text. Hendel actually makes a formal comparison between Gen 6 and the Greek tradition regarding the motive of the Trojan War. Although this suggestion helps us to understand how the Greeks would have read Gen 6, it does little (or nothing) to educate us as to how the Hebrews did (Ronald S. Hendel, "Of Demigods and the Deluge: toward an Interpretation of Genesis 6:1-4," *JBL* 106, no. 1 [1987]: 12-26).

[27]The phrase "men of the name" is related to several ancient idioms coming out of Mesopotamia, all of which are related to preserving one's name for posterity. To be a person of "name" was to be famous. And a primary means of fame in the ancient world was military exploits (Richter, *The Deuteronomistic History and the Name Theology*, pp. 127-205).

[28]The LXX (the early Greek translation of the Hebrew text of the Old Testament) translates the Hebrew word *nĕpilîm* as "giants" (Greek *gigantes*).

[29]Cf. Num 14:3, 43; 2 Kings 19:7; Is 3:25; 37:7; Jer 19:7; 20:4; Ezek 5:12; 11:10; Hos 7:16; 13:16; Amos 7:17; cf. Gen 43:18; Judg 4:16; 1 Kings 20:25; and H. Seebass, "נָפַל *nāpal*," *TDOT*, 9:494.

[30]It has long been recognized that the genre of Gen 2–11 is a bit peculiar, at least from our modern perspective. I believe the best explanation is that this material is truly archaic. Plausibly the oldest material we have in the Bible, Gen 2–11 probably began as oral tradition that was narrowed over the centuries in order to communicate the redemptive truths critical to the biblical authors in the most concise fashion possible.

[31]The proposed biblical dating emerges from a chronological benchmark found in Solomon's account of the building of the temple. According to 1 Kings 6:1, Solomon began construction in his fourth regnal year. As we can confirm Solomon's ascension year as c. 970 B.C. from

contemporaneous records out of Mesopotamia, this places the date of the temple in 966 B.C. Solomon claims that this is 480 years after the exodus, which places the exodus at 1446 B.C. When the records in Ex 12:40; Gen 47:9; Gen 25:26; Gen 21:5; Gen 12:4 are compared, we come up with a date for Abraham c. 2000 B.C. But keep in mind that it is entirely possible that Solomon's 480 years (12 x 40) is a stylized number and not intended to communicate "hard" chronological data.

[32]For details on these urban features as well as diagrams and images see Amihai Mazar, *Archaeology of the Land of the Bible: 10,000-586 B.C.E.* (New York: Doubleday, 1990), pp. 174-231; cf. *Harper-Collins Concise Atlas of the Bible*, pp. 52-53.

[33]Mari was an extremely important city in the nineteenth and eighteenth centuries B.C. The more than 20,000 documents recovered from its palace archives include a detailed correspondence between government officials within the city and those on the frontier. Much of this correspondence deals with how to administrate the nomadic populace in a fashion that would not exacerbate tribal factions or violate territorial allotments while protecting the interests of the crown. An introduction to the Mari period may be found in Roaf's *Cultural Atlas of Mesopotamia*, pp. 114-19.

[34]See Dan Fleming, "Genesis in History and Tradition: The Syrian Background of Israel's Ancestors, Reprise" in *The Future of Biblical Archaeology: The Proceedings of a Symposium, August 12-14, 2001*, ed. James K. Hoffmeier and Alan Millard (Grand Rapids: Eerdmans, 2004).

[35]*Archaeology of the Land of the Bible*, p. 225.

[36]"In summary, from the MB Age on there was no region of the Levant that had not been influenced by the Amorite language and culture in various ways and various degrees. Their cultural and linguistic influence was a lasting one. . . . It is equally clear that the Amorite populations were themselves drastically modified by the various cultures into which they became integrated in the later phases of the Bronze Age, so that eventually they ceased to exist as a distinct cultural group" (George Mendenhall, "Amorites," *ABD*, 1:202).

[37]See Moshe Weinfeld, "The Covenant of Grant in the Old Testament and in the ANE," *JAOS* 90 (1970): 184-203, and "בְּרִית bĕrît," *TDOT*, 2:270-72). Although many have attempted to identify these royal grants as entirely promissory (no obligations involved), further research into the secular profile of these patron/client agreements demonstrates that mutuality was still present (see chapter three, "The Concept of Covenant," n. 34; Gary Knoppers, "Ancient Near Eastern Royal Grants and the Davidic Covenant: A Parallel?" *JAOS* 116, no. 4 [1996]: 670-97).

[38]The name *Sarai* seems to be an older, Amorite version of *Sarah*, as is demonstrated by female names found in Ugaritic and Amorite texts (Victor Hamilton, *The Book of Genesis 1-17*, NICOT [Grand Rapids: Eerdmans, 1990], p. 476; E. A. Speiser, *Genesis*, AB [Garden City, N.Y.: Doubleday, 1964], p. 125 n. 15).

[39]For images see Philip J. King, "Circumcision: Who Did It, Who Didn't and Why?" *BAR* 32, no. 4 (July/August 2006): 48-55. Cf. Geraldine Pinch, "Private Life in Ancient Egypt," *CANE*, 1:377-78.

[40]Pinch, "Private Life in Ancient Egypt," and Herman te Velde, "Theology, Priests, and Worship in Ancient Egypt," *CANE*, 3:1733.

[41]For a variety of views on baptism in an accessible format, see Thomas J. Nettles et al., *Understanding Four Views On Baptism* (Grand Rapids: Zondervan, 2000).

Chapter 7: Moses and the Tabernacle

[1]See chapter six, "Noah and Abraham," n. 31.

[2]I am indebted to my colleague Lawson G. Stone for the following chart which communicates the discrepancy indicated above.

Wilderness	40 years	E.g. Deut. 1:3
Conquest up to Josh 14	5 or 7 years	Cf. Josh. 14:7, 10
Joshua Post-conquest	X (45 years?)	
Post-Joshua Period	Y	
Judges	410 years	
Eli	40 years	1 Sam 4:18, LXX gives only 20 years
Career of Samuel	20+?	
Saul	Z	
David	40 years	1 Kings 2:11
Solomon to Temple	4 years	1 Kings 6:1
Total	559 years + X + Y + Z	

X= the undetermined number of years after Joshua—ninety years? Period Y= the unknown period from Joshua's death to the first judge. Although we don't know the length of the apostasy before the first judge, it must have been long enough for the legacy of that whole generation to be lost. Z is the reign of Saul, which we don't know from Old Testament sources. If the New Testament reference is accepted, we have forty years for Saul. (Lawson G. Stone, "Doing the Numbers: The Challenge of Old Testament Chronology," unpublished paper, 2007).

[3]For maps of these trade routes, see *The HarperCollins Concise Atlas of the Bible*, pp. 15, 37.

[4]"Under the Akkad Empire (2371-2191 B.C.), a decent slave fetched 10-15 silver shekels, though the price dropped slightly to 10 shekels during the Third Dynasty of Ur (2113-2006 B.C.). In the second millennium B.C., during the early Babylonian period, the price of slaves rose to about 20 shekels, as we know from the Laws of Hammurabi and documents from Mari and elsewhere from the 19th and 18th centuries B.C. By the 14th and 13th centuries B.C., at Nuzi and Ugarit, the price crept up to 30 shekels and sometimes more. Another five hundred years later, Assyrian slave markets demanded 50 to 60 shekels for slaves; and under the Persian Empire (fifth and fourth centuries B.C.), soaring inflation pushed prices up to 90 and 120 shekels" (Kenneth Kitchen, "Patriarchal Age: Myth or History?" *BAR* 21, no. 2 [March/April 1995]: 52).

[5]Ibid.; cf. the Laws of Hammurabi, sections 116, 214 and 252; G. Boyer, *Archives Royales de Mari VIII* (Paris: Imprimerie Nationale, 1958), p. 23; and M. Van De Mieroop, *Archiv für Orientforschung* 34 (1987): 10, 11.

[6]The Papyrus Brooklyn 35.1446 lists the servants in a large Egyptian household in 1740 B.C., seventy-nine total. Over forty of those servants have Semitic names. Such evidence indicates that Semites made up a large segment of the slave immigrant working-class in the Middle Bronze Period (James K. Hoffmeier, *Israel in Egypt*, p. 61; cf. *The Harper Atlas of the Bible*, p. 36).

[7]See chapter six, "Abraham's real time." The name of this group derives from two Egyptian words, *hekau khasut*, meaning "foreign rulers." These were Semites, and their arrival in Egypt was part of the second-millennium spread of "Amorite" culture. The Hyksos settled in the eastern Delta and founded a local dynasty, designated in Egyptian history as the Fifteenth Dynasty (Mazar, *Archaeology of the Land of the Bible*, pp. 191-92).

[8]See *HarperCollins Concise Atlas of the Bible*, pp. 18-19 and Hoffmeier, *Israel in Egypt*, pp. 83-95 for details and images.

[9]Hoffmeier states: "Throughout the millennia, Egypt's lush Delta was like a magnet to the pastoral nomads of the Sinai and Canaan. . . . As early as Dynasty I the pharaoh had to defend Egypt's borders and commercial interests in Sinai from troublesome Bedouin" (*Israel in Egypt*, pp. 53-54).

[10]The epigraphic evidence for this forceful immigration, and the defenses Egypt designed to resist it, includes the The Instruction of Merikare (Tenth Dynasty) and The Prophecy of Neferti (Twelfth Dynasty). The former speaks of the ongoing problem with "the miserable Asiatic" in

the Delta and a resulting plan to build canals ("the Dividing Waters") to augment the eastern defense system. The latter speaks of the Semites in poetic and prophetic terms: "[a] strange bird will reproduce in the marsh of the Delta, having made its nest by the people; the people have caused it (the bird) to approach because of want. . . . One will build the 'Walls of the Ruler,' life prosperity and health, to prevent Asiatics from going down into Egypt. They beg for water in the customary manner in order to let their flocks drink" (Hoffmeier, *Israel in Egypt*, pp. 58-59). There is also unequivocal evidence that the Middle Bronze trade connection between Egypt and Phoenician Byblos was so significant that there were Semitic enclaves in the Delta region and Egyptian officials permanently appointed to Byblos and its environs (Mazar, *Archaeology of the Land of the Bible*, pp. 214-18; cf. the Egyptian tale of Wen-Amon, Arnold and Beyer, *Readings from the ANE*, pp. 212-14).

[11]Along this wadi is one of the primary highways east out of Egypt. Seventy-one ancient sites have been excavated here, mostly villages and campsites, although five could be classified as cities. Twenty-one of them show Middle Bronze II Levantine materials. "The comparison of materials . . . suggest that during Egypt's Second Intermediate Period, Semitic-speaking peoples at opposite ends of the socioeconomic spectrum resided in Egypt" (Hoffmeier, *Israel in Egypt*, pp. 65-68).

[12]Although the exact location of "Goshen" is unknown, the Bible makes it clear that it may be found in the eastern delta, was suitable for flocks and was associated with "the land of Rameses" (Gen 47:11). The Wadi Tumilat is also in the eastern Nile delta and had long supported Semitic pastoralists. I suspect that the two regions overlap; I. Rabinowitz has made a linguistic argument which makes this specific connection ("Aramaic Inscriptions of the Fifth Century B.C. from a North-Arab Shrine in Egypt," *JNES* 15 [1956]: 1-9, esp. 5).

[13]See n. 7. Regarding the Hyksos capital city, Avaris, Donald Redford states: "The domestic and cultic character of the quadrants excavated owed nothing to Egyptian culture, being wholly of northern, Levantine inspiration. . . . The extent of Asiatic occupation in the Delta in the 17th and 16th centuries B.C. as revealed by recent archaeological work, is confined to the eastern Bubasite branch of the Nile and the Wadi Tumilat, thus the eastern fringe of the Delta" (*Egypt, Canaan, and Israel in Ancient Times* [Princeton, N.J.: Princeton University Press, 1992], p. 115).

[14]Hoffmeier reports that beginning in the early part of the Eighteenth Dynasty and extending until the accession of Rameses II (when many date the exodus), Egypt was "teeming" with Semites who were utilized as a slave populace (*Israel in Egypt*, pp. 112-16). For images see Hoffmeier, "Out of Egypt: The Archaeological Context of the Exodus," *BAR* 33, no. 1 (January/February 2007): 30-41.

[15]A very accessible and well-illustrated article that reviews the external evidence for the exodus in comparison to the Bible's testimony is Kevin D. Miller's "Did the Exodus Never Happen?" *Christianity Today*, September 7, 1998, pp. 44-51.

[16]Hoffmeier, *Israel in Egypt*, pp. 117-19.

[17]See Hoffmeier on the practice of adopting the "children of the chieftains" during the New Kingdom era (*Israel in Egypt*, pp. 142-43).

[18]It is significant that the nature and order of the plagues may be related to the annual inundation of the Nile River. When the inundation did not go well, the steady agricultural cycle the Nile fostered was thrown into very predictable disarray. The first nine of the ten plagues follow the order of those predictable problems of nature (James Hoffmeier, "The Plagues of Egypt," *ABD*, 2:374-78). As the Egyptians understood that it was the divine power of the Pharaoh that kept the Nile in line, the fact that Yahweh disrupted the inundation effectively demonstrated that he was greater than Pharaoh and his power superseded that of Egypt's gods.

[19]Jon D. Levenson, *Sinai and Zion: An Entry into the Jewish Bible*, p. 23.

[20]See *HarperCollins Concise Atlas*, pp. 34-35 for details. For a thorough discussion of the Num 33 itinerary, see Charles Krahmalkov, "Exodus Itinerary Confirmed by Egyptian Evidence," *BAR* 20, no. 5 (September/October 1994): 54-62, 79. Although we cannot be sure that present-day Jebel Musa (Arabic for "Mountain of Moses") is indeed the Sinai of Israel's wanderings, Jebel Musa is certainly a likely location. Tradition has long identified this as the correct spot as is evident from the Monastery of St. Catherine, built at the foot of the mountain in the fourth century A.D. as Helena's Chapel.

[21]G.R. Osborne, "Type, Typology," *Evangelical Dictionary of Theology*, Walter A. Elwell, ed. (Grand Rapids: Baker, 1984), pp. 1117-18.

[22]Ibid.

[23]Lev 16 describes the Day of Atonement as an annual ritual designed to purify the sanctuary by sprinkling it with the blood of two communal sin offerings (one for the priesthood and one for the people) and to purify the people by laying their sins upon a "scapegoat," who was then driven out of the camp and into the wilderness.

[24]Walter C. Kaiser, "Exodus," *The Expositor's Bible Commentary*, 2:467.

[25]W. S. LaSor, D. A. Hubbard and F. W. Bush offer a helpful summary of the various categories of Mosaic sacrifice in *Old Testament Survey*, 2nd ed. (Grand Rapids: Eerdmans, 1996), p. 83. It is important to realize that out of the eight categories listed, only one involved the complete holocaust of the sacrificial victim. In contrast to what most Christians typically imagine, the bulk of the sacrificed animal was normally returned to the worshipper so that he and his family might feast together in God's presence. In other words, the act of sacrifice was usually a time of joyous fellowship with one's family and one's God at the holy site. These holy days were truly "holidays." In fact, throughout the law code of Deuteronomy, which is focused on proper worship of Yahweh at the central holy site, the repeated command is to "eat" and to "rejoice" in Yahweh's presence (Deut 12:7, 12, 18; 14:26; 16:11, 14; 26:10-11; 27:7). God was not interested in taking from these people the little they had; rather, he was interested in them bringing a portion of what he had given them into his presence so that he might enjoy their joy with them.

[26]The Hebrew for "tabernacle" is the noun *miškān*, which derives from the verb *šākan*, meaning "to dwell." Thus, the word "tabernacle" literally means "the place of dwelling," and Ex 25:8 reads: "let them construct a sanctuary *[miškān]* for me, so that I may dwell *[šākantî]* among them." The word play is obvious. Noting that the Greek equivalent for Hebrew *šākan* is *skēnoō* (σκηνόω), note a similar wordplay in Jn 1:14: "And the Word became flesh and *eskēnōsen* [ἐσκήνωσεν "tablernacled/dwelt"] among us."

[27]For a detailed treatment of Paul's use of "the law," "the works of the law," etc., see James D. G. Dunn, *Jesus, Paul, and the Law: Studies in Mark and Galatians* (Louisville, Ky.: Westminster John Knox Press, 1990), and Scott Hafemann, *Paul, Moses, and the History of Israel* (Peabody, Mass.: Hendrickson, 1996).

[28]See David Daube, *The New Testament and Rabbinic Judaism* (Peabody, Mass.: Hendrickson, 1956), pp. 55-62; cf. Jacob Neusner, *The Way of Torah: An Introduction to Judaism* (Belmont, Calif.: Wadsworth, 1993), pp. 64-74.

[29]Hafemann, *Paul, Moses*, pp. 132-33.

[30]William J. Dumbrell makes the statement that "though Israel would prove unworthy, it will come as no surprise, given the nature of (God) that the ideals of the Sinai covenant will not be jettisoned, but will find new expression in the . . . new covenant" (*Faith of Israel: A Theological Survey of the Old Testament*, 2nd ed. [Grand Rapids: Baker Academic, 2002] p. 41). Scott Hafemann adds to this by saying that Jesus is "the divinely promised answer to the perennial problem of Israel's heard-hearted rebellion against Yahweh" (Hafemann, *Paul, Moses*, p. 129). That in him "a

harmony between God's laws and the inward desires . . . the ability to *keep* the Law, as a result of having a transformed nature" becomes possible (ibid., pp. 131-32). Thus, whereas the law is just and it taught us our sin, in Christ we are able to change and truly fulfill God's law.

Chapter 8: David and the Monarchy

[1]For details and images regarding the post-exilic, Jewish community see *The HarperCollins Concise Atlas of the Bible*, ed. James B. Pritchard (San Francisco: HarperSanFrancisco, 1991), pp. 90-103. For a more exhaustive treatment, see *The Oxford History of the Biblical World*, ed. Michael D. Coogan (New York: Oxford University Press, 1998), pp. 276-387.

[2]For a synopsis of this transition, see the *HarperCollins Concise Atlas*, pp. 44-48. For a technical treatment see Amihai Mazar, *Archaeology of the Land of the Bible: 10,000-586 B.C.E.* (New York: Doubleday, 1990), pp. 295-402, and Israel Finkelstein and Nadav Na'aman, eds., *From Nomadism to Monarchy: Archaeological and Historical Aspects of Early Israel* (Jerusalem: Israel Exploration Society, 1994).

[3]See the previous note and Robert Wilson, "Reconstructing Israel's History: An Anthropological Perspective on Israelite Society in the Period of the Judges," in *Sociological Approaches to the Old Testament*, Guides to Biblical Scholarship (Philadelphia: Fortress Press, 1984), pp. 30-53. Much of the conflict associated with such a transition involves the fact that individual tribal leaders would have to surrender some of their power to the new monarch and his government. In addition, the unavoidable reality was that one of the tribes—by virtue of their kinship to the king— would gain a favored status. Prior to Saul, there had been several self-aborting attempts toward monarchy in Israel. The paradigmatic example is the story of Gideon and his son, Abimelech, in Judg 8:22–9:57.

[4]See *HALOT* s.v. "מָשַׁח," pp. 643-44 and K. Seybold "מָשַׁח" *TDOT* ix: 49-54. Cf. Roland de Vaux's chapter on coronation rites, *Ancient Israel: Its Life and Institutions*, pp. 102-7.

[5]I would like to thank my colleague Bill Arnold for this particular insight. See his commentary *1 and 2 Samuel*, NIV Application Commentary (Grand Rapids: Zondervan, 2003), p. 230.

[6]Note that the tribe of Benjamin was one of the smaller tribes and centrally located within Israel. This may have added to Saul's political attractiveness in that the other tribal leaders did not see Benjamin as a substantial threat to their personal power and influence. Thus, although Saul was indeed a northerner, at least he was a southern northerner! Note as well that the book of Judges sets us up for suspicion regarding Saul's potential success by its regular condemnation of the moral character and political loyalty of this particular tribe. In contrast, the book of Ruth demonstrates that even in the era of the judges, integrity mattered. And Ruth is, of course, *David's* ancestress.

[7]Assaf Yassar-Landau argues for a land-based migration. He argues that as the "Sea Peoples" were from post-collapse culture of Mycanaea, they were unable to organize the resources necessary for a large-scale sea migration. ("One if by Sea . . . Two if by Land: How Did the Philistines Get to Canaan?" *BAR* 29, no. 2 [March/April]). See Tristan Barako's critique in the same article (ibid.).

[8]Two of the collections in the book of Psalms are attributed to David, Ps 3–41 and Ps 51–71; and seventy-three times we read that an individual psalm was *lĕdāwîd*, meaning "belonging to" or "dedicated to David." Although this designation does not necessarily indicate that David *wrote* all (or any) of these psalms, it is clear that the Israelite people associated him with the best of their earliest temple music. See Bernard W. Anderson, *Out of the Depths* (Philadelphia: Westminster Press, 1983), pp. 28-36.

[9]This term is unique in the Old Testament and may be translated "the man-in-between, a certain man-in-between (the ranks)." This might be a generic term for infantryman (thus, Goliath is simply being identified as a member of the Philistine infantry), or as Roland de Vaux argued

years ago, this phrase might specifically mean "champion." The latter would indicate that Goliath was the one who always stepped forward for this sort of contest (Kyle McCarter, *1 Samuel*, AB 8 [Garden City, N.Y.: Doubleday, 1980], pp. 290-91 n. 4a).

[10]This sort of single-champion combat was uncommon practice among the Israelites, but was quite common among the Mycaneans and Greeks from whom the Philistines descended. A famous Greek example would be the contest of Hector and Ajax during the Trojan War.

[11]An interesting discussion of Goliath's height, weight, armor and giant warriors in the ancient Near East is Clyde E. Billington's "Goliath and the Exodus Giants: How Tall Were They?" *JETS* 50, no. 3 (September 2007): 480-508, and J. Daniel Hays response, "The Height of Goliath," 509-17.

[12]We should not underestimate the ancient slingers. These were prized military men, and reports from the ancient world indicate that a well-hurled stone could travel well over a hundred miles an hour. For an image see Yigael Yadin, *The Art of Warfare in Biblical Lands: In the Light of Archaeological Study* (New York: McGraw-Hill, 1963), p. 364.

[13]We know this because of the records of Nebuchadnezzar II. When the Babylonian king first conquered Jerusalem in 598 B.C., he deposed the Israelite monarch, Jehoiakin, who had rebelled against him and replaced him with his relative Zedekiah (2 Kings 24:17). Nebuchadnezzar speaks of Zedekiah as: *šarra ša libbīšu,* "a king of his heart." The Babylonian Chronicles, *ABC* #5:11-13 (p. 102); cf. McCarter, *1 Samuel,* p. 229, and Phil Long, *Reign and Rejection* (Atlanta: Scholars Press, 1989), pp. 92-93.

[14]I have written on this dialogue in *The Deuteronomistic History and the Name Theology: lĕšakkēn šĕmô šām in the Bible and the Ancient Near East,* BZAW 318 (Berlin: Walter de Gruyter, 2002), pp. 69-75. Significant to the exchange between Yahweh and David is the fact that in the world of the ancient Near East, kingship and temple building were inextricably linked. As the servant of the gods and the conduit through which the gods interacted with the nation, prominent among a king's royal duties was the building and maintenance of the patron deity's temple. Thus, it was customary for the newly crowned king, especially a usurper (which David was), to celebrate his ascension by building or refurbishing a temple for the deity who had assisted him in the successful acquisition of the throne. According to Thorkild Jacobsen, one motivation behind such temple-building was to ensure the presence (and patronage) of the deity. For the new king, the divine presence meant the security of his throne (see Thorkild Jacobsen, *Treasures of Darkness* [New Haven, Conn.: Yale University Press, 1976], pp. 14-16). With this lens, we see that David's passion for temple-building was probably something less than selfless piety, and Yahweh's harsh response to David begins to make sense. David is being rebuked for attempting to manipulate Yahweh and for patterning his kingship according to the model of neighboring nations. But note that even in the midst of this rebuke, Yahweh does answer David's real concern—the security of his throne.

[15]See n. 4 in this chapter.

[16]Here is another wonderful story of redemption. Solomon was *Bathsheba's* son. David's most public failure was his adultery with this woman, and his most self-serving, politically corrupt action as king was his conspiracy to orchestrate the death of her innocent (and loyal) husband. Yet God takes this union, disciplines it and redeems it. As a result, it is Bathsheba's son who inherits David's throne.

[17]For images and details see chapter two, "Cherubim," *HarperCollins Concise Atlas,* pp. 52-55, and Victor Hurowitz, "Inside Solomon's Temple," *BR* 10, no. 2 (April 1994): 24-37, 50.

[18]Walter Bruggemann, *First and Second Samuel,* Interpretation (Louisville, Ky.: John Knox Press, 1990), p. 330.

[19]Baal was the god of fertility and storm, and as Canaan was dependent upon thunderstorms for their dry-farming economy, these two roles are closely associated. He is typically depicted as walking astride the mountains, his right arm raised wielding a weapon, and his left hand grasping a lightening bolt. He wears a helmet with the horns of a bull-calf. He is associated with Asherah the Canaanite goddess of fertility. See Daniel Fleming, "If El Is a Bull, Who Is a Calf?: Reflections on Religion in Second-Millennium Syria-Palestine," *Eretz Israel* 26 (1999): 23-27.; "K. G. Jung, "Baal," *ISBE*, 1:377-78; and A. H. W. Curtis, "Canaanite Gods and Religion," *DOTHB*, pp. 132-42.

[20]Syncretism is defined as "the process by which elements of one religion are assimilated into another religion resulting in a change in the fundamental tenets or nature of those religions. It is the union of two or more opposite beliefs, so that the synthesized form is a new thing" (S. R. Imbac, "Syncretism," in *Evangelical Dictionary of Theology*, Walter Elwell, ed. [Grand Rapids: Baker, 1984], p. 1162).

Chapter 9: The New Covenant and the Return of the King

[1]Cyrus is reported to have marked his capture of Babylon by grasping the hands of the statue of the national deity, Marduk, and announcing that he would allow his new subjects the opportunity to live their lives according to their established cultural norms and religions. This level of cultural tolerance was unheard of in the preceding generations of Babylonian and Assyrian rule and was welcomed with both joy and loyalty. The latter, of course, was Cyrus' goal. His more generous approach to domestic policy resulted in a more content, more loyal, less disruptive populace (see T. Cuyler Young Jr.'s summary, "Cyrus," *ABD*, 1:1231-32).

[2]Years ago John Bright estimated that the restored community was less than a tenth the size of preexilic Jerusalem. He states that Judah's population, which probably exceeded 250,000 in the eighth century, and was possibly half that after the deportation of 597, was scarcely above 20,000 after the first exiles returned, "and must have been sparse indeed in the intervening years" (*A History of Israel*, 3rd ed. [Philadelphia: Westminster Press, 1981], p. 344).

[3]The only exception to this was the brief and conflicted period of the Hasmonean revolt and monarchy from 142-63 B.C. (*HarperCollins Concise Atlas of the Bible*, ed. James B. Pritchard [New York: HarperSanFrancisco, 1991], pp. 100-101; cf. 1 and 2 Maccabees).

[4]See Neh 8:1-8 in which Ezra's reading of the Scripture must be *translated* to the Jews as they no longer understood the Hebrew of the text.

[5]See Mordechai Cogan's discussion in his chapter, "Into Exile," in *The Oxford History of the Biblical World*, ed. Michael D. Coogan (New York: Oxford University Press, 1998), pp. 269-75.

[6]See chapter eight, "David and the Monarchy," n. 4.

[7]Jon D. Levenson offers exceptional insight in his *The Death and Resurrection of the Beloved Son: The Transformation of Child Sacrifice in Judaism and Christianity* (New Haven, Conn.: Yale University Press, 1993).

[8]See chapter seven, "Moses and the Tabernacle," n. 26.

[9]See chapter five, "God's Final Intent," pp. 119-36.

Frequently Asked Questions

[1]See chapter seven, pp. 166-88.

[2]One accessible discussion of this extensive topic is Brevard Childs, *Old Testament Theology in a Canonical Context* (Philadelphia: Fortress Press, 1986), pp. 84-91.

[3]Although with each covenantal administration there is overlap regarding stipulations, there is change as well. One example is the Abrahamic covenant, in which it was a crime of sizable pro-

portions to kill Canaanites . . . even when provoked. This is evident in the story of the seduction of Dinah by the prince of Shechem. Here the prince of Shechem "lay with her by force" (Gen 34:2) and then begged Jacob to give Dinah to him as a wife. The brothers conferred with their father and told the people of Shechem that they would allow Dinah to marry the prince if all the men of the city agreed to be circumcised. But this was only a ruse. The Shechemites agreed to the proposal, and while they were recovering from their mass circumcision, Simeon and Levi burst upon the city and slew the men, retrieved their sister and lead their brothers in looting the city (Gen 34). Because of these actions, Simeon and Levi lost their inheritance (Gen 49:5-7). And the honor of their birth order fell to the fourth-born, Judah. Now consider this story in contrast to the story of Joshua's conquest of Canaan under the Mosaic covenant. Here, because God had instituted his theocracy and, therefore, the enemies of Israel had become the enemies of God, and Canaan was God's territory, it was *righteousness* to slay Canaanites.

[4]In this era of redemptive history, Yahweh's sovereign reign over all creation was uniquely identified with an earthly polity: the nation of Israel. Thus, at this stage of redemptive history, to be a member of God's people on this earth, one had to be incorporated into the life of national Israel. I realize that this articulation of God's rule in the Mosaic era may challenge some articulations of the same (cf. George Eldon Ladd, *The Presence of the Future* [Grand Rapids: Eerdmans, 1974]), but it highlights a decisive change between old and new. With the new covenant the theocracy of Israel ends, and the earthly counterpart of God's kingdom becomes a transpolitical, transcultural community in which there is no particular locus of God's rule—that because his reign is being exercised from heaven. What we look forward to in the "not yet," however, is the reinstitution of theocracy on this planet. God will once again rule from the New Jerusalem ("and the throne of God and of the Lamb will be in it, and his bondservants shall serve him" Rev 22:3), and all those who choose not to be incorporated into this polity will once again be excluded from the kingdom of God.

[5]Even though the New Testament and Old Testament share terminology, we should not assume that the office of the prophet in the Old Testament is equivalent to the office in the New Testament. As defined in Deut 13:1-5; 18:9-22, the prophetic office in the Old Testament was both a civil and religious appointment, and the authority of the Old Testament prophet was enormous. The prophets were understood as God's messengers, who had stood in his very throne room, received his message, and were delivering it (as would a diplomat) to God's vassal king and people (see Theodore Mullen, "Divine Assembly," *ABD*, 2:214-17 and 1 Kings 22:1-40; Is 6; Jer 23:18, 22; Amos 3:7, 8; Mal 3:1). The Old Testament prophet was an extension of Moses in his or her contemporary setting (Deut 18:18-22). They actually added to the canon. In contrast, the New Testament office of prophet is only a religious appointment, and the New Testament prophet is never compared to Moses in terms of authority and rank.

[6]Cf. chapter seven, "Moses and the Tabernacle," p.166-88.

[7]Perhaps the most important question in this mix is whether or not a Jewish Christian has a different entryway into the new covenant. The New Testament clearly announces that admission to the covenant is the same for Jew and Gentile—belief in Jesus Christ. As the Jewish apostle Peter said to a first-century Jewish audience in Acts 4:12, "there is salvation in no one else; for there is no other name under heaven that has been given among men by which we must be saved."

GLOSSARY

anthropomorphic: Suggesting human characteristics for deity, animals or inanimate things. See pp. 93-94.

archaeology: The study of the material remains of a culture.

Assyria: An ancient Mesopotamian nation responsible for the fall of the northern kingdom of Israel in 722 B.C., and an important source for covenant documents in the ancient Near East. See figure 2.3 and pp. 56-58, 66-68, 77-90.

Babylonia: An ancient Mesopotamian nation responsible for the fall and exile of the southern kingdom of Israel in 586 B.C. See figure 2.3 and pp. 56-58, 66-68, 206-9.

bĕrît: The Hebrew word for "covenant." See figure 3.1 and pp. 70-91.

bêt 'āb: The Hebrew phrase for "father's household," which was the standard family unit in ancient Israel. These were "extended" families in that these households included as many as three generations, up to thirty persons. See figure 1.1 and pp. 25-37.

bureaucratic: The typical cultural form of Western, urban society in which the state stands at the center of the society and serves as the individual's link to the legal and economic structures of that community. See pp. 25ff.

Canaan/Palestine: One of the three major regions of the ancient Near East in which the nation of Israel settled. See figures 2.4-2.8 and pp. 58-60.

cherubim: Known throughout the ancient Near East, these composite, semi-divine creatures were understood as the guardians of sacred spaces and were therefore posted as sentries at the entrances of palaces, throne rooms and temples. See pp. 119-25 and figure 5.3.

corvée labor: Unpaid labor required by a king of his citizens in lieu of (or in addition to) taxes; often utilized for governmental building projects. See p. 205.

Egypt: One of the three major regions of the ancient Near East in which the nation of Egypt may be found. This is the land of Joseph's sojourn, the slavery of the Israelites, and Moses' deliverance of the same. See figures 2.2, 2.4, 2.6 and pp. 60-64.

epigraphy: The study of the written remains of a culture, i.e., inscriptions.

Ezra: An important post-exilic scribe and priest who helped to restore the Jewish community in and around Jerusalem. See Ezra 7, figure 9.1 and pp. 209-11.

father's household: The basic term for "household" or "family" in ancient Israelite society; in Hebrew *bêt ʾāb*. See figure 1.1 and pp. 25-37.

Fertile Crescent: The crescent-shaped, watered region of the ancient Near East in which all of the Old Testament narratives occur. See figure 2.2.

Goshen: The region in the eastern Nile Delta in which Pharaoh settles Joseph's family. Probably to be associated with the archaeologically identified Wadi Tumilat region as an area of heavy Semitic settlement in the Middle Bronze period. See figures 2.7 and 7.4, and pp. 53, 62, 171-72.

Haran: Identified in Genesis 11:31 as the "mid-way" point of Abraham's migration into Canaan, this large and important second-millennium-B.C. urban center was located along the major travel routes from Mesopotamia into Canaan. See figure 2.4 and pp. 26-27, 53, 57-59.

Hasmonean Monarchy: A brief period of independent Jewish rule in Palestine from 142-63 B.C., initiated by the Maccabean Revolt (see the apocryphal books of 1 and 2 Maccabees). This was Israel's only era of national independence after the fall of the southern kingdom to Babylonia. See figure 2.1 (timeline) and p. 49.

hermeneutics: The science of interpreting Scripture.

Hittite: The Hittite Empire occupied Anatolia and northern Syria from c. 1400–1200 B.C. The discovery of an archive of treaty documents in their capital city in the early part of the twentieth century spurred the modern study of ancient Near Eastern covenants and covenant-making. See pp. 74-90 and figure 3.1.

Holy of Holies: This is the innermost and most sacred precinct of the tabernacle and temple's tripartite structure. It was understood as the place in which God sat enthroned "above the cherubim." See figures 5.1, 5.2, 5.4, 5.5 and pp. 120-29, 180-83.

inalienable land law: The biblical law found in Leviticus 25:13-28 insuring that the family land remained within the lineage. Thus, if a parcel of land had been sold outside the clan, it was the responsibility of one's nearest kinsman to buy it back, and if this was not possible, the land was to revert back to its original owner in the year of jubilee. See pp. 33-34.

Iron I Age: The archaeological period in Palestine dating from c. 1200-1000 B.C., this is the age of Israel's judges and the emergence of the monarchy.

Iron II Age: The archaeological period in Palestine dating from c. 1000-586 B.C., this is the period of Israel's monarchy through the destruction of the southern kingdom.

Late Bronze Age: The archaeological period in Palestine dating from c. 1550-1200 B.C., this is the period of Israel's exodus from Egypt and settlement in the land.

levirate law: The biblical law found in Deuteronomy 25:5-10 dictating that when a man's brother died before he had produced an heir, it was the responsibility of the living brother to marry the young widow and to father a child in his brother's name. See pp. 31-33, 40-42.

Mesopotamia: One of the three major regions of the ancient Near East in which the nations of Sumer, Assyria and Babylonia may be found. See figure 2.2 and pages 56-58.

Messiah: From the Hebrew verb *māšaḥ*, "to anoint," this term was reserved for an individual who was chosen, divinely empowered and publicly announced (by anointing) as a leader. Thus, it literally means "one who is anointed" and was frequently employed to speak of the promised offspring of David who would rule and restore Israel. See pp. 196, 203, 208, 214-15.

Middle Bronze Age: The archaeological period in the ancient Near East dating from c. 2000-1550 B.C., this is the period of Israel's patriarchs. See pp. 157-59, 171-72.

Nebuchadnezzar II: The Babylonian king who conquered and exiled the southern kingdom of Israel in 586 B.C. See pp. 67, 201, and chap. 8 n. 13.

Nehemiah: An important post-exilic figure who led the last corps of Jewish exiles from Babylonia home to Jerusalem to assist in rebuilding the city. See Nehemiah 1–2, figure 9.1 and pp. 209-11.

parity treaty: An international agreement ("covenant") made between equals. See pp. 73-75, 79, 91, and chap. 3 n. 33.

patriarchal: Having to do with the authority and centrality of the oldest living male member of a family in a tribal society. See figure 1.1 and pp. 25-27.

patrilineal: Having to do with tracing ancestral descent through the male line in a tribal society. See pp. 28-31.

patrilocal: Having to do with the living space of the family unit being built around the oldest male in a tribal society. See pp. 34-39.

Red Sea/Reed Sea: The body of water through which the Israelites crossed in their flight for freedom from Egypt. See figure 2.7, p. 63 and chap. 2 n. 14.

Samaria: The capital of the northern kingdom first built during Omri's reign in the ninth century B.C. and destroyed by the Assyrians in 722 B.C. See figures 2.1 and 2.10, and p. 66.

Septuagint: Abbreviated as LXX, this Greek version of the Old Testament was translated from the Hebrew between the third and first centuries B.C.

Sumer: Identified by many as "the cradle of civilization," this ancient Mesopotamian nation is the locale of Abraham's hometown, the city of Ur, and the source of the "Sumerian King's List." See figures 2.2 and 2.3, and pp. 56-59.

suzerain/vassal treaty: An international agreement ("covenant") made between a greater (suzerain) and lesser (vassal) king. See figure 3.1 and pp. 73-88.

suzerain: A king or state that exercises dominion over a lesser king or state. See figure 3.1 and pp. 73-88.

syncretism: The process by which elements of one religion are assimilated into another religion, resulting in a change in the fundamental tenets or nature of those religions. See p. 206 and chap. 8 n. 21.

theocracy: Literally means "government by God" and is descriptive of the government in the nation of Israel during the Mosaic covenant. The three human officers of this theocratic government in Israel were the prophet, the priest and the king. But the true sovereign of Israel was Yahweh. See pp. 175-76, 191, 227-31.

tribal: A society in which the family is the axis of the community and an individual's link to the legal and economic structures of that society is through the family. See figure 1.1 and pp. 25-39.

type/typology: An event or person in one era of redemptive history that has a specific parallel (an *antitype*) in another era of redemptive history. A type is *not* an allegory. Typology interprets the Bible through the lens of types and has to do with the principal of analogous fulfillment. See pp. 178-83.

Ur: Identified in Genesis 11:28, 31 as Abraham's city of origin. This ancient Mesopotamian city was the political hub of lower Mesopotamia in the late third millennium B.C. See figure 6.7 and pp. 53, 140, 158-59.

vassal: A king or state that owes allegiance to and is dependent upon a more powerful king or state. See figure 3.1 and pp. 73-88.

Via Maris: "The way of the Sea" was a well-traveled, ancient highway that ran along the coast of Canaan and served to connect Egypt, Syria and Mesopotamia. See figure 7.3 and pp. 60, 169.

Vulgate: This Latin version of the Old Testament was translated from the Hebrew in the fifth century A.D. See p. 93.

Scripture Index

Genesis
1, *93, 94, 95, 96, 97, 98, 99, 100, 102, 103, 104, 105, 109, 112, 129, 148, 242, 243*
1–2, *93, 118*
1–3, *114*
1–5, *49*
1–11, *140*
1–17, *247*
1:1, *95, 147*
1:1–2:3, *93*
1:2, *95, 96, 143, 242*
1:6, *147*
1:6-9, *143*
1:24-31, *98*
1:26, *109*
1:26-27, *107*
1:26-28, *102*
1:28-30, *148*
1:31, *102*
2, *93, 94, 103, 245*
2–3, *94*
2–11, *246*
2:1, *102*
2:1-3, *102, 104*
2:2-3, *105*
2:3, *93*
2:4, *93, 243*
2:7, *93, 107*
2:8, *93*
2:8-9, *57*
2:10, *127*
2:15, *103*
2:16-17, *104*
2:17, *106*
2:18, *109*
2:18-25, *103*
2:21, *78*
2:22, *93*
2:23, *109*
2:24, *38*
3, *106, 111, 112, 129*
3:8, *103*

3:15, *110, 216*
3:16, *108, 109*
3:17-18, *110*
3:19, *111*
3:20, *108*
3:23-24, *112*
4–5, *152*
4:7, *109*
5, *151, 154*
5:1-3, *107*
5:1–6:4, *154*
5:3, *107*
5:29, *138*
5:32, *51*
6, *137, 153, 245, 246*
6–9, *142, 146*
6–11, *52*
6:1-4, *151, 152, 153, 154, 246*
6:3, *143*
6:4, *153*
6:5, *137, 152, 154*
6:5-7, *52*
6:11, *137*
6:13-22, *143*
6:17, *143*
6:18, *143*
7:10-11, *147*
7:10-24, *143*
7:11, *143*
8:4, *58*
8:6-12, *245*
9:1, *148*
9:1-4, *148*
9:1-17, *148*
9:2, *148*
9:3, *148*
9:4, *149*
9:5-7, *149*
9:6, *107, 149*
9:8-16, *149*
9:18-27, *150*
9:24-27, *149*
9:27, *150*
11, *154*

11:1-3, *58*
11:10-32, *154*
11:26-32, *27*
11:27, *51*
11:28, *259*
11:31, *53, 256, 259*
12, *154, 159, 162*
12–50, *52*
12:1, *53*
12:1-3, *78, 159, 177*
12:2, *159*
12:3, *159*
12:4, *247*
13:5-6, *28*
13:11, *28*
14, *43*
14:14, *43*
15, *159, 161, 162*
15:1, *162, 165*
15:1-6, *160*
15:5, *160*
15:6, *159*
15:7, *161*
15:8, *78, 161*
15:9, *78*
15:9-10, *78*
15:9-12, *161*
15:12, *78*
15:17, *78*
15:17-21, *84*
15:17-18, *162*
15:18, *60, 65, 79, 161*
17, *162, 163*
17:1-4, *163*
17:7, *164*
19:1-11, *193*
21:5, *247*
23:1-20, *37*
24, *26, 70*
24:28, *236*
25:9-10, *37*
25:26, *247*
26:26-33, *70*
28:10–31:55, *53*
31:43-54, *70*

34, *254*
34:2, *254*
34:14-17, *163*
35, *28*
35:3, *243*
36, *28*
36:6-8, *235*
37:17, *60, 169*
37:18-22, *71*
37:28, *170*
37:30, *71*
38, *32*
38:6-11, *32*
38:6-26, *27*
38:9, *32*
38:14, *32*
38:18, *32*
38:24, *27*
38:25-26, *33*
41:14, *170*
41:42, *170*
43:18, *246*
43:33, *29*
45:26, *61*
45:28, *62*
46:27, *53, 62*
46:34, *171*
47:9, *247*
47:11, *249*
47:30, *37*
49:5-7, *254*
49:29-32, *37*
50:13, *37*
50:25, *37*

Exodus
1:5, *53*
1:8, *53, 171*
1:9-10, *172, 173*
1:9-14, *171*
1:11, *173*
1:22, *171*
2:24, *82*
4:24-31, *163*
6:28, *243*

12:35-36, *173*
12:35-37, *174*
12:37, *177*
12:38, *82*
12:40, *247*
13:17, *62, 63*
13:18, *238*
14:2, *238*
19–32, *175*
19:1, *63*
19:1–23:19, *82, 240*
19:4, *82, 175*
19:5-6, *83*
19:6, *88*
20, *87*
20:4-6, *86*
20:8-11, *105*
20:10, *187*
20:12, *226*
21:32, *236*
23:19, *187*
24, *89*
24:3, *88*
24:3-8, *84*
24:5-8, *88*
24:7, *84*
25–26, *120*
25:8, *120, 179, 182, 250*
25:18-21, *122*
25:18-25, *123*
25:21, *84*
25:22, *122, 124*
26:31-33, *120*
28:31-35, *181*
29:45, *181*
31:14-16, *105*
32, *206*
32:15, *84, 87*
32:16, *241*
34:29-33, *108*
35:3, *187*
36–37, *120*
36:8-13, *120*
37:1-9, *122*
40, *222*
40:20, *84*

Leviticus
1:1-4, *182*
4:35, *182*
16:2, *182*
18:30, *187*
25, *42*
25:13-28, *33, 257*
25:28, *34*
25:47-55, *236*
27:4, *236*

Numbers
2:2-4, *237*
2:17, *237*
3:1, *243*
3:40-51, *237*
7:11-89, *237*
7:89, *122*
10:1-28, *237*
10:11, *63*
13:22, *152*
13:28, *152*
13:33, *152*
14, *64*
14:3, *246*
14:43, *246*
15:38-39, *226*
26:33, *28*
27:1-11, *28*
33, *250*
36:1-12, *28*

Deuteronomy
1–3, *84*
1:2, *64*
1:34-46, *64*
2:3, *64*
4:11, *78*
4:26, *84*
5:6, *84*
5:7-21, *84*
5:23, *78*
9:2, *152*
10:5, *84*
10:17-18, *27*
11:23, *60*
12–26, *84*

12:7, *250*
12:12, *250*
12:18, *250*
13:1-5, *254*
14:26, *250*
16:11, *250*
16:14, *250*
17, *87, 203, 204*
17–18, *176*
17:14-20, *195*
17:18-19, *88, 195*
18:9-22, *254*
18:18-22, *254*
21:17, *29*
21:19, *235*
24:19-21, *30*
25, *42*
25:5-10, *31, 41, 257*
26:10-11, *250*
27, *241*
27:7, *250*
27:11—28:68, *84*
28, *241*
28:1-14, *86*
28:15-68, *86*
30:19-20, *84, 87*
31:10-12, *84*
31:11, *87*
31:28, *84*

Joshua
1:4, *60*
1:13, *104*
1:13-15, *104*
7:14-15, *234*
8:30-35, *84*
9–10, *70, 75, 76*
9:11, *75*
9:12-14, *75*
9:15, *75*
9:16-21, *76*
9:23-27, *76*
10:4, *76*
10:6, *76*
10:7-10, *76*
11:23, *104*
14, *248*

14:15, *104*
15:13-14, *152*
17:3-6, *28*
21:11, *152*

Judges
1:20, *152*
4:16, *246*
8:22–9:57, *251*
19, *193*
19:22, *193*
19:27-30, *194*
21:25, *194*

Ruth
1:11-13, *41*
1:13-14, *41*
1:16-17, *41*
2:3, *42*
2:20, *42*
3:12, *71*
4:6, *42*

1 Samuel
1–8, *194*
1:5, *29*
4:4, *122*
4:18, *248*
6:2, *122*
8, *65, 195, 203*
8:7, *195*
8:9-18, *205*
8:22, *197*
9:1-2, *196*
9:16, *196*
9:25-26, *37*
13:5-14, *198*
13:14, *201*
15:1-35, *198*
15:24-31, *198*
16:1, *30, 197*
16:1-13, *199*
16:7, *30, 199*
16:14, *199*
16:14-23, *199*
17, *199*
17:34-36, *200*

17:37, *200*
17:45-46, *201*
17:47, *201*
28:24, *36*
31, *198*
31:1-3, *198*

2 Samuel
6:2, *124*
7, *190, 201, 202, 203,
    213, 216*
7:1, *105*
7:11-16, *203*
7:14, *151*
7:14-16, *203*
7:16, *203*
12, *176*
12:1-4, *176*
22:11, *122*

1 Kings
2:11, *248*
5:15, *76*
6, *125*
6:1, *166, 167, 246,
    248*
6:23-29, *122*
6:29, *126*
6:29-35, *125*
6:32, *126*
6:32-35, *120*
6:35, *126*
7:15-26, *126*
7:36, *126*
8, *222*
8:6-7, *122*
9:11, *205*
10:14–11:8, *204*
11:11, *204*
11:26-40, *204*
12:1-21, *205*
12:6-7, *205*
12:10-11, *205*
12:16, *204*
12:19, *204*
12:25-33, *204*
12:26-29, *206*

13:34, *206*
17:19, *37*
20:25, *246*
22:1-40, *254*

2 Kings
7:1, *236*
7:16, *236*
7:18, *236*
8:1-6, *34*
17, *206*
19:7, *246*
19:15, *124*
22, *241*
23:2, *87*
24–25, *206*
24:17, *252*

1 Chronicles
13:6, *124*
28:2, *124*

Ezra
3:10-13, *211*
7, *256*

Nehemiah
1–2, *258*
8:1-8, *253*
10:31, *187*
13:1, *87*
13:15-22, *187*

Job
1:6, *151*
2:1, *151*
38:8-11, *143, 145*

Psalms
2:7, *151, 214*
3–41, *251*
8, *108*
18:10-11, *122*
51–71, *251*
80:1, *124*
82:6, *151*
90:4, *243*

99:1, *124*
104:2, *108*
126:1-3, *209*

Song of Solomon
3:4, *236*
8:2, *236*

Isaiah
3:25, *246*
6, *254*
9, *215*
9:2, *207*
9:5-6, *215*
9:6, *215*
9:6-7, *207, 211*
10:8, *215*
11:1, *211*
11:9, *224*
11:10, *211*
14:3-23, *96*
14:9-14, *243*
24:1, *242*
34:11, *96*
37:7, *246*
37:16, *124*
40:1-11, *209*
43:1, *24*
44:9-20, *107*
45:1-7, *209*
45:18, *242*
60:19, *108*
64:6, *117*
66:12, *127*

Jeremiah
4:23, *96*
4:23-27, *242*
16:20, *107*
19:7, *246*
20:4, *246*
23:18, *254*
23:22, *254*
25:11-13, *209*
31:31-33, *185, 186*
32:6-44, *34*
34:17-20, *84*

34:18-22, *77*

Ezekiel
1:5-11, *122*
5:12, *246*
11:10, *246*
11:22-25, *244*
24:25-27, *244*
28:11-19, *96*
28:12-15, *243*
37:1-14, *209*
37:21-28, *207*
37:27, *181*
40–48, *126*
43:7, *126*
45:11, *236*
47, *126*
47:8, *126*
47:9, *127*
47:10, *126*
47:12, *127*
48:35, *126, 181*

Hosea
1:2, *43*
2:5, *236*
2:12, *44, 236*
3:1, *44*
3:2, *45, 236*
7:16, *246*
8:10, *215*
13:16, *246*

Amos
3:7, *254*
3:8, *254*
7:17, *246*

Malachi
3:1, *254*

Matthew
1, *28*
1:1, *212*
1:2-17, *50*
1:17, *50*
1:20-21, *212*

1:23, *216*
3, *214*
3:1-3, *213*
3:13-17, *214*
4:1-11, *134*
5–7, *184*
5:17-48, *184*
5:18, *185*
7:27, *226*
8:27, *146*
12:1-9, *228*
12:10, *226*
13, *217, 222*
13:24-30, *218*
13:31-32, *218*
13:33, *218*
13:36-52, *219*
17:2, *108*
19:3-9, *228*
20:28, *45*
22:30, *152*
22:36-40, *226*
23:23-25, *188*
24:36-39, *153*
24:37-39, *138*
26:27-28, *89*
27:22-25, *84*
28:3, *108*

Mark
7, *188*
16:19, *228*

Luke
1:68, *24*
2:7, *37*
3:23-38, *50*
3:27, *50*
3:38, *107*
10:30-37, *226*
15:29, *71*

John
1, *242*

1:1, *216*
1:1-18, *242*
1:14, *182, 216, 221,
250*
1:29, *214*
2:19-21, *227*
2:21, *221*
3:16, *217*
5:24, *219*
13:36-37, *39*
14:1-2, *39*
14:1-3, *39*
14:23, *181*

Acts
1:13, *37*
2, *221*
2:2-4, *221*
4:12, *254*
10, *225*
10:15, *228*

Romans
3:9-18, *117*
5:6-8, *183*
5:12-19, *136*
5:14, *106*
5:19, *119*
5:21, *119*
7:12, *184*
8, *114, 115*
8:19-23, *114*
8:21, *127*
8:23, *219*
8:29, *216, 219*
9:13, *240*
10:9, *135, 164*
10:9-13, *220*

1 Corinthians
3:16, *222*
6:19, *222*
7:19, *228*
12:28, *228*

15:22, *106, 135*
15:45, *106, 136*

2 Corinthians
1:22, *219*
6:16, *181*
10:4, *230*

Galatians
3:1-9, *161*
3:13, *24*
3:24, *185*
3:24-25, *186*
3:26-29, *220, 232*
3:29, *17*
5:14, *227*

Ephesians
2:19, *222*
2:19-22, *227*
4:11, *228*
6:10-19, *230*
6:15-17, *230*

Colossians
1:13-15, *46*
1:15-20, *216*
2:16-17, *227*

1 Timothy
2:5, *217*
3, *228*

2 Timothy
2:11-13, *220*

Hebrews
1:1-2, *217*
1:3, *186*
2:17, *227*
4:14–5:10, *183*
7:1-28, *183*
8:1, *228*
9:11-28, *183*

9:13-15, *89*
9:15-22, *239*
9:24-26, *227*
10:1, *185*
10:19-23, *183*
11:8-10, *221*

1 Peter
1:18-19, *24, 46*
1:23, *219*
2:5, *222*
2:9-10, *175*
2:10, *82, 89*
3:18-22, *147*
3:21, *179*

2 Peter
3:7, *118*

Jude
1:6, *151, 245*

Revelation
4:5-11, *122*
11:15, *219*
12:12, *96*
19–22, *219*
19:11-21, *231*
21–22, *127, 129*
21:1, *147, 223, 230*
21:1-5, *127*
21:1–22:5, *220*
21:3, *128, 181, 183,
224*
21:5, *127*
21:10-11, *108*
21:16-17, *244*
21:22-23, *224*
21:22-27, *128, 129*
21:27, *223*
22:1-5, *128*
22:3, *133, 254*
22:4, *129*
22:5, *108*

Finding the Textbook You Need

The IVP Academic Textbook Selector

is an online tool for instantly finding the IVP books

suitable for over 250 courses across 24 disciplines.

---

ivpacademic.com